THE STORY OF
CHICHESTER

PHILIP MacDOUGALL

SUTTON PUBLISHING

Sutton Publishing Limited
Phoenix Mill · Thrupp · Stroud
Gloucestershire · GL5 2BU

First published 2004

Title page photograph: East Street, 30 July 1904.
Bathed in bright sunlight, hundreds of
Cicestrians patiently await the arrival of King
Edward VII. The lining of the street with flags
and bunting was typical of how the city
celebrated numerous royal events and national
occasions.

British Library Cataloguing in Publication Data
A catalogue record for this book is available from the
British Library.

ISBN 0-7509-3760-2

Typeset in 10.5/13.5pt Photina.
Typesetting and origination by
Sutton Publishing Limited.
Printed and bound in England by
J.H. Haynes & Co. Ltd, Sparkford.

A factory outing, *c.* 1920. A fleet of Southdown coaches gathers outside Shippam's city centre factory.
These trips were an annual event (see p. 175).

CONTENTS

Introduction & Acknowledgements

For a publication on Chichester, this book may appear slightly unusual. Given the town's considerable connections with the Roman Empire, I have said relatively little about the Romans in Chichester. This was deliberate. Much is currently available on this era of the town's history and I did not wish to duplicate that which can easily be found in any bookshop. Instead, I chose to concentrate on other aspects of Chichester and the influence of Roman archaeological remains upon the modern-day town. Apart from this deliberate omission, much that is new will be found in the book. This applies in particular to the Georgian period onward where I have used a good deal of original material to present an interpretation of the town that differs substantially from that of other writers. In addition, the final chapter expresses my concerns for the future of Chichester. To some, the ideas expressed may appear controversial. If nothing else, however, they may help generate a debate as to where the city is going and whether this is entirely the best route for all those who live and work within the confines of the present-day Chichester city area.

In particular I wish to express thanks to Stephanie, my partner and research assistant. She diligently carried out a number of interviews on my behalf. In turn, both of us would like to thank the following for allowing us to interview them: June Arnold, Douglas Cecil, Joyce Taylor, and Alan and Cecily Williams.

Further thanks are also due to Judith Hills and Doreen Turner for the loan of photographs. The *Chichester Observer*, the Chichester Museum and the West Sussex Record Office were also kind enough to grant permission for reproduction of photographs in this book. Throughout, these pictures have been individually acknowledged. All other photographs and illustrations have been drawn from my own collection.

Finally, I would like to thank the staff of Chichester Library, Chichester Museum and the West Sussex Record Office for their untiring efforts in various enquiries connected with the writing of this book. In particular, a special thanks must be given to Simon Kitchin, an assistant curator of the museum, who gave a great deal of his time in the searching-out of a particularly good selection of photographs from the museum archives.

Opposite, above: Faces in the crowd, June 1911. Chichester is celebrating the coronation of George V, which took place on 22 June. Unusually, this photograph is of those who attended the city's festivities – here the crowd is enjoying an open-air comical performance.

Opposite, below: King George V, himself, came to Chichester in August 1913 and officially reopened the West Sussex Hospital. It was one of many royal visits to the city, with the hospital acquiring its status as 'Royal' as a result of this occasion.

A late nineteenth-century view of the Council House. Standing in North Street, it is one of many fine Georgian buildings that help make Chichester such a distinctive and interesting city.

1

To the Victor the Spoils

History does not record the moment in which Earl Roger de Montgomery, a distant ancestor of Lord Montgomery of Alamein, first set eyes upon the town of Chichester – nor does it record his feelings. A French-speaking Norman baron, he had been present at the Battle of Hastings (1066), leading a division of mercenary French. Supposedly he had helped ensure Duke William's victory by killing a giant of an Englishman who, at a pivotal moment, was causing panic among the Norman knights. Richly rewarded for his efforts, Roger de Montgomery received numerous estates on the west side of Sussex – these including the township of Chichester.

In fact, Earl Roger, in acquiring these spoils of war, had become the most powerful and richest man in the county of Sussex. Apart from the wealth that these properties brought, he was also required to hold this side of the county against any of William's enemies. To clarify the extent of his authority, and those of neighbouring lords, Sussex was divided into separate administrative areas known as rapes, the outline of these areas approximately replicating similar divisions of the county that had been adopted by the Saxons. In origin, however, the term 'rape' has not been clearly identified, although it could also have been borrowed from the Saxons, possibly derived from the word 'hrepp', which itself refers to an administrative area. Under King William, five separate rapes were created: Arundel, Bramber, Lewes, Pevensey and Hastings. Chichester, which was of fairly limited importance in those early years of the second millennium, fell inside the rape of Arundel. Only in later years, and as a result of acquiring much greater importance, did the city give its name to an administrative rape. However, this was not until about 1265, Chichester by that time having been entirely transformed.

It is possible that on first glimpsing the town of Chichester, Earl Roger may have been greatly impressed. For one of a warlike background, it was, from a distance, a magnificent sight. Of approximately 100 acres in area, Chichester was then fully enclosed by a solid-looking masonry wall that, itself, was fronted by a broad, dry moat. Furthermore, along the wall, and at regular intervals, a number of bastions poked out, these preventing an attacker finding any blind spots. Even at that time, however, these walls were over 800 years old, having been built by the Romans. Closer inspection would have shown that, in spite of some apparent efforts at repair work, the walls were still in need of further attention and would, at that time, not have been in a position to fend off a determined enemy attack.

The wall had originally been built during the late third century, a need having then arisen to defend the town against increasing incursions made by Germanic seaborne pirates. Of flint construction, rising to a height of approximately 11ft, it had a uniform width of 8ft at the base and which was reduced at a more raised level to 6ft through the use of two internal scarcements or ledges. Its total length was a little over 1 mile 810yd. While the internal core of the wall consisted of rubble, the outer wall was of carefully coursed pieces of large flint held in place by a yellow mortar. Providing the wall with some additional strength was an internal rampart. This not only secured the wall from heavy battering by catapulted stones but also served as a walkway. Furthermore, the rampart, having been built at the same time as the wall, had been used to assist in constructing its upper layers, the builders being able to use the rampart in place of scaffolding.

It seems likely that a total of twenty-seven bastions were then positioned along the wall and spaced at distances of approximately 100yd. Also of flint construction, they had been added to the wall towards the end of the fourth century, some 100 years after the wall itself had been completed. Of interest was the particular method used in their construction. The Roman engineer responsible had appreciated that the digging of foundations for the bastions might well have undermined the strength of the wall, causing it to collapse. To prevent this, none of the bastions were provided with foundations at the

The walls of Chichester, which date to the late third century. Prior to the construction of these walls, the Romans had defended the town through construction of two sets of ditches that approximately followed the area of the wall. The stretch of wall in this photograph is the section that runs alongside the Bishop's Palace Gardens.

The horseshoe-shaped bastions were a later addition to the wall and constructed during the late fourth century.

point where they were attached to the wall. Instead, they were designed as independent structures and subsequently attached to the wall through the use of a flint in-fill. While the Romans used the bastions as a platform for their giant crossbow-like devices known as *ballistae*, the Normans were to use them in a much less imaginative way, simply lining them with archers.

Whatever feelings Earl Roger may have developed about the strength of the wall that now surrounded his acquired township, there can be no doubt that, in previous years, it had certainly performed the task for which it had been built. According to the *Anglo-Saxon Chronicle*, an annalistic history of Britain that first appeared during the reign of King Alfred (849–99), the wall was successful in fending off a determined attack by the much-feared Vikings. According to the anonymous monk who put together this part of the *Chronicle*, and referring to the year 895, 'The Danish Army went up plundering in Sussex nigh Chichester; but the townsmen put them to flight, and slew many hundreds of them, and took some of their ships.' Little further detail of the battle is known, although it is believed that not only townsmen but many others from the surrounding area were involved, Chichester merely serving as a rallying point. One further supposition has also been made, this being that the final battle, as described, took place close to Kingley Vale.

Of course, to ensure that the wall could be successfully used in such a strategy, previous effort must also have been expended on its repair and upkeep. Furthermore, it would have been kept in a more or less constant state of repair, the fear of the Vikings being not merely restricted to the reign of King Alfred. Under Ethelred (978–1016), the threat returned and Chichester must once again have been threatened. The *Anglo-Saxon Chronicle* provides the evidence, with the writer referring to the year 994: 'Thence they advanced, and brought the greatest evil that ever an army could do, in burning and plundering and manslaughter, not only on the sea-coast in Essex, but in Kent and in Sussex and in Hampshire.' Six years later the situation had not improved: '. . . everywhere in Sussex, and in Hampshire, and also in Berkshire, they plundered and burned.'

On entering the town through one of its gates, four in number and each sited at one of the cardinal points of the compass, Earl Roger may have met with his first disappointment – the gates themselves. These were less than impressive. Simple in design and lacking any form of ornamentation, they were little more than archways cut through the wall. This, at least, is the assumption that can be made from the archaeological evidence, there being nothing to suggest that the gates might have once possessed the thrusting drum towers typical of other Roman towns.

If Earl Roger had approached Chichester from the east, or Arundel side, he would have noticed one strange feature of the town. This was a vast elliptical depression that was made even more noticeable by having within its area large amounts of collapsed rubble mixed with iron nails. The Norman invaders themselves

The enclosing walls of Chichester do not represent the town's earliest defences. Prior to the arrival of the Romans, earlier inhabitants of the area had constructed a line of defensive banks and ditches that covered the main approaches from the South Downs. The most impressive is the Devil's Dyke, which is seen here at a point to the south of West Stoke village.

The Roman Eastgate as depicted by S.H. Grimm in 1782. By this time a postern gate, 4ft wide, had been added. Unfortunately, none of the gateways into the city now survive, the Eastgate demolished only one year after Grimm had completed his engraving.

would not have been aware of the significance of this structure, but nowadays we know it to have been the old Roman amphitheatre. At its longest point it was 185ft in length and at its shortest axis 150ft across. The collapsed rubble, much of which had been used to help keep the city wall in repair, was the remains of the inner wall of the amphitheatre, this used to support the raised tiers of wooden seats that surrounded the performance area. It was here, from the first century onwards, that excited crowds, having poured through the south and east gates of the city, were entertained by gladiators in combat.

Having passed through one of the four gates, Earl Roger would then have entered a town that clearly showed the vicissitudes of mixed fortune. With a population of only about 1,200, little of the town appeared occupied. Such housing as existed was strung along the main streets, which began and ended at the city gates. These had been the pride of the city in Roman times with North, South, West and East Streets once lined with numerous buildings of stone. On the north side of West Street (opposite the future cathedral) had stood the baths (an important local meeting place) and the forum (a centre for local government and justice). Under the site of the present-day cathedral there is evidence of another magnificent stone building, while at the junction of Lion Street and North Street stood a temple dedicated to Neptune and Minerva. However, as these, and many other substantial buildings, had collapsed, the stonework had been reused either in the town wall or to provide more makeshift buildings. The exception to all this was towards the centre of the town where a few administrative and religious buildings dating to the late Saxon period were of a more solid construction. Among them must have been a building for the manufacture of coins; Chichester was designated a mint during the reign of King Athelstan (924–39) with coins continuing to be produced not only during the reign of the Conqueror (1066–87) but as late as that of King John (1199–1216). From coins produced at Chichester, we also know the names of some of those responsible for their striking, with Brunman, Edwine and Godwine being contemporaries of Earl Roger.

Of the various religious buildings in tenth-century Chichester, the first thing that needs to be said was that the town did not then possess a cathedral. Instead, this honour had been bestowed upon Selsey some time around the year 680. Even in those days Selsey was a fairly isolated community and the choice appears a strange one. That it came about was a simple product of economics. The Church, during the seventh century, possessed little land within the walls of Chichester for construction of such buildings, while at Selsey, St Wilfrid, the exiled Bishop of Northumbria, was given a considerable area of land to maintain himself. Only in later years did the Church begin to acquire a sufficiency of land within Chichester, this eventually to be used for the construction of the new cathedral. In the meantime, Christians of the town may well have had the choice of two churches in which to worship: St Olave's and All Saints'. In addition there was a monastery and a nunnery, both of which had either a church or chapel.

The monastery, dedicated to St Peter, stood on the south side of West Street. Little is known of its origins, or even its later history, although it might well have been in existence as early as the year 956. A charter, supposedly of that year, refers to 'brethren residing at Chichester', these possibly the monks of St Peter's monastery. It is upon the site of the monastic church that the present-day cathedral now rests.

Also within this same area of the city stood the nunnery. According to a Benedictine catalogue of monastic foundations once held at Glastonbury Abbey, the nunnery was originally founded in 653, a date that is generally considered to be impossibly early. Little more, however, is known of the nunnery and it probably ceased to exist shortly after the Conquest. Possibly, it

St Olave's Church in North Street. The structure shows little external evidence of possible Saxon origins.

too was subsumed into the cathedral, with the nuns transferred to a more distant location.

The existence of the two churches in Chichester at this time must be treated with a good deal of caution. In the case of St Olave's, this must appear a somewhat strange statement, since the former church of that name, to be found in North Street, frequently displays a wooden notice that uncompromisingly states the building to be of Saxon origin. The problem, however, is that there is no definite proof. The position of the church is unhelpful, squeezed between various shops, and this prevents a proper examination of its external walls. In addition, the church has seen not only partial rebuilding during the Middle Ages but heavy restoration during the nineteenth century. Furthermore, the interior of the building has been completely plastered and covered with whitewash, this further hiding valuable architectural clues. In fact, the strongest visible evidence of a Saxon date is that of the blocked south door, which is tall and narrow and generally shaped in the Saxon style. But this is hardly

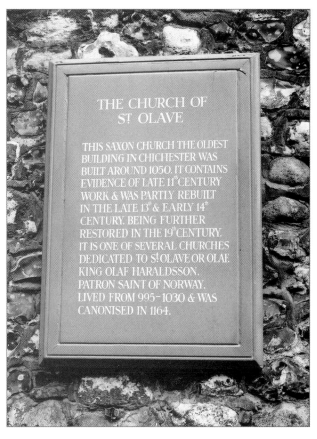

The Saxon origins of St Olave, according to this regularly displayed notice, are seemingly beyond doubt.

proof positive. If there is definite evidence of Saxon origin, it probably exists in the undercroft that lies beneath the floor of the chancel. Discovered in 1851, but subsequently made inaccessible, the undercroft walls are apparently rich in reused Roman tiles, a practice frequently adopted by Saxon builders. One further clue is the dedicatory name. St Olave was King Olave Haroldson of Norway (1016–30), who fought alongside King Ethelred against the Danes. Although he was recognised as a saint as early as 1030, his cult did not immediately reach this country. This might serve as an indication of the church being of a much later date, if it were not for the presence of a Scandinavian community in Chichester during the late Saxon period. It may well have been this influence that led to the building of the church. The presence of this community continued under Earl Roger, with the shipmaster, Ketel Esterman, almost certainly of Scandinavian origin, holding property on the east side of the town.

Further uncertainty surrounds All Saints' Church in the Pallants. Known to have existed by about the beginning of the thirteenth century, it is possibly the one church in Chichester referred to in the pages of the Domesday Book. That there is confusion results from the reference being an indirect one, appearing not under an entry for the city of Chichester but for Pagham Hundred. This was an area of Sussex owned by the Archbishop of Canterbury, with the Hundred, for reasons now impossible to discover, also possessing property in the Pallants. As a result, a simple entry in this section of the Domesday Book, to 'a church in Chichester which pays 64d' has been

Rumboldswyke church, which may also be a church with Saxon origins. Although Rumboldswyke was once a parish outside the city of Chichester, it was incorporated into the city during the late nineteenth century.

assumed to be All Saints. It is unlikely that this assumption will ever be placed beyond dispute, especially as the existing Church of All Saints, located in West Pallant, is of much later construction.

A further Saxon church may also have existed in the village of Rumboldswyke, an area that has subsequently become a suburb of the town. It has been suggested that the church, now dedicated to St Mary, may well have been originally dedicated to St Rumbold, a seventh-century notable. If so, this would account for the rather unusual name held by this area of Chichester. However, by the thirteenth century, when assessments were made for papal taxation ('Peter's Pence'), the church was clearly dedicated to 'Our Lady of Wyke', this rather undermining the possibility of a dedication to St Rumbold. The age of this church is difficult to determine as, together with St Olave's, it has been considerably altered over the years. Again, much of this happened in the nineteenth century, a result of rebuildings and additions undertaken in 1866 and 1890. Perhaps the most significant alteration was on the earlier occasion when the original chancel arch was removed, this apparently built entirely of Roman brick. Similarly, the throwing-out of the north aisle at that time resulted in the removal of the original north wall, with partial reconstruction of the south wall also undertaken. Again, Roman brickwork appears to have been removed. This leaves the assessment of the church as a Saxon building constructed of reused Roman masonry dependent upon the sporadic existence of herringbone Roman brickwork in the south wall of the chancel and those parts of the nave walls that remain unaltered. As for Rumboldswyke in general at this time, the Domesday Book of 1087 simply states, 'Hugh holds Rumboldswyke from the Earl [Roger], and Warin from him. Five free men held it as five manors. Then it answered for 9 hides; now for 6 hides. Land for 9 ploughs. In Lordship 1 plough; 6 villagers and 2 smallholders with 2 ploughs. One slave. [Value], then and now 100s; when acquired 40s.'

While the centre of the town may be said to have regained some of its former affluence, this cannot be said of those areas immediately beyond the central crossing-point of its four major roads. Even in Roman times, these outer areas of the town would not have been particularly rich, consisting primarily of timber-framed buildings occupied by artisans, labourers and poorer merchants. However, the occupancy of this area in Roman times had, at the very least, been planned, a standard grid-pattern of metalled and cambered roads clearly indicating where housing was permissible. Upon the departure of the Romans all this slowly changed, so that by the time of Earl Roger's arrival, the outer part of the town was best avoided. Much of it, indeed, was unoccupied or long since converted into small farm holdings. The limited amount of housing that existed was mainly hut-like structures that often ignored the earlier road pattern established by the Romans. Well, perhaps not ignored. Often these structures had been built on top of the earlier roads, these providing a useful floor for the new enclosure. It was because of this that, beyond the central roads of the town, the original road pattern has been lost, replaced by that maze of streets that can cause such confusion to those visiting or newly settled in the town.

The mound in Priory Park that represents the site of a motte and bailey castle built shortly after the Conquest. The castle itself was demolished during the reign of Henry III.

Yet Chichester had potential. Those ancient Roman roads that ran through the city gates and on towards London and other major towns were still among the most usable roads in the kingdom. This was bound to ensure that Chichester would remain a trading centre, a fact upon which Earl Roger was to build. However, the newly arrived owner of the town was to go much further, introducing a number of new buildings and generally encouraging an expansion of trade. These were the factors that were to transform Chichester and ensure that by the late thirteenth century it was to become the centre of its own administrative area upon the introduction of a sixth rape to the county of Sussex.

It was to the defence of Chichester that Earl Roger was to give much of his attention, sanctioning construction of a motte-and-bailey castle. This was a simple affair, one of several similar fortifications built across West Sussex (others were constructed at Arundel, Bramber and Lewes) with each having as its ultimate aim that of subduing the local population to the rule of their new Norman overlords. In design, these castles were quite simple, little more than a tall wooden tower set upon a mound (or motte) that was surrounded by a ditch, and a wooden palisade surrounding a larger enclosed area (the bailey). At Chichester, the new castle was positioned adjacent to the north-east section of the town wall on a mound that is still easily detectable within the grounds of Priory Park. As for the bailey, this was formed out of an area partly protected by the original Roman walls, together with a newly erected wall to the west and south of the motte.

At the time of its construction, the tower on its motte would have been the tallest building in the area. Adding to its high visibility was the likelihood, in keeping with the common practice in these years, of the structure being brightly painted, the normal choice being red, green or blue. This, however, was not to fulfil some aesthetic whim, but to ensure that its grim presence could not go ignored. For the purpose of providing the necessary land for the building of the castle, a previously semi-inhabited area had to be cleared, this doubtless causing a lot of local misery and further resentment towards the Norman invader. Evidence for this is based on the sudden truncating of a number of streets that would previously have terminated only upon reaching the outer wall of the city.

On only a few occasions was the castle put into a state of readiness for war. In 1193 an expected attack by the forces of Prince John, who at that time was attempting to remove Richard I from the throne, led to the castle being fully provisioned and five knights added to its garrison. The threatened attack never materialised. Given that at this period the castle was in much need of repair, it would doubtless have fallen quite easily. During the year 1195 attempts were made to improve its overall condition but there were limits to the level of improvement that could be made. Its timber walls were much decayed and the real solution would have been its reconstruction in stone. Rather than pursue this particular course of action, it was decided that the castle itself should be demolished. This was a decision taken in 1216 and at a time when the country was being threatened by a French invasion. While Chichester castle, in an improved state, might well have contributed to the defence of the nation, in its then state it was nothing but a liability. In fact, this was soon shown to be the case, with the castle captured by the French before the demolition order could be carried out. Only after the castle's recapture in 1217 was it finally demolished, this work carried out by Philip d'Albini.

A much more important addition to the town, and the one that was to have a lasting influence upon its prosperity, was the translation of the see from Selsey to Chichester. This took place in 1075, following a decree that bishoprics should be removed from villages to towns. To permit the early fulfilment of these instructions, St Peter's was given the task of performing all diocesan duties while at the same time, or very shortly afterwards, work began on constructing the new cathedral. Eventually, given that St Peter's

Church stood inside the area set aside for the new church, this former monastic church was demolished. The first Bishop of Chichester, as a result of his consecration in 1070, was Stigand, a favourite of King William I, having served for many years as his chaplain.

This first cathedral, which was not dedicated until 1108, would eventually consist of a three-storey nave that led into a choir that was partly situated under the central crossing. Pushing out from the crossing on the north and south sides were transepts, these housing several small chapels. Further to the east was the presbytery, surrounded by a walkway that gave access to three further chapels, each having rounded or apsidal endings. In keeping with the technical knowledge of the age, the architectural work would have been characterised by heavy round arches set upon massive cylindrical shafts.

Earl Roger had made construction of the cathedral possible through the granting to the church of considerable additional land within the south-west quadrant of the city. Furthermore, he must frequently have gazed upon the new edifice as it steadily took shape. Yet he was never to see the building completed, witnessing only construction of the presbytery and crossing,

these being as much as was likely to have been completed by the time of his death in 1094. At that time, the Earldom of Chichester passed to his son, Hugh de Bellesme.

It was as a result of the death of Earl Roger, or more accurately, as a result of his foreseen death, that one additional building was bestowed upon the town. This was St Cyriac's chapel, a chantry house supporting a single priest who had the task of praying for the soul of the dead earl. The building, which stood between Chapel Street and North Street, was not particularly large, but did survive into the nineteenth century. By that stage it had long since lost its original function and had seen more recent usage as a barn. The site, however, is still easily pinpointed: a car park behind the newly rebuilt Chapel Street clinic.

The appearance of the original cathedral can best be appreciated by an examination of the nave where the four eastern-most bays date to the early eleventh century. Such an appreciation is particularly enhanced by this nineteenth-century print as it also shows the cathedral in an earlier and uncluttered state.

2

A Centre of Trade and Prosperity

While Earl Roger and his successors helped bring prosperity to Chichester, they only did so if it also brought a degree of benefit to them. It is for this reason that the feudal overlords did much to encourage the growth of the town, with the Domesday Book recording that under Earl Roger alone, the city of Chichester increased in size by some sixty properties. As the town grew, the Earl's appointed administrator, the reeve, would not only be in a position to collect more taxes for the king but also the increased amounts of money that would go directly to the overlord. This latter income was primarily raised through ground rent on many of the properties in the town.

The right to levy ground rent resulted from the overlord having been gifted the city and its lands by the king. A nominal rent could be charged on many properties, although tenement owners were still free to sell and rent the property as they pleased. Lying outside this arrangement, however, were those areas of the city held either directly by the Church or an alternative overlord. Consequently, ground rent was not chargeable upon land occupied by the cathedral and parish churches. Furthermore, the Pallants being part of Pagham Hundred, ground rents in this area of the city were paid to the Archbishop of Canterbury. Another source of income for the feudal overlord was the raising of money through fines, a result of actions taken by the court leet, a combined civil and criminal court. The overlord's appointed reeve was the court judge and he had the power to fine or imprison. Specifically, the court leet had various policing powers that included summary justice for minor misdemeanours, while individuals might also call upon this same court to execute and witness the signing of deeds. In addition, and providing a further source of income, the feudal overlord had the right to levy tolls upon merchandise entering the city.

Opposed to the vast amounts of power wielded by the feudal overlord were the merchants of Chichester. They wished to reduce this authority, allowing larger proportions of the city's wealth to be ploughed back into the city. To achieve this, a bargain had first to be struck with the king, leading to the issuing of a royal charter that would empower the burgesses of the city to assume the right to levy ground rent, tolls and fines.

The merchants of Chichester, from an early point in time, were united into one single body known as a guild. Given the subsequent importance of this body to the history of the city, it would not be unreasonable to set down here both its founding date and the circumstances under which it was formed. Neither, unfortunately, is possible. The earliest reference to it does not appear until 1135: the Guild had an already existing authority that was confirmed in a charter of that year and issued by King Stephen (1135–54). It is the first royal charter known to refer specifically to Chichester and confirms rights already possessed by the Merchant Guild since, at least, the time of William I (1066–87). The exact nature of these rights is unclear but must have been connected with the regulation of trade, members of the Guild possessing unfettered rights to buy and sell within the area enclosed by the wall. In addition, they probably had the right to control the number of apprentices that might be appointed within the city. Despite its general vagueness, this is an important document and for this reason is reproduced in full:

> Stephen, King of the English, to the Bishop of Chichester and reeves, greeting. I direct that my burgesses [citizens with full municipal rights] of Chichester shall well, honourably and quietly possess their customs and rights of Borough and Merchant Guild as they enjoyed them in the best manner, honourably and quietly, in the time of King William my grandfather, and afterwards in the time of my Uncles and in the time of Earl Roger. And I prohibit that, on pain of forfeiture to me, no one shall do them any injury.

A further charter of July 1155, granted by Henry II, enhanced these original powers. In particular it restricted the retailing of cloth within the city to only those merchants who were members of the Guild. At the time, cloth was the main produce of the town and a source of wealth for many of its citizens.

The arrangements confirmed in these charters undoubtedly provided local merchants with a number of important advantages. Yet, for the merchants of Chichester, it was not enough. The Guild was striving for something much more important: the right to collect the king's taxes and levy their own fees and tolls. However, this was not to be achieved for almost a century, eventually being granted by Henry III (1216–72) in 1226. The new arrangement would come at a price: the merchants would have to pay an annual sum, known as a fee farm, allowing a newly created corporation to retain rents, fines and taxes. Unfortunately, the particular charter that heralded this arrangement no longer exists and it is only by reference to later charters that it is possible to get a more complete picture of the terms of the agreement. By the early fourteenth century the mayor and citizens of Chichester were making an annual payment of £32 to the Exchequer.

It was the earlier charter of 1226 that appears to have directly led to the appointment of Chichester's first mayor. The individual concerned was Emery de Rouen and he appears to have held office for the period 1239 to 1242. Elected by the town's merchants, he headed the Common Council of the Corporation, a body composed of the most senior members of the Guild. It was this body that was eventually to appoint the town's bailiff, an official who superseded the reeve. Having gained responsibility for the collection of taxes, fines and tolls, the corporation determined upon the best use of this money. While it was directed to outcomes that improved the city's trading prospects, so generally benefiting the merchants of the city, it frequently happened that the general populace also gained. Thus, the council's concern with the maintenance of roads, general policing of the city and the removal of nuisances had a common advantage to all.

A building of some importance at this time was the Guildhall, the meeting place of the Guild. The undercroft of this building still remains, incorrectly referred to as a crypt. Situated on the west side of South Street and only a stone's throw from the Market Cross, it currently serves as a restaurant. Although much of the building was demolished in 1396, the undercroft was retained when accommodation for the vicars choral of the cathedral was built immediately above. It was this original Guildhall that became the hub of much of the town's economic and political activities, with the mayor and corporation using the building for their regular meetings. In effect, it had become Chichester's town (or city) hall, whilst also continuing to serve the more general needs of the Guild.

The undercroft, with its twelfth-century vaulting and circular piers, provides a clue as to the flavour of the rest of the building. This would have been a suitably impressive structure, if somewhat small by later standards. Above the undercroft would have been the main building, used by both the Guild and Common Council for their meetings. A chapel would have led out of the hall while a kitchen and further storerooms would have been situated nearby. Completing the complex were stables, a garderobe (or privy) and rooms for various officials.

That the Merchant Guild chose to abandon the original Guildhall in 1396 is probably a result of a greater separation of the Guild from the governance of the town. The Common Council of the Corporation was, or was about to become, a completely separate body, while the Merchant Guild reformed itself into a religious body known as the Guild of St George. This reorganisation appears to have been completed in 1446 and at a time when the affairs of the Guild were being administered by a master and four elected wardens. In a charter of that year, the Guild of St George was empowered to acquire land to an annual value of £10. The revenue accruing from this land was to be used to maintain a chaplain to say mass in the chapel of St George within the cathedral. The Guild, however, was eventually dissolved in 1547 with the city acquiring the lands that it had held. Primarily these were 'Portefield' (modern-day Portfield) and 'Gyldenfild' (now crossed by Guilden Road). However, even before partial demolition of the Guildhall in 1396, the corporation had already acquired a new Guildhall, situated in North Street and adjacent to St Peter North Street. First referred to in 1304, the new Guildhall continued in use until replaced by Grey Friars in 1541.

The interior of the
undercroft as it
appeared during the
1950s.

The merchants who dominated the Guild and corporation would mostly have had their businesses and houses in the north-east quadrant of the city. This was the business and market area and was also the site of the second Guildhall. Along the east side of North Street was the Butchers' Shambles, while various tenements and shops are known to have existed along East Street and a second street, known as Vico Borum, which ran north from East Street. A further pointer to the area's affluence was the existence of a number of small churches, which survived on gifts bestowed by the local populace. Also in this quadrant was St Mary's Hospital.

An unusual feature of the south-east quadrant was that it was dominated by the Pallants, an area under the jurisdiction of the Archbishop of Canterbury. This meant that the corporation was not empowered to act in this area, a cause of frequent controversy. In 1495, for instance, Mayor Richard Exton attempted to make an arrest there. Apparently he entered the Pallants with four representatives of the city. Upon this information being passed to the Archbishop of Canterbury he expressed his immediate annoyance, accusing the mayor of acting illegally. The south-east quadrant, including the Pallants, was also a trading area, with various shops and tenements existing on the south-east side of East Street. In this quadrant, too, was situated the city gaol with an adjoining forge, while both the Franciscan and Dominican Friars established themselves in the same area.

The two remaining quadrants were significantly different from those to the east. The south-west quadrant fell, in almost its entirety, under the jurisdiction of the Bishop of Chichester. It was here that the cathedral and precinct had been established. Because of this, only a limited amount of trading activity had been established in this area. In 1205, the bishop had obtained permission from King John to build a number of shops, 12ft in breadth, around the walls of the cemetery. A further contrast was the north-west quadrant, which, throughout the entire Middle Ages, remained relatively undeveloped. Much of it was open farmland or gardens with a number of small barns also recorded. One example of an agricultural building was a granary owned by the dean that was first recorded in 1246 and situated alongside West Lane (now Tower Street). It was perhaps the cathedral's association with this area that resulted in travelling bell founders using a site close to West Lane for the casting of bells for the cathedral during the fourteenth century.

The actual limits of the city were, at that time, delineated by the wall and surrounding ditch. The suburbs that developed beyond the wall from the twelfth century onwards fell completely outside the jurisdiction of the corporation, and remained under the authority of the appointed overlord. These various settlements were formed close to the city gates and followed the course of the various roads, but only a little is known about them. They generated their own parish churches (St Pancras and St Bartholomew) while a forge is mentioned in 1239 as existing just outside the Westgate.

Evidence of further occupation has also been revealed by more recent archaeological surveys. The most recent, conducted in 2000 (in advance of the construction of retirement homes in the Avenue de Chartres), revealed the site of a short-lived medieval kiln that specialised in the production of roof tiles and chimney pots. Using archaeomagnetic dating, the archaeologists at the site were able to prove that the kiln ceased to be used at some time during the mid-thirteenth century. A second pottery kiln, also in use during the thirteenth century was uncovered during the 1960s. This stood close to Northgate. The existence of the two kilns, both immediately outside the city walls, would seem to support suggestions, made by Schofield and Vince, that Chichester was subject to a primitive form of town planning whereby the more obnoxious and dangerous trades were removed to these extramural areas.

A further area that should be mentioned, also existing on the north side of the city wall, is that of the Broyle. An area of enclosed woodland that was reserved for hunting, it effectively prevented more general outward expansion on this side of the wall. Originally held by the king, the Broyle was gifted to Bishop Ralph Neville (1224–44) in 1229. In 1377, and again in 1385, the cutting of wider city ditches meant that some properties close to the walls had to be removed.

Essential to the prosperity of Chichester had been the right to hold both a weekly market and an annual fair. A regular market at Chichester was certainly being held in the twelfth century but probably had a much earlier origin. The right to the market, as laid down by royal charter, was in the hands of the feudal overlord until 1316 when it passed to the corporation. Markets were held on Wednesdays and Saturdays (as they still are today). The latter was a more general occasion, local merchants selling a range of wares. The Wednesday market was more specialised. This was an occasion for the sale of livestock, with different parts of the main streets sectioned off for the sale of various farm animals.

The clue as to the site of the original market and where the differing sections of the market were once located can be discerned from names given to some of the city's parish churches. In particular, the long-since-demolished church of St Peter in the Market stood in East Street close to the intersection with North Street. This was the key market area, with the market spreading along North and East Streets and encompassing part of St Martin's. The first clue for such a conclusion is that of the former parish church that stands immediately to the north of East Street and known as St Andrew Oxmarket. Here would once have existed an area set aside for the sale of the medieval economy's chief beast of burden. A little further to the north can be found the shell of one more parish church, that of St Martin. This was once known as St Martin in the Pig Market. Furthermore, and for reasons not unrelated, the road in which the church stood, St Martin Street, was once known as Hog Lane.

The regularity of the market made it an occasion popular only with local traders. Fairs, on the other hand, were much grander, drawing traders and entertainers from much further afield. A particularly popular fair would even see traders from overseas, with rarely obtainable spices and other merchandise uniquely available for purchase on such occasions. At Chichester, there appears to have been a number of fairs eventually established, of which the earliest and most important was the Sloe Fair. Named because of a sloe tree in a field near the Northgate where it was held, it took place, at that time, on 6 October and the eight days immediately following. Henry I (1100–35) had granted this fair to Ralph Luffa, Bishop of Chichester (1091–1123). Another local fair that was under the patronage of the bishop was that of the Feast and Morrow of St Lawrence the Martyr (9–11 August). Henry I had granted this fair to Bishop Seffrid Pelochin (1125–47). Two other fairs also appear to have an early prominence, these granted to the original overlords of the city before acquisition by the corporation. They were held on the days surrounding the Feast of St Michaelmas (29–30 September) and St James (24–5 July).

A particular advantage to the patron of a fair was the right to establish a court that administered justice during the period of the fair. Primarily aimed at offences connected with trading, it often took on a wider jurisdiction, with all other courts in the town suspended. The patron retained fines levied. Known as 'pie powder' courts, in reference to the dusty-footed merchants who often attended them (*pied poudre*), their establishment by the bishop during the period of his two fairs was occasionally challenged by the corporation. In 1407, the then mayor of Chichester, Thomas Pacchyng, sought a boycott of the bishop's court, which led to only two merchants bringing cases before it. Even so, Pacchyng was sufficiently incensed by these two merchants' disregard for his instructions that one of them was subsequently imprisoned.

Also helping to stimulate trade was Chichester's status as a port, through which merchants were obliged to send their goods for export. The extent of the port area roughly followed the coastline of the rape of Chichester with merchants who used any of these harbours having to pay duty. In the case of wool exports, of which considerable amounts passed through the port in the thirteenth century, such duties were paid direct to the government. In the case of wheat and other commodities, this benefited the town more directly as it was paid to the corporation. At one time the Crown appointed its own customs officials for the collection of taxes in connection with wool and hides but in 1339 the corporation also assumed this duty. Of interest is that Emery de Rouen, the first mayor of Chichester, was also the first reported exporter of goods from the city. In that year he gained a licence to export wool, bacon and cheese to Flanders.

A particular drain on the city's economy was the need to expend relatively large sums of money on the upkeep of the walls. At one time this would have had little impact on the citizenry of the town, as funds for the maintenance of the walls were taken out of the general taxes and fees raised by the feudal overlord. However, the corporation had generally fewer funds to call upon and was frequently in difficulty when it came to the repair of the walls. On a number of occasions special

The upkeep of the city walls was a considerable burden on the medieval economy. However, the wall, of which this section running alongside Jubilee Park is a particularly fine example, was essential to the defence of the city.

arrangements had to be made. In 1261 the corporation was granted the right of murage, a special tax for the upkeep of the defensive walls. In 1339, Edward III, having ordered a survey of the walls, ordered that they be put into a state of defence. More recent archaeological evidence (based on excavations carried out in 1968) revealed that, during the reign of Edward III, at least one part of the wall had to be extensively reconstructed: it reached to a height of no more than 4ft, while the original Roman embankments had collapsed over it. It was these repairs that the corporation had been asked to undertake, but they were unable to meet the cost. On this occasion, the dean and chapter of the cathedral agreed to make up the shortfall. Further extensive work upon the walls was undertaken in 1378 when a new ditch, 50ft wide, was dug around the city, with the inner lip approximately 40ft from the wall.

Undermining the early economic progress of the town had been three major fires that had ravaged the town during the twelfth century. Only limited documentary evidence exists as to the true impact of these fires but it is known that each was fairly extensive. Perhaps the least damaging was that of 1160, this appearing to be restricted to the market area. Much more extensive were those of 1114 and 1187. On these two occasions, fire quickly spread across the numerous tenements and small workshops that dominated the east side of the city. Also engulfed by the fire on both occasions was the cathedral, while the bishop's palace was partially destroyed by the fire of 1187. Surprisingly, given the amount of excavations undertaken by archaeologists within the city area, little physical evidence of these fires appears to have come to light.

Another factor that would have impinged on the prosperity of the town was the Black Death of 1348. Although there is no directly recorded evidence, it is likely to have struck Chichester and probably caused a high level of devastation. The poll tax returns of 1380 provide a certain amount of indirect evidence. Although not particularly accurate, they show that within the area of the city wall only 250 individual payments were made. This is indicative of a sharp fall in population. While children, beggars and churchmen were not expected to pay the tax, it is clear that a much larger number of payments should have been made if the population had stood at anything like the earlier Domesday-period estimate of 1,200. Indeed, this low figure of 250 poll tax payments suggests that the population at that time stood at less than 800. If this is correct, then the Black Death was responsible for a demographic crisis within the city, some 30 per cent or more of the population dying from the hideous disease.

Furthermore, a number of additional events in the fourteenth century also collectively served as a brake on Chichester's economic progress, including a period of high taxation (as a result of wars with Scotland and France) and a series of poor harvests (leading to widespread famine). Only at the beginning of the fifteenth century did matters begin to improve. However, as will shortly be noted, such improvements were slow in pace and were invariably confined to a small minority of merchants and highly skilled artisans.

3

The Town Spiritual

Medieval Chichester was well served spiritually. The area of the city within the walls was divided into nine separate parishes, each having its own church or place of prayer. This was a quite remarkable arrangement, given that the population of the town never exceeded two thousand during the entire medieval period. Furthermore, immediately outside the walls were a further two parishes, not including the adjacent village of Rumboldswyke.

Of the parish churches either already in existence or eventually to be built, the mother church was commonly accepted to be St Peter. This was the original monastic church that had been sacrificed for construction of the cathedral. Having, at some point, thrown its doors open to the wider population of the town, it had acquired clear parochial duties that continued until its final demolition. In recognition of this, a parish altar was incorporated into the nave of the cathedral, also dedicated to St Peter and serving the needs of a parish that encompassed the immediate area either side of South Street.

Given, therefore, the close connection between the mother church of St Peter and the cathedral, it seems not unreasonable to begin this survey of spiritual Chichester with a return to the cathedral and progress in its construction in the three centuries that followed Earl Roger de Montgomery's death. In stating that construction of the cathedral had begun shortly after translation of the see to Chichester in 1075, I am dependent upon evidence adduced by the noted cathedral historian Tim Tatton-Brown. In contrast to many of those who have previously written about the cathedral, he suggests that the original Norman building was close to completion by the time of Bishop Ralph Luffa (1091–1123). Earlier historians had taken a distinctly different view, considering that no work was undertaken on the cathedral during the time of Bishop Stigand (1070–87), believing that such work was fundamentally the work of Bishop Luffa. As for the subsequent history of the cathedral, there is a more general agreement.

Consecration of the cathedral took place in 1108; a stone commemorating that ceremony embedded in the wall of the building. A neat supposition

A general view of the cathedral from West Street. While the core of the building is Norman, much else dates to the later years of the Middle Ages. The tower and spire were constructed during the nineteenth century.

would be that this date represents completion of the first cathedral, consisting of the presbytery, transepts, a tower over the crossing and a four-bay nave; these have been previously described, and were completed in the heavy Romanesque style that was characteristic of the age. However, there can be no certainty that this was the situation, with work still going on to complete the nave following consecration. But in accepting Tim Tatton-Brown's conclusions, it is also necessary to reassess the role of Bishop Luffa. He must no longer be seen as the man responsible for overseeing the entire construction of the original cathedral. Instead, he was merely responsible for ensuring that Stigand's great plans were brought to a conclusion.

Yet Bishop Luffa was still a major contributor. He comes into his own just six years after the dedication ceremony and as a result of a serious fire. This appears to have broken out on 5 May 1114 and probably took its greatest toll on the high-pitched roof that covered the nave, transepts and chancel. Bishop Luffa, therefore, is seen as the man responsible for the full restoration of the cathedral following the fire. Furthermore, it is generally accepted that he went a lot further, extending the nave by a further four bays and overseeing work upon the two western towers that could only be constructed on final completion of the nave. This is based on the supposition, again supported by Tim Tatton-Brown, that the Norman cathedral was built in two distinct phases, as evidenced by a clear break in the outer wall face of the clerestory where there is a difference in the coursing of the masonry. The logic, therefore, is that Bishop Luffa continued to pursue the original plan as possibly set down by Bishop Stigand.

One problem does present itself. Why, if the building had been substantially completed by the time of Bishop Luffa's death in 1123, was it a further sixty-one years before the cathedral was rededicated? In the intervening period there was certainly reconstruction work underway. However, this was of a relatively limited nature, consisting of repairs made necessary by uneven settlement and an extension to the Lady Chapel. Whatever the reason, the rededication of Chichester cathedral did not take place until October 1184.

Again disaster quickly struck. Just three years later, in October 1187, a fire once again started in the cathedral, also engulfing much of the city. If anything, damage to the cathedral was more severe than in the previous fire. Building work had to be recommenced but this time there was a marked difference. Because of the more extensive nature of the damage, part of the existing stonework had to be entirely replaced. This is most noticeable in the nave where the original upper storey, or clerestory, must have been either extensively disfigured or destroyed. Instead of merely replacing this feature with a duplicate of that which had previously existed, it was not only heightened but provided with pointed arches flanked by slender columns of Purbeck marble. These contrasted sharply with the earlier rounded style that continued to prevail elsewhere in the nave. Another change introduced at this point was the greater use of stone vaulting in the roof, thus helping to reduce the risk of a further fire.

It is possible that the fire of 1187 inflicted greatest damage to the east end of the cathedral. Leastways, it is here, following that particular fire, that the most extensive rebuilding work was undertaken. In particular, the two-bay retrochoir was constructed, regarded by many as the finest part of the cathedral. Built in a stage of transition between Romanesque and Gothic, it is in perfect harmony with the rest of the building. Beyond the retrochoir, the original ambulatory east end and apsidal chapels were replaced by a square east end with square chapels. These chapels were dedicated to John the Baptist and Mary Magdalene and were constructed either side of the Lady Chapel. As to how much of this work had been completed by 1199, the date of the cathedral's reconsecration, this is debatable. However, on 12 September, the building was dedicated to the Holy Trinity.

Even before this rededication a further disaster had struck the cathedral, with the collapse of two towers in 1195. Confusion exists as to which two towers were concerned, there being little documentary evidence to provide confirmation. At one time it was believed that it was the central tower over the crossing and the south-west tower. However, it is now generally believed to have been the two towers to the west. The earlier belief that the central tower had collapsed was based upon this tower having received much attention at the beginning of the thirteenth century, the arches at the crossing taken down and rebuilt from

Detail of the two-bay retro-choir of the cathedral, perfectly blending the rounded Norman style with the emerging pointed Gothic style. While the arcade is round arched, the gallery has two pointed arches overset by a round arch.

The nave of the cathedral, 1920s.

below the spring. This seems an excessive amount of work for the strengthening of what was then a short stubby tower that rose only a little above the cathedral roofline. It could also have been indicative of an early plan, to be fulfilled in later years, of a heightening of the tower and the building of a spire.

The reason for the collapse of the two towers, accepting the assumption that it was the twin towers at the west end, was probably twofold. To begin with, the earlier fire may well have weakened their structural integrity. A second factor, even more worrying than a further outbreak of fire, was the poor nature of the ground upon which the cathedral was built. Situated on top of numerous remains from the earlier Roman city, including walls, pavements and various trenches and ditches, it was constantly shifting, resulting in parts of the cathedral settling to a depth of 2ft 6in. Not surprisingly, this would have had most impact upon those parts of the cathedral that required the greatest amount of downward thrust to secure stability.

Alongside the frequent rebuilding works necessitated by the more obvious disasters, much attention was also given to the additional damage to the fabric caused by the ongoing settlement. The lengthy period of time taken to reconstruct the east end following the fire of 1114 is certainly associated with the general repairs on the fabric of the building brought about by uneven settlement. By that time, there was a clear lean to the south of 2ft. The new work undertaken by Bishop Luffa, in which he had extended the nave by four bays, had had to counter such problems. To try and prevent further subsidence, the quality of masonry had been greatly improved. More strikingly, however, the new work had to be built on a line slightly to the south of the existing nave in order to create the impression of a building in harmony with itself. Indeed, these early difficulties can be readily appreciated by anyone visiting the cathedral and looking up towards the triforium of the nave: the lean to the south is obvious. The later four-bay addition stands noticeably straight compared with the earlier four bays. A further indicator of the early-day problems of settlement can be seen from the greater thickness of the late twelfth-century columns compared with the more slender, but less useful, columns of the early eleventh century.

It was also ground settlement that led to considerable buttressing of the building having to be undertaken. In particular, the massive outward thrust placed upon the walls as a result of the introduction of stone vaulting saw use of flying buttresses, transmitting the thrust across the aisle to a buttress pier. To prevent a further lean to the south, particular attention was given to the south-side transept, this developed as a solid immovable object that would help prevent further movement. To achieve this, massive stone buttresses were added to its west face and east corner (with similar work, for purposes of symmetry, undertaken on the north transept).

The rebuilding of the collapsed south-west tower, too, was turned into a means of further stabilising the cathedral, the tower being given considerable buttressing on its south and south-west sides. However, in spite of this, both west towers continued to demonstrate weaknesses to their inner corners and were subject to further subsidence problems during years to come.

Statue of Bishop
Richard de Wych
(St Richard), located
close to the cathedral's
west door. In his left
hand, the sainted bishop
holds a scourge, a sign
of self-discipline.

A turning point in the prosperity of the cathedral was to be reached in the
mid-thirteenth century; this was marked in 1245 with the election of the
48-year-old Richard de Wych (*c.* 1197–1253) to the office of bishop. A man
with friends in certain high places, de Wych had undergone a meteoric career
rise, having been ordained into the church only two years earlier. Previous to

his formal entry into the church, de Wych had spent most of his youth at Oxford University, gaining a doctorate in canon law. Remaining at the university and rising to the position of chancellor, he eventually came to the attention of Edmund of Abingdon, then Archbishop of Canterbury. In 1237 he was invited by the archbishop to become his chancellor, a position he continued to hold until Edmund's death seven years later. It was then that de Wych chose to seek ordination, this taking place in 1245. That he was appointed, in such a short time, to the office of bishop, had much to do with politics: the Church at that time required the newly appointed office holder to have little to lose by a clash with the nation's overpowerful monarch, Henry III (1216–72).

At that time a crisis had engulfed the church at Chichester. The canons of the local diocese had chosen to elect the king's nominee, Robert Passelewe, one of Henry III's favoured administrators, to the office of bishop. Pope Innocent IV, who was required to confirm all such appointments, felt disinclined to accept the king's nominee, having already clashed with Henry on a number of other matters. The choice of Richard de Wych, the nominee of Boniface, the new Archbishop of Canterbury, was looked upon much more favourably, with his consecration taking place on 5 March 1245. This was a clear snub to Henry III, and it would have been easy to predict that the affair was far from over. The king, who had been enjoying the income of the vacant bishopric, refused de Wych access to the various estates of the diocese. Instead, the new bishop had to find temporary residence in a small ecclesiastical palace that belonged to the Archbishop of Canterbury, at West Tarring.

The dispute over the diocese of Chichester was partially resolved two years later when Henry III, having been threatened with excommunication, finally acceded to the wishes of the Archbishop of Canterbury and allowed de Wych to assume the full rights of office. That the matter was only partially resolved was a result of the King's refusing to part with the income that he had collected from Chichester during the two years in which the bishop had been in exile in West Tarring. Nor was it a matter that de Wych chose to forget, especially as the money was still unreturned at the time of his death. In his will, the Bishop of Chichester laid it upon the executors that they demand from the king 'the fruits of the bishopric of Chichester, which he for two years took unjustly and which of right belong to me, and payment of which I shall also seek in the Court of the Most High unless he has fully satisfied my executors'. Only at the time of his translation to sainthood in 1276 was this money repaid, a task undertaken by Edward I when he gave the cathedral £583 0s 4d, stated to have been 'lent' by the bishop to Henry III.

However, it was not the eventual payment of this withheld money that was the primary means of enhancing the funds available for repairing and improving the fabric of the cathedral. Instead, it resulted from the translation, in due course, of the deceased de Wych from simple bishop to fully fledged saint. Again, this must be seen in the context of the Church's worldly need, the cathedral community at Chichester having much to gain from the ability of one of its number to claim a position on the right hand of God. A sainted bishop, carefully entombed, could draw many thousands of pilgrims to the church, each required to make an offering out of respect to the man they had come to venerate.

To ensure a maximisation of these offerings, each pilgrim was eventually to be shown three sites within the cathedral, each deserving of a separate gift. These were the chapels of St Edmund and St Mary Magdalene, together with the retrochoir. The first represented the original place of burial; the chapel of St Edmund situated on the north side of the cathedral and built by de Wych as the chosen site for his tomb. Following the former bishop's canonisation in January 1262, plans were made for a magnificent jewel-encrusted shrine to be placed in the retrochoir, immediately behind the high altar. Upon completion of this in 1276, the body of St Richard de Wych (minus its head) was translated to the new shrine, King Edward I being among those present on this occasion. As for the saint's head, this was enshrined in a silver reliquary placed in the chapel of St Mary Magdalene. In later years, the chapel was to be specially decorated, with frescoes on the left side, where the head was placed, depicting the life of St Richard. A further financial advantage that accrued from the new arrangement was that of having two focal dates upon which pilgrimages were encouraged: 3 April and 16 June. The first was the saint's feast day, the date of his death (or heavenly birthday). The second was the Feast of the Translation, the day that his body was removed to the new shrine. For those who made a pilgrimage on these occasions, and as a means of further encouraging offerings, a remission of sins was allowed. For a pilgrimage made on the feast day, the remission was for one year and one Lent's penance; for a pilgrimage on the Feast of the Translation, the allowed remission was forty days.

To gain elevation to sainthood a few formalities had been required. Prior to his death, Bishop de Wych had already gained an outstanding reputation for good pastoral work within his diocese while also living fairly frugally. In addition, he was heavily involved in the collection of funds in support of the seventh crusade to the Holy Land. It was much of this that underpinned his subsequent promotion to sainthood, with an outline of the evidence presented to Pope Urban IV given by Odo of Chateauroux, Cardinal-bishop of Tusculum, in a sermon during the second half of the thirteenth century: 'Forty witnesses attested that the blessed Richard was steadfast in his humility, nine that he did not have any regard for fine clothes or expensive horses or trappings. Instead, he behaved as if he were one of his own clergy. Nineteen witnesses stated that he was kind and merciful to the poor. He did not let anyone praise or flatter him.'

Yet, to become a saint, something more than a good reputation and the undertaking of services to the Church was required. This something was a need to be associated with miracles. No saint could exist without a super-natural connection. In the case of Richard de Wych, an amazing collection of stories was soon being circulated, these telling of how the mere mention of his name or the touching of his clothing would cure not only a range of ailments but brought life to those thought to be dead. Again, Odo of Chateauroux supplies some details: 'He calmed a storm. He caused bread and even beans to increase so that he could give them to the poor. A sick man who lay down on the bishop's bed in the hope of a cure soon recovered his health. Another recovered the sight of an eye when the bishop touched it. As did a woman.' Friar Ralph Bocking, a contemporary of the bishop who went on to write his hagiography, adds detail to one particular miracle. Taking place alongside the bishop's original tomb in the chapel of St Edmund, it concerned John Stokes, a man paralysed for six years. Stokes, who had come to the cathedral in search of a cure, fell into a deep sleep during which time he dreamed that the future saint had told him 'to get up and walk'. Upon awaking, Stokes found himself completely cured. Other similar miracles, were also said to have taken place alongside the bishop's tomb. These were carefully broadcast, ensuring that those who made a pilgrimage to the shrine would make even larger offerings.

As for de Wych's real worth as a saint, this needs to be seriously reconsidered. If early Christianity was based on turning the other cheek and the seeking of humane solutions to existing problems, then he was no obvious model. As one of England's leading advocates of crusades to the Holy Land, he was clearly signalling the right of those who claimed to be Christians to kill and mutilate all who stood in their way. Compare this with the views of Bishop Bell during the war against Nazi Germany (discussed in Chapter 11). Furthermore, the 'goodly' Bishop de Wych would have known that a peaceful solution to the problem of the Holy Land was not impossible. In the year 1229 an accord had been struck between the Christian and Muslim worlds, permitting both religions access to their respective holy sites in the city of Jerusalem. Working towards the renewal of such an accord would have been much more worthy of a future saint. Another downside to the character of St Richard was that he had been an anti-Semite. In laying down rules for the governance of the diocese of Chichester, the bishop in his seventy-first statute, ordered that Jews 'should build no new synagogues'. Furthermore, and a clear precursor of later treatment of Jews in early-twentieth-century Europe, was his instruction 'that they should wear a prominent badge' and that Christians were forbidden 'to live with them'. All that can be offered in de Wych's defence is that his anti-Semitic views were generally in line with those of medieval Christianity. However, for the extensive Jewish trading community that was actually established in Chichester during these years, such orders must have been highly disturbing. Indeed, de Wych could have learnt much from that far more worthy saint, St Francis of Assissi, the words of whose prayer simply state,

> O Master, grant that I may never seek
> So much to be consoled as to console,
> To be understood as to understand,
> To be loved, as to love, with all my soul.

During his seven years as Bishop of Chichester, de Wych had certainly given considerable thought to the cathedral. He oversaw work on the construction of the first of a series of chapels built to the north and south of the nave, the first of these being that dedicated to St Edmund. To ensure that this work could continue, he had also encouraged others to bestow gifts upon the cathedral while his own will had left a bequest of £40. However, it was the arrival of ever-greater sums, a result of his canonisation, that ensured the introduction of more ambitious schemes. Chief among these was an extension of the Lady Chapel, together with construction of a new central tower and spire, all undertaken during the late thirteenth century. At the beginning of the next century the south transept was remodelled and provided with a considerably larger south window. Finally, the detached 107ft bell tower was added between 1375 and 1430, the structure built in two stages.

Apart from new works, a great deal of the cathedral's monetary resources continued to be directed to the problems created by subsidence. To give further strength to the south transept, now seen as a giant buttress in its own right, a sacristy was added to the east side of the transept, this helping to create greater stability. The subsequent insertion of a large window in the transept counteracted some of the earlier stability work, resulting in even-heavier buttressing

The large window of the south transept, which dates to about 1330. Its introduction considerably undermined the strength of the building, resulting in the need for extensive buttressing.

having to be added. Unfortunately, similar attention was not given to a further strengthening of the crossing piers under the new tower; the immense weight of both this and the spire was to take its toll 600 years later. However, attention was given to one further problem created by subsidence: the uneven roofline of the choir and nave. To overcome a peculiar series of curves that had resulted from differential sinkage, the whole length of wall was heightened through the use of projecting brackets, or corbels, upon which the new straight-topped roof rested. Again, a visit to the cathedral allows the extent of the problem to be appreciated. By viewing the upper wall of the nave from the exterior, it will be seen that the pattern of stonework still shows evidence of the dramatic shifting that had taken place. As for when the straightening of the roof was carried out, this was probably towards the end of the thirteenth century.

With the construction of a cathedral at Chichester, a number of ancillary buildings also became necessary. Chiefly, these were to house those variously serving the cathedral, providing both residential and administrative areas. Such buildings were all to be located in the south-west quadrant of the city and upon that area of land that lay between the new cathedral and the city

wall. Within this area, the largest single unit of land was set aside for the bishop, being situated on the western side. Here, some time during the early to mid-twelfth century, construction began on a palace building that would serve both as a residence for the bishop and as a seat for diocesan administration. Little of that original building remains other than the outside wall of the kitchen, which displays two blocked windows and a blocked door, all dating to the twelfth century. However, the fire of 1187, which destroyed much of the palace, necessitated considerable reconstruction, which was undertaken by Bishop Seffrid II (1180–1204). Of this building, the chapel, two-storey hall and kitchen still remain. The kitchen is of particular note, one of its walls having served the earlier, fire-damaged building. Within the kitchen is to be found a quite exceptional hammerbeam roof. The chapel, which stands immediately to the south-west of the cathedral, diagonally opposite the south-west tower of the cathedral, clearly dates to about the year 1200, although the windows are a later insertion of about 1320.

Elsewhere upon this land acquired by the church in this south-west quadrant of the city was a cemetery situated to the north-east, while to the south and east was an area of housing for those who made up the cathedral chapter. The size of each house carefully reflected the status of each individual, with the dean, responsible for administering the affairs of the cathedral, having the largest of these houses. However, it must be assumed that the original medieval accommodation given to this particular office-holder was demolished in the eighteenth century, the current house for the dean having

Above, left: An example of the heavy buttressing, in the form of a flying buttress, that became necessary upon the insertion of the new north transept window.

Above, right: With the introduction of this large window to the north transept, further buttressing had also to be added to the north side of the cathedral. The window itself supposedly dates to the episcopacy of William Rede (1369–85) and is a compromise in design. In part, it looks back to the earlier Decorated style while introducing the straighter lines normally associated with the Perpendicular style.

been built in 1725. The other chief
dignitaries of the chapter were the
precentor (who oversaw the choir),
the chancellor (responsible for the
day-to-day running of the cathedral)
and the treasurer (who safeguarded
the cathedral's finances and treasure). They, however, even if ordained,
were not expected to officiate at any
of the cathedral services. Instead,
these were duties performed by the
canons, or latterly, the vicars choral.
The former made up the majority of
the chapter and were responsible for
both electing and working with the
dean. Those who were resident in
Chichester were allowed accommodation, with examples of some of these
houses still to be seen. These include
the Wiccamical Prebendary and the
Chantry. Originally, it was the canons
who led the majority of divine services at the cathedral but this was
eventually to prove impractical. In
particular, this was a result of their
small number but also because many
were either non-resident or frequently absent from the city on other
business. It was for this reason that
the vicars choral were introduced,
these originally substituting for the
canons and given accommodation by
the canons for whom they were dep-

Further evidence, this
time from an early
nineteenth-century
engraving, of
buttressing to the north
side of the cathedral.

utising. However, a necessary increase in their numbers led, towards the end
of the fourteenth century, to the building of Vicar's Close, a set of terraced
houses that is estimated to have had about twenty-eight chambers – reflecting
the approximate number of vicars choral at this time.

Further features of the medieval precinct that deserve notice are both its
cloisters and the enclosing wall. The cloisters were added in about 1400 and
are in the Decorated style. Unlike many other cathedrals, the cloisters built at
Chichester did not serve the needs of an attached monastery. Instead, they
must be seen as an elaborate covered walkway that connected the cathedral
to the residencies of the precinct. As for the enclosing wall, this was designed
to bring about a more complete separation of the chapter and other members
of the cathedral from the ordinary citizens of the town. Of particular note is
the fifteenth-century gatehouse leading to the palace and which had attached
to it, prior to its demolition in 1608–9, the Bishop's Prison.

More now needs to be said about the role of the dean within medieval Chichester. Apart from duties associated with the cathedral, he also had a wider role in the city. As chief administrator of the cathedral, he also oversaw the altar of St Peter, which was in the nave. Since this represented the mother church of the city, it was here that all other clergy of the city could be summoned by the dean to appear before the bishop. Through the bishop, the dean also had a general unspecified authority over many of the churches in the city, together with the Hospital of St Mary. However, this authority did not extend to the Church of All Saints, which was under the ownership and jurisdiction of the Archbishop of Canterbury. As for the various monastic communities, they took their authority direct from the pope and were also not beholden to the dean.

Specifically, the eight parishes within the wall (setting aside St Peter's as represented by the altar in the cathedral nave) were those of All Saints in the Pallant, St Andrew Oxmarket, St Olave, St Peter the Less, St Martin, St Peter in the Market and St Peter sub Castro. Immediately beyond the city were the parishes of St Bartholomew and St Pancras. Slightly further distant was St Mary's in the village of Rumboldswyke.

It has already been noted that the churches of St Olave and All Saints had Saxon origins. Both were considerably altered during the thirteenth century,

The Bishop's Palace. In origin the Palace is twelfth century but over the centuries it has undergone a good many changes and alterations.

with this and further adaptations removing most of the evidence as to their genesis. They are two of the three medieval churches of Chichester that have survived into the twenty-first century. Both are of a very simple style, having neither aisles nor lavish patterned stonework to enhance any original doors and windows. Of note in St Olave's, however, is a fourteenth-century piscina, described by Nairn and Pevsner as having 'all the humanity that is missing from the Decorated part of the cathedral'. The other surviving medieval church is that of St Andrew Oxmarket, another unaisled church that is predominantly thirteenth century. In his account of the little churches of Chichester, Lindsay Fleming states,

> St Andrew's, a plain well-lighted building of dignified proportions, is built of flint and stone rendered with rough-cast, serviceable but not handsome, so that one is hardly prepared for the pleasant interior. The arrangement of the windows, the height of the roof (now boarded but once with open timbering), and the restrained memorials on the walls, are principal factors in this agreeable impression.

An archaeological exploration of the church of St Andrew Oxmarket has revealed that the footings of the church are actually earlier than the building above ground, suggesting that the original church was built some time during the twelfth century. As a result of bomb damage in 1943 the church finally ceased to serve the needs of its parishioners and was declared redundant in 1953. Since then it has been transformed into an arts centre.

All Saints in the Pallant. Now in the hands of the Red Cross, this former parish church dates to the thirteenth century and is as simple in design as any medieval church could be.

A further group of medieval churches have, over the years, been lost to the city and their parishes amalgamated. The earliest of these to disappear was that of St Peter in the Market, its particular parish recorded in 1229 as numbering but two people. In that year Ralph, Bishop of Chichester petitioned Henry III to demolish the church and have the two parishioners attached to the Hospital of St Mary. Even though this request was granted, the church may well have survived into the fifteenth century, rededicated as that of St Mary in the Market. Such a possibility arises from the financial records of the hospital, which refer to a chapel of that name, which required repairs to its chancel in 1402. A second demolished church was that of St Peter sub Castro, standing at the eastern corner of Guildhall Street and Priory Road. A small, oblong building, it was demolished in 1574, its former parish having already been united with the parish of St Peter the Less. The third church to disappear during the Middle Ages was that of All Saints in the Pallants, which stood at the corner of Baffin's Lane and East Pallant. Little is known of the church other than that it was mentioned in 1199 and 1289, probably ceasing to exist soon after then.

Two further medieval churches survived into the twentieth century: those of St Martin and St Peter the Less. The former, which probably dates to about 1260 and described as 'in the Pig Market', stood in the north-east corner of St Martin's Square and was demolished in 1906, a tablet marking the site that it occupied. It was slightly larger than the churches so far described, possessing not only a nave and chancel but also a bell tower. A further feature of the church, brought to light at the time of its demolition, was that it had a thirteenth-century wall-painting of a bishop with mitre and crozier, believed to depict St Richard of Chichester. As for the church of St Peter the Less, which stood in North Street, this was demolished in 1957. Originally constructed in the thirteenth century, it possessed at that time only a nave and

In 1957, following the closure of St Peter the Less Church in North Street, the keys of the church were fused into this York Road gateway.

chancel. During the following century, however, it was provided with a south aisle and tower, making it the largest of Chichester's medieval churches. By the time of its demolition, various alterations and changes had been brought about, with little of the original church remaining.

Beyond the city walls were the churches of St Bartholomew (immediately beyond Westgate), St Pancras (beyond Eastgate) and St Mary (Rumboldswyke). While the first two both date to the thirteenth century, the longer-established Church of St Mary witnessed many changes during that century. Among such alterations were the addition of lancet windows and a south doorway with roll mouldings. As regards St Pancras, a first reference to the church appears in papal taxation accounts for the year 1291. In common with the other churches of Chichester, St Pancras was of a fairly simple design, consisting of a small nave and chancel. Today, however, there are no remains of that original church. Similarly, present-day St Bartholomew's Church reflects nothing of its medieval origins. In style, however,

Detail of the memorial stone that was placed into the wall of the former church of St Martin's following its partial demolition in 1906.

The public garden, which lies beyond this closed gate, represents the site of the former church of St Martin's, once known as St Martin in the Pig Market.

St Bartholomew's was very different from all the other parish churches of the area, as it replicated in design the circular style of the Holy Sepulchre in Jerusalem. For this reason, St Bartholomew's was alternatively known as St Sepulchre's.

Within the city there were also a number of other religious bodies represented, of which the most important was the monastic order of Franciscans. The Franciscans, better known as the Grey Friars because of the distinctive colour of their habit, first came to Chichester in 1230, having acquired land in the area of St Martin's Square. Immediately they set about clearing the site of existing structures and erecting a series of buildings suited to their own needs. By 1253 the order, in Chichester, consisted of twenty-six brethren. The subsequent availability of land upon which the castle had once stood resulted in the Franciscans abandoning the area of St Martin's and moving to a new site.

The former site of the first Franciscan monastery was at that time given over to the warden and brethren of St Mary's Hospital. This was an already-established institution in Chichester, the hospital having been founded in the twelfth century, most probably by William, a dean of the cathedral (1158–72). At that time it had been located on the corner of South and East Streets, close to the present Market Cross. Despite a long-held assumption that the hospital had actually been founded in 1158, the first verifiable evidence of its existence is reference to 'the Hospital' in Bishop Ralph's petition of 1229, in which he sought to demolish the Church of St Peter in the Market and transfer its parishioners to the hospital.

Upon moving to the new site, in about 1253, the hospital probably made use of existing buildings left by the Franciscans. In 1285 Edward I gave a licence confirming the hospital to be in possession of this land: '. . . the Prior and brethren of the Hospital of St Mary Cicestre to retain a plot in the City of Cicestre where the Friars Minor of Cicestre used to dwell, which Henry de Chikehull lately gave them in franc almoin before his death.' It was shortly after that work began on construction of a large hall with a chapel at its east end. This was a characteristic feature of medieval hospitals. The hall was where the sick could be tended, while the position of the chapel allowed them to celebrate divine service in comfort. Prior to construction of the new hall, a public footway extending out from St Martin's Church had to be blocked; it appears that the new building would otherwise have straddled the footpath. In 1290, to allow this, Edward I granted the appropriate permission.

Construction of the new hall appears to have been carried out between 1290 and 1300. Still in existence, and unique in Britain as the only example of a still-inhabited medieval hospital, it has the general appearance of a towerless church. It is aisled with flint walls and timber framing, the walls once breached by a series of tiny, single-light windows, similar to one still existing on the south side. Separating the hall from the chapel is an oak screen bearing similarities in style to the window of the cathedral's Lady Chapel, the two completed within a few years of each other. Within the chapel there is also a piscina, similar in many respects to the piscina of St Olave's in North Street.

A view of the inner workings of the hospital is made possible from a series of manuscripts held by the University Library at Oxford, these being transcriptions made in 1725 of earlier documents held by the dean and chapter of the cathedral. Among these documents is one that refers to the dress and general conduct of the brothers and sisters of the hospital:

> . . . let the males be cropped below the ear; or the hair of the women be cut off back to the middle of the neck, and thenceforward they must be addressed by the name of brother and sister. If a brother, under the instigation of the devil, fall into immorality, out of which scandal arises, or if he be disobedient to the superior, or if he strike or wound the brethren or clients, or commit any other grievous irregularity, then, if he proves incorrigible, he must be punished severely, and removed from the society like a diseased sheep, lest he contaminate the rest. But let this be done not with cruelty and a tempest of words, but with gentleness and compassion.

The hospital itself served as a temporary home for the sick and infirm, with the brothers and sisters acting as nurses:

> Let everything that he requires be administered to him as the means at the disposal of the House may permit; and if he has anything of his own let the Prior take charge both of it and of his clothes, until he is restored to health; then let them be given back to him without diminution, and let him depart, unless, of his own accord, he offer the whole, or part, to the house. If he die in the House, let his goods be distributed as he has disposed of them. If he die intestate, let his property be kept for a year in the House, so that if any friend of the deceased shall come and prove that he has a claim upon it, justice may not be denied to him. If no one claims within the year, let it be merged into the property of the Hospital.

In addition, the hospital also acted as a night refuge for impoverished travellers:

> In regard to the poor people who are received late at night, and go forth early in the morning, let the Prior take care that their feet are washed, and, as far as possible, their necessities attended to. Care must be taken that they do not annoy the sick, they do not pilfer, that they behave respectfully in word and deed. The sexes must be separated.

In general, it was the various religious bodies that existed in Chichester that took responsibility for the sick and infirm. The Franciscans would certainly have undertaken such duties on that same site later occupied by St Mary's Hospital, while a second religious order, the Dominicans (or Black Friars), established a monastery on the south side of East Street close to Eastgate, which also possessed a hospital. They apparently reached Chichester some

time around 1280, making use at this time of existing buildings. With additional land purchased for them by Queen Eleanor, consort of Edward I, they went on to construct a church in about the year 1300. The Dominicans were never a large order in the town, with only twenty-one friar preachers attached to the house in 1324. However, they did attract a good deal of royal attention, with both Edward I and Edward II visiting the monastery and making donations.

Outside the city, and also administered by those in holy orders, existed three small hospitals for the care of lepers: Westhampnett, Rumboldswyke and Stockbridge. The placing of these particular hospitals at a discreet distance from the city is a reflection of the fear that leprosy generated. It was a progressive disease that exhibited quite horrific symptoms; those considered to have contracted it were excluded from the city and placed in isolation. To ensure further that they had no contact with the general community, those suffering from leprosy had a bell placed round their necks.

Another hospital, that of St James and St Mary Magdalene, was situated close to the River Lavant about a mile east of the city, with its inmates drawn more generally from 'the infirm of Chichester'. Founded, it is generally believed, by Queen Maud, consort to Henry I, it was under the charge of a chaplain or master and several brethren. Inmates, of whom there were eight, were given a weekly allowance of money and expected to attend regular

St Mary's Hospital. Founded in the twelfth century, it was situated within the city's affluent merchant quarter.

divine service. During the 1980s and 1990s, archaeological surveys of the hospital site revealed a total of 330 burials. The majority had certainly died from leprosy, but a significant number had died of other causes, so confirming this to be a general hospital.

The Franciscans, prior to moving to the site of the vacated castle, had the gift confirmed by a patent of Henry III. Dated 15 October, it gave to the Franciscans 'a certain place in Chichester which is called the old castle site to inhabit'. Soon afterwards, they set about constructing a new church. This particular building, now more commonly known as the Guildhall, made considerable use of stone from the partially demolished castle. It is a building that raises one important question. It has often been asserted that the structure represents only the choir of a much larger church. However, there is no evidence of a nave or transept having ever been built. Instead, the Franciscans may only have made use of the building as seen. Attached to it on the north side was a cloister that gave access to a refectory, kitchen, chapter room, dormitory, infirmary and guesthouse.

One final religious order that also had a presence in Chichester was the Knight Hospitallers of St John. St Richard, given that it was a military order dedicated to the overthrow of Islam, would have particularly favoured it. Unlike the Franciscans and Dominicans they brought little benefit to Chichester, using the land they owned in Little London to generate money for the continuance of the Holy War. Those who joined the order were expected to bestow all their wealth upon it while committing the rest of their lives to its main objective. It is likely that the original owner of the land that came to be possessed by the order might himself have joined it under such conditions. This, of necessity, would have resulted in the individual moving to one of its military bases strung across the Levant or, following the loss of the Holy Land, the successive island bases of Rhodes and Malta.

4

The Reformation

Throughout the late Middle Ages, the Church in Chichester was rarely free of controversy and bitterness. Mostly, the issue was that of reform, with Chichester invariably acting as a vanguard of conservatism. Nevertheless, the cathedral precincts must have frequently rung with the loud and forceful voices of the reform-minded, vehemently arguing with the majority who opposed them. Such disputes must have first taken place during the early fourteenth century, a time when the views of John Wyclif began to take hold. A good many Chichester clerics at this time became enamoured with his opposition to the worldliness of the Church, Wyclif having questioned the lives of luxury that many of their colleagues appeared to enjoy.

Within this debate, Chichester was clearly on the side of the establishment. One particular bishop, Robert Rede (1397–1415), made considerable efforts to suppress the Lollards, the name given to the reformists who favoured the views of Wyclif. However, he proved only partially successful. A second bishop who also opposed the Lollards, Reginald Peacock (1450–9), went one step too far. Instead of condemning them out of hand, he chose to debate with them. Furthermore, instead of conducting these discussions with his opponents in Latin, he chose to use the medium of English. It was something that the Lollards themselves greatly favoured. However, for the Church establishment, it was quite unacceptable, giving the ordinary folk of the day an opportunity to understand and enter this same debate. It was as a result of this decision on Peacock's part that he was accused of heresy, suffering the double indignity of imprisonment and removal from office.

Religious reform was only one of several problems that confronted the Church in Chichester. Among other things, corruption was rife. Many of the minor office-holders took advantage of a laxity in administration, with huge sums of money either misused or diverted into the pockets of those who formed the chapter. During the time of Bishop Rede, one of the canons, besides stealing money from the treasury, also appropriated for his own use materials intended for the repair of the cathedral. Within the city, priests of some of the parishes allowed their cures to fall into a state of destitution, leaving them to the care of poorly paid vicars, while they themselves resided elsewhere.

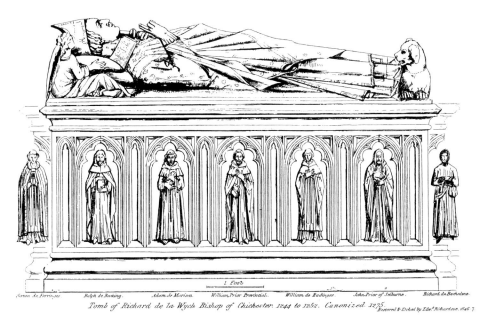

Simon de Ferringes.   Ralph de Bocking.   Adam de Marisca.   William, Prior Provincial.   William de Badinges.   John, Prior of Selburne.   Richard de Bartelone.

Tomb of Richard de la Wych, Bishop of Chichester. 1244 to 1252. Canonized 1275.
Restored & Etched by Edw.d Richardson. 1846. ?

A medieval bishop's tomb. Located in the cathedral, this tomb (which was restored in 1846) was once believed to be that of Bishop de Wych. However, it is now thought more likely to be that of Bishop Adam Molyneux (who was murdered in Portsmouth) with the effigy that of Bishop John Langton (1305–1337). (*West Sussex Record Office*)

Causing equal pain for the more spiritually minded were the activities of Adam Molyneux, another of Chichester's controversial bishops. In 1450, because of his immense unpopularity, he was murdered at Portsmouth. He was heavily involved in national affairs, having been one of the leaders at court and holding the office of Lord Privy Seal. Many believed that it was his counsel that resulted in the loss of large amounts of territory in France. Under the instruction of Henry VI, he had been sent to Portsmouth to pay the sailors of the fleet, but the money he handed out was much less than expected. This, and the fact that he was generally disliked, led to the killing. A mob of sailors marched upon the chapel of the Domus Dei where he was in prayer, dragging him out of the building before kicking and stabbing him to death.

A period of temporary respite descended upon the cathedral and its administration during the time the Bishop's Palace was occupied by Edward Story (1478–1503). Free of religious controversy and more removed from affairs of state, he was able to direct much of his time to the needs of the diocese and cathedral city. Out of these concerns were created two enduring memorials to his name: the Prebendal School and Market Cross.

The first of these emerged out of an already-existing school that may well have dated back to the founding of the cathedral. In these early times, the purpose of the school had been that of simply housing and teaching the cathedral choristers. These were usually drawn from local boys aged between 10 and 14, who boarded at the school and were expected to attend the regular daily services. In return, and without having to pay any fees, they received a rudimentary form of education that had, as its emphasis, song and voice training. Older fee-paying scholars who benefited from a wider curriculum that included Latin, grammar, rhetoric and logic, were later to join the younger choristers. This latter group were charged a fee of 8*d* a

The Prebendal School, early twentieth century. The original school building is the light coloured one towards the centre. Although retaining the Gothic style, the building was remodelled in 1830. Despite this, there is considerable internal evidence of its medieval origins, including blocked thirteenth-century east and west windows.

quarter, with most of this amount going to the master in charge. Some scholars, usually drawn from further afield, would also board at the school, paying an additional fee of approximately one shilling per week. As for the original location of the school, this is unknown. However, by the mid-fifteenth century it had been transferred to the site of the flint-fronted, Gothic-styled building that represents the face of the modern-day school.

At the time of the appointment of Bishop Story, it is likely that the school was one of several ineffectual institutions that appeared to surround the cathedral in that period. In fact, Story made a point of highlighting the shortcomings of local education in a preamble to statutes drawn up for the new school:

> Looking upon the no slight ignorance of the priests under our charge, and the excessive predominance of wicked priests, on account of the rarity of good Ministers of Christ in our Diocese of Chichester appointed as they too often are without sufficient piety, inasmuch as from causes of this kind very many evils arise because as the sacred page bears witness in the 6th of St Luke, 'If the blind should lead the blind, they both fall into the ditch'.

It is for this reason that he set about organising the new school, 'believing that an increase in grammatical knowledge would be the best remedy' against many of the evils existing in the diocese.

His main objective, apart from ensuring a high quality of education, was that of placing the school on a sound financial footing. To this end, he

Vicars Close. Although re-fronted in the eighteenth century, these houses, on the west side of Vicars Close, were built in the fifteenth century to house the Vicars Choral.

conferred upon John Wykley, the first master of the school, together with his successors, the prebendaryship of Highleigh. The prebendaries, of which there were several attached to the cathedral, had previously been held only by canons. Each prebendary came with an endowment of land, or *prebenda*, this ensuring each respective canon a degree of financial security. In return for this, the master of the school was not to charge fees to any of the scholars, so making the institution, if only temporarily, a free school. At the same time, Story purchased from the dean and chapter a building in West Street, then known as 'Furley' (but previously 'Ladynporch') to accommodate the master of the school.

In establishing the new foundation, Bishop Story laid down a series of regulations that covered its general organisation. Dated February 1498, they first tackled the procedure by which new masters were to be appointed. Of particular importance was that any such appointee was to be a 'priest well and sufficiently instructed in Grammar, and other Literature, and apt in teaching'. However, in later years the necessity of being a priest was repealed, with the first lay master appointed as early as 1550. The procedure of appointing the new master had to be undertaken by the dean and chapter within thirty days of a vacancy occurring.

Of interest are details of the school day also laid down by the regulations, which declared that the scholars should

be within our aforesaid Grammar School by five or very soon after but in winter before six no reasonable cause preventing . . . and afterwards when the bell shall have rung for full morning Mass to be celebrated within the chapel of St Gregory in our Cathedral Church of Chichester we will that the said 'Grammatici' and other Scholars above named collectively and individually should be present at the same morning Mass or at least in the elevation of the Body of Christ in the same Mass, and then peacefully and soberly should return to the Grammar School . . . and shall say the Psalm 'Deus Misereeatur' with the 'Gloria', 'Kyrie Eleison', 'Pater Noster', 'Ave Maria' etc.

The second important contribution made by Bishop Story to modern-day Chichester was that of the stone market cross that stands at the intersection of the city's four main streets. It replaced an earlier wooden cross that had been erected on the same site by Bishop Rede (1369–85). The new cross was not only a much grander affair but it had a very specific purpose, that of helping the poor of the area gain a regular income.

The cross, by way of its situation, was at the very heart of the regular twice-weekly markets. All around it, the various market traders competed with one another to establish their stalls in this prime location. Having entered the city and set up a stall, each of these traders was subject to a number of dues and tolls that was imposed upon them by the corporation. Yet, not all traders could afford these payments, with the market cross an attempt to redress the difficulty. Under the terms of its foundation, the cross was to be available for use only by the poor, with those trading under its shelter to be completely free of any form of charge.

It seems likely that the cross was built in 1501, a deed made out in December of that year implying it had already been constructed. It is this deed that provides virtually all that is known of the cross at this early point in time. According to this document, Story purchased the land for erection

One of Chichester's most familiar landmarks is that of the cross, given to the city by Bishop Story in 1501. This is a representation of the cross as it might have appeared towards the beginning of the eighteenth century. The artist, Owen Brown Carter (1806–59) painted the scene in 1843.

Detail of one of the heraldic shields that surround the cross.

of the cross from the city corporation, 'for which ground the said Reverend Father has given ten pounds of lawful money of England'. In return for this payment, the corporation would cease to have any interest in that parcel of land and would not 'interrupt, vex nor trouble any of the poor people that shall hereafter stand or sell any chaffer within the cross'.

Beyond this, little more is known. The cross was certainly constructed of Caen stone, one of the most favoured building materials of the age. Yet, as to its cost, the length of time it took to build and its original appearance, little more than guesswork is possible. As regards appearance it has, over the years, undergone a number of alterations. For one thing, there was no clock on the original cross, while the upper section was removed and replaced in the seventeenth century. Furthermore, the eight niches above each of the arches were likely to have been filled with stone figures. These were removed in 1642/3 and no documentary evidence remains as to who or what they might have been. A possible clue, that of a bishop's mitre positioned under the niches, suggests that each might have held a representation of a former bishop, one of them possibly Edward Story himself.

The bitterness and controversy that had so marked the ecclesiastical side of Chichester during much of the fifteenth century returned just thirty years after Bishop Story's death. The roots of this lay in the immense changes wrought by Henry VIII as a result of his desire to annul his marriage to Catherine of Aragon. In achieving this, Henry not only broke with Rome but established himself at the head of the Church of England. It was a move that Robert Sherburne, who had been appointed to the see in 1508, found quite unacceptable. Although willing to obey the king, he could not disregard the principles that had dominated his life from birth. In 1534, he placed his beliefs on record, writing in these terms to Thomas Cromwell, the king's principal secretary, protesting against, 'the king's most dreadful commandment concerning (among other things) the uniting of the Supreme head of the Church of England with the Imperial Crown of the realm; and also the abolishing and secluding out of this realm the enormities and abuses of the Bishop of Rome's authority, usurped within the same'.

Not wishing to overplay his hand, Sherburne, who was on the point of death, resigned in 1536. It was a wise move. In that same year two members of the cathedral

House of the Wiccamical Prebendaries, St Richard's Walk. Probably a fourteenth-century building, it was allocated to the holders of four prebendaries created by Bishop Robert Sherburne (1505–36). As well as creating these particular prebendaries, Sherburne also left his mark on the cathedral building, as it was during his episco pacy that the painted panels of the north and south transepts were added, together with the screen behind the high altar.

chapter were beheaded at Tyburn for holding views that failed to coincide with those of the king. The luckless pair were George Croft, the chancellor, and John Collins, a canon who held the Bursalis prebendaryship.

Under the next three bishops, Richard Sampson (1536–43), George Daye (1543–52) and John Scory (1552–4), these religious differences within the city continued to deepen. Each of those bishops was opposed to the ever-more-radical changes that were now taking place, with both Daye and Scory finding themselves removed from office. For Daye, it was because of his opposition to the new English-language prayer book and the removal of church finery, while Scory was unfortunate enough to agree with these things, but at a time when Queen Mary (1553–8), a renowned ultra-Catholic, ascended the throne.

For the ordinary citizens of Chichester, the comings and goings of these various bishops might have been possible to ignore. More noticeable, however, were the physical changes taking place within the city. In October 1538, as a result of direct instructions from the king, properties of the city's monastic orders were seized. In the case of the Franciscan friary in the grounds of the former castle, this not only provided the government with a sizeable amount of property but also 141oz of silver, which was promptly sold. The Dominicans, by contrast, were much poorer: upon payment of their debts and the need to redeem much of their plate, there was insufficient left to pay the administrative costs connected with the closing of their monastery. The buildings that once belonged to the Franciscans and Dominicans, having

The former chapel of the Franciscan monastery, Priory Park, 1920s. A survivor of the Reformation, it was subsequently acquired by the city corporation as their Guildhall. Nowadays, it is in the hands of the city museum and is frequently open to visitors. A visitor today, during any summer's weekend, would normally be confronted with a very similar view to that seen here.

Interior of St Mary's Hospital, early twentieth century. This shows the original thirteenth-century building.

fallen into government hands, were quickly released for rent or purchase. The Franciscan monastery subsequently fell into the hands of the corporation, the chapel itself becoming the Guildhall. The former Dominican friary was taken over by Edward Milet, a yeoman of Westminster, who initially took on a 21-year lease at a payment of 20s a year. Nothing, however, now remains of it. Less significant, taking place in 1540, was government confiscation of property in Little London belonging to the Knights of the Order of St John.

As for the seven Franciscan and seven Dominican friars who were made homeless upon the dissolution of their respective monasteries, they were treated relatively well. They were each given a small annual pension and licensed to act as ordinary secular clergy. Because of this, many were able to settle locally, with several of the friars appointed to the smaller parishes in the diocese of Chichester. Among them was William Styles, a former Franciscan, who became both a chantry priest at the cathedral and rector of nearby St Pancras.

Fortunately, the king's lust for church property did not extend as far as the two surviving hospitals of the city, St James and St Magdalene together with that of St Mary. In common with most other religious institutions in the town, both hospitals had witnessed a period of mismanagement during the fourteenth century. This was highlighted in 1442, when the dean of the cathedral carried out an inspection of the two hospitals, recording of St Mary's that it then had only two brothers and two sisters to oversee the needs of the inmates. In earlier years, the inmates had been regularly defrauded of their weekly sustenance payments, which were kept by the brethren for other purposes. At St James and St Magdalene, the dean revealed that the inmates had all secured admission by bribing the master, while six of the eight brethren were married and usually spent the nights at home.

That the two hospitals survived the even more rigorous inspections overseen by Thomas Cromwell in the late 1530s was down to both having

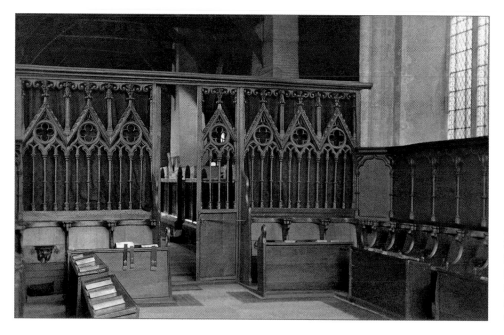

A view of the chapel, St Mary's Hospital. On the left is seen one of a remarkable collection of misericords (choir stall carvings) that exist within the chapel.

been thoroughly overhauled a few years earlier. In the case of St Mary's, this was undertaken in 1528 when the reform-minded dean, William Flesh-monger, drew up a fresh set of regulations. These limited the number of inmates to five poor and infirm, with each entitled to a room, garden and 8*d* a week. In return they were expected to live a quiet and sober life and to learn, should they not already know, the Lord's Prayer, Salutation and Creed. Placed under the charge of the *custos*, a residentiary canon of the cathedral with a stipend of £8 a year, the financial accounts were to be submitted annually to the dean and chapter for inspection. A priest was also to visit the hospital once a month to ensure that masses were being said.

The cathedral, together with the parish churches, also underwent consider-able change during the middle years of the sixteenth century. A major target of 1538 was the shrine of St Richard; the royal commissioners sent to Chichester received comprehensive instructions from the king:

> We willing such superstitious abuses and idolatries to be taken away, command you with all convenient diligence to repair unto the said cathedral church of Chichester and there to take down that shrine and bones of that Bishop called St Richard within the same, with all the silver, gold, jewels aforesaid, to be safely and surely conveyed and brought into our Tower of London, there to be bestowed as we shall further determine at your arrival. And also that you will see that both places where the same shrine stands to be razed and defaced even to the very ground. . . .

The visit of the commissioners saw the comprehensive demolition of the shrine behind the high altar and the removal from the chapel of St Mary Magdalene of the silver casket that had contained the saint's head. At the same time a second shrine, a tomb situated in the Lady Chapel and thought to be that of Bishop Gilbert (1288–1305), was also broken up. Despite the efforts of the commissioners to eradicate completely everything associated with shrine-worship at Chichester, two reminders still remain of the existence of these once-hallowed sites. In the Lady Chapel, part of the original screen that once belonged to the shrine of St Richard has been merged into the ironwork of the gate, while St Mary Magdalene's chapel still contains a cusped trefoiled recess in the north wall, which formerly contained the head of the saint.

A further target emerged during the 1540s: that of the chantries. Endowed by individuals for the holding of masses for their souls, a number had been established in the cathedral. With the suppression of these chapels, carried out at Chichester during the reign of Edward VI, a small group of unemployed clerics was created. However, the government was not unsympathetic to their situation, granting to these individuals a pension that was not far short of their original earnings. Among them was William Styles (the former Franciscan who now had two pensions as well as the 'living' of St Pancras) and a certain Nicholas Hickett. The latter was a man whose fortunes would eventually be revived and of whom more will be said.

It was also during the reign of Edward that the city's parish churches were most affected by the reformist movement. Already they had seen a number of changes, including the introduction of English into the litany, an injunction against placing candles before images or pictures and a requirement that each should display a version of the Bible in English. While these fairly limited reforms had been imposed upon them during the reign of King Henry, the nature of the changes under Edward VI was more extreme. A series of decrees eventually resulted in the wholesale destruction of church fineries, such as elaborate crosses, church plate and statues. It was also required that large stone altars should be torn out and replaced by simple tables that were supposed to resemble the one used in the Last Supper, this certainly undertaken in the cathedral (including the altar of the subdeanery) in 1550. That these decrees were obeyed in the parish churches of Chichester cannot be stated with equal certainty. However, there is evidence of a large wooden rood screen having once existed at St Andrew's Oxmarket, this also likely to have been removed some time around 1550.

A further crisis for the church occurred with the accession of Queen Mary in 1553. After twenty years during which the authority of Rome was rejected, the faithful were now expected to

All Saints in the Pallant, one of three medieval churches that have survived into the twenty-first century. The other two are St Olave's and St Andrew Oxmarket.

return to the fold. While some, including the former priest Nicholas Hickett, were happy at such a prospect, others were prepared to die for the Protestant cause. Indeed, Chichester, during this period, witnessed the burning of two Protestant martyrs, an act that was heralded by the return of George Daye to the Bishop's Palace. Having been removed from the see in 1552, he had a number of personal scores to settle, made easier by the command of his royal patron, who expected him to root out all those of Protestant persuasion and replace them with dedicated Romanists. The two Protestants he chose to burn were Thomas Iveson and Richard Hook, both of whom met their fate (probably in the cathedral precincts) during 1555. Neither were residents of Chichester, Iveson coming from Godstone and Hook from Alfriston.

Among the clergy who suffered upon Daye's return to episcopal office was John Lloyd, the subdeanery vicar. In 1554 he was unceremoniously removed and replaced by Hickett. However, Lloyd's demise was quite civilised, in that he was allowed a pension. One who narrowly missed removal was Bartholomew Trahern, appointed dean in November 1551. Using his position to bring a number of committed Protestants to the city, he was himself unable to adapt to the conservative leanings of the city. For this reason he resigned office just a few months before the accession of Queen Mary and subsequently fled the country. Apart from Hickett, a great number of other pensioned cathedral-chantry priests were provided with new positions during the reign of Queen Mary, several of them raised to the chapter through the allowance of a prebendary. It was in this way, too, that others of good Catholic record were also introduced into Chichester, among them Robert Oking, given the title of Prebend of Highleigh upon his acceptance of the mastership of Prebendal School.

This renewed Catholic ascendancy did not last long. Elizabeth succeeded Mary in 1558, with the new queen seeking to bring about reconciliation rather than a new round of burnings and deprivations. Admittedly, a number of removals were made in Chichester, but these were fairly minimal. Among them was Hickett, deprived of the subdeanery through the restoration of John Lloyd. However, it would be difficult to see this action as one of punishment, for Hickett was transferred to the parish and living of Pulborough. It was here that he served the remaining twenty-seven years of his life, a mute but committed Catholic. Upon his death, mindful of his time at Chichester, he willed to Dr Alban Langdale (former archdeacon of Chichester and a one-time leading Catholic in the diocese) his best robe. One who remained in place was William Styles, the former Franciscan friar and chantry priest. Having been appointed to the parsonage of St Pancras in 1543, he remained there until his death in 1568.

Within the parish churches it was turn and turn about. Under Queen Mary, Latin services, mass and stone altars had all been restored while possession of an English-language Bible was discouraged. Well, at least that was the theory. However, the fact that her reign lasted a mere five years meant that few of the city churches were in a position to carry out the more expensive dictates of replacing the many lost images or purchasing a new altar. The accession of Queen Elizabeth immediately put a stop to all this, with a further enactment

St Peter the Less, North Street. In contrast to All Saints in the Pallant, St Peter the Less is one of two medieval churches that were demolished during the twentieth century. (*Photo courtesy Chichester District Museum*)

requiring that, once again, all churches should provide 'at the charge of the parishes, one book of the whole bible together with a copy of "the Paraphrases of Erasmus" also in English'. However, proof that these various government demands, whether made by a Catholic or Protestant monarch, were having limited impact, can be seen from the locally held records of the dean's court. Fairly complete for the late sixteenth century, they show that the churchwardens for St Andrew Oxmarket had to be frequently reminded of the need to purchase the *Paraphrases*, an English translation of the gospels with explanatory notes. Despite such reminders, a purchase was not to be finally made until 1639, some eighty-one years after the instruction to do so was first issued!

One reason for the early reluctance to purchase a copy of the *Paraphrases* may have stemmed from the views of one of the leading parishioners of St Andrew's, William Bullacker. He was a die-hard Catholic who, as a result of marriage, first moved to Chichester in 1571. His wife, Elizabeth, was the daughter of John Diggons, a three-times mayor of the city; the marriage ceremony took place at the subdeanery altar in the north aisle of the cathedral. Bullacker, a noted academic who produced the first English grammar, was rapidly accepted into the local community, becoming a churchwarden at

St Andrew's in 1576. This, in itself, must say something about the views of the local parishioners, for in selecting him as churchwarden, they had chosen a man who, in the previous year, had been excommunicated for his Catholic beliefs. Furthermore, during his time as churchwarden (1576–9), he steadfastly refused to take communion.

The issue of Holy Communion was an important indicator of Catholic feeling. Under the laws of Queen Elizabeth attendance at church was compulsory, but not the act of receiving the sacrament. As a result, many Catholics were quite happy to give an outward show of obedience providing they did not have to take the final steps towards the altar. It was not only Bullacker and his family who shied away from this particular commitment: a number of others did so as well. In 1591 it was recorded that three members of St Andrew's parish were brought before the dean for failing to take communion, with this number increasing to eleven in 1601. A much more serious offender from the parish of St Andrew's was Joan Ipsley, presented to the dean as a recusant (one who failed to attend any services), the penalty for this act being a fine. Her husband, as it happens, was then churchwarden and the man responsible for informing on her.

Within the city generally, and especially among the elderly, there was a distinct reluctance to abandon the ancient traditions. During their inspection of Chichester's eight parish churches in 1569, members of the archiepiscopal visitation were shocked to find older members of the various congregations still in possession of rosaries, and taking Latin primers to Sunday service. Apparently, matters were no different in the cathedral, where there is further evidence of worshippers hoping for a return to the old faith. In particular, the wording of wills frequently mentions, with a degree of reverence, the name of St Richard. In 1586 John Large, who described himself as 'a poore man of the citie of Chichester', complained of certain unacceptable practices:

> In the cathedral church there stands the passion of Christ (as it is called), even whole, saving that about two or three years past, it was washed over with some white colours; but since that time some well wishers of that [Roman Catholic] way (of which there are too many) have taken some pains that it is almost as bright as ever it was. And besides also there are monstrous and idolatrous monuments in the high cross. I call them idolatrous because the common people are used to doing reverence unto them. . . .

The Chichester that witnessed the events of the Reformation was a city that was also undergoing considerable change. A slow but steady period of increasing prosperity characterised the fifteenth century, with the population of the city growing quite considerably. Perhaps, indeed, it had nearly doubled since the low point of the mid-fourteenth century that had been brought about by the Black Death. Such an estimate is based on the subsidy returns of 1524, these listing the names of all 301 individuals in Chichester who paid that tax. Unlike the earlier poll tax, fewer lay adults were expected to pay this particular levy, it being restricted to property owners or those benefiting from wage-derived employment. In other words, with few exceptions, and unlike the poll tax, it did not include women. For this reason, the figure of 301 represents only a small proportion of Chichester's total population at that time. To reach a reasonable assessment of a likely population level, women, children, non-wage-earners and laymen all have to be added. While any resulting figure has to be little more than an educated guess, it does not seem reasonable to place it at less than 1,200.

Further use can also be made of the 1524 subsidy returns as they provide a good deal of information about the city's more affluent citizens. For one thing, it is clear that the most sought-after houses were only those that either fronted the four main streets or had been built within the Pallants. Not one single taxable person lived outside this area. Living in West Street, for instance, was John Cresweller, a former mayor and Chichester's most affluent citizen. The returns assess his property and goods to have had a value of £200. Indeed, his level of affluence was well beyond that of any other single citizen, Cressweller possessing some 15 per cent of the city's taxable wealth. A glance at the subsidy roll shows that, after him, the next most affluent were John Boys, Robd Bowyar, John Moleyns, William Bradbrigge, John Hardham and John Cartar. The first three of these lived in East Street, the others in North Street; all were assessed as having property close to the value of £40. Furthermore, they were also among the most respected of the town: William Bradbrigge was the current mayor and Boys, Bowyar and Moleyns had also held mayoral office.

Another interesting detail that can be drawn from the subsidy roll is that the town was becoming increasingly cosmopolitan, as a consequence of trading connections. In all, the Chichester of 1524 had within its ranks eighteen Frenchmen, six Dutch and a Scot. It is likely that all were permanently resident in the city and had been joined by their families. Because of their alien status, each had to pay double the tax paid by those born in England.

It would be good if similar details could be provided on the city's less affluent and impoverished: those who lived behind the fine houses that lined the main streets. All that can be said of them is that they existed. It was to them, or at least to those who were unable to care for themselves, that a number of charitable bodies and institutions devoted much of their time. Among these, of course, was St Mary's Hospital and, prior to their dissolution, the monastic Dominicans and Franciscans. Another body with an interest in helping the poor was that of the Guild of St George, the body that had grown out of the original Merchant Guild. In keeping with its original constitution, it made regular payments to a number of the aged and infirm of the city. More prosaic was a further benefaction, the guild annually purchasing for use on the feast day of St George (23 April) a quarter cask of choice wine. However, this was not exclusively reserved for members of the guild, as the wine was to be taken to the city cross and shared with the general populace. Unfortunately, with the dissolution of the guild in 1547, this rather pleasant occasion ceased to occur.

Despite the economic strides made during the fifteenth century, Chichester failed to achieve real prosperity when compared to other centres of trade. For this reason, the city was specifically mentioned in an act of 1540 for the 're-edifying' of decayed towns. However, matters do not appear to have improved by the end of the century, when an expression of concern was placed on record by an anonymous petitioner to the Treasurer of England. The petitioner was particularly concerned that the city was fast decaying and that poverty was continuing to increase. As a solution he made several proposals, one of which was the development of the nearby harbour, which was of sufficient size to accommodate 300 ships of about 100 tons safely. Further damaging the city's fortunes was a return of the plague in 1563. It is not impossible that there had been other plague years in the sixteenth century, but a simple lack of documented evidence prevents the making of a more definite statement. However, for the year 1563 we are on firmer ground, thanks to the existence of church registers for the parishes of St Pancras, All Saints and St Andrew. Between them, they show that there were 167 burials in that year, massively in excess of the ten or so burials that might normally have been expected. As proof that this increased mortality was due to plague, Neville Osborne, a medical doctor and historian, notes that the majority of these deaths (136) occurred during the autumn of that year, thus satisfying the criteria for a diagnosis of plague:

> Namely, when an excessive number of burials showed more than 50 per cent in any successive three months in the plague season, June to October, plague is suggested; if more than 60 per cent of the annual total occur in July to September, plague is almost certainly the cause. Although the latter criterion is not quite met, the 136 or 82 per cent in August to October is acceptable.

It must be further assumed that this high number of deaths was not simply restricted to these three parishes, and that the other parishes are also likely to have been subject to a similar catastrophe. If so, then approximately 25 per cent of the city's population would have been taken in that one year.

An upturn in the fortunes of Chichester appears to have taken place in the last two decades of the century. In part, this was through trading developments that were to see local merchants beginning to exploit more positively the extensive farmland of western Sussex. In addition, a new industry emerged: that of needle-making. As a consequence of this cottage industry centred upon the parish of St Pancras, the area was to become the largest manufacturing centre for needles in England. By the end of the century it appears to have occupied the vast majority of houses in the parish.

A final insight into the city at this time can be gained from an examination of the seven coroners' inquests that took place during the reign of Elizabeth I. The holding of an inquest was requisite in the case of all sudden and unexplained deaths but was mostly likely to occur where a homicide was suspected. This was certainly the situation with respect to the inquests held in Chichester, where each involved a suspected unlawful death. The person responsible for the carrying-out of these inquests, the city coroner, was a further officer who was elected by the Common Council of the Corporation. As such, he held jurisdiction only within the area of the city.

If these seven inquests represent anything like a complete picture, then they demonstrate the town to have been fairly law-abiding, but by no means a stranger to occasional outbreaks of violence. On 8 September 1578, for instance, John Gilbert of Apuldram, possibly returning from the town market, fell into an argument with a local shoe-mender, accused of killing him with a shovel that he may well have purchased earlier that day. An equally violent death on 25 March 1587 befell William Reeves, a carpenter of Singleton. He was stabbed to death on Broyle Heath, attacked by George Tilley also of Singleton. Both men were subsequently tried, John Gilbert found not guilty while George Tilley was found guilty of the reduced charge of manslaughter.

The annual and highly popular Sloe Fair also witnessed at least one exceptionally violent episode. During the evening of 12 October 1597 a quarrel took place within the grounds of the fair, resulting in the death of John Kennet, a tanner from Petworth. The man responsible, Thomas Tapper, a soldier from Portsmouth, had taken a rapier to him, striking him about the neck and chest. The outcome was Tapper's appearance before the assize court where he was sentenced to be branded on the left hand. An identical sentence was also handed out during the following year to Ralph Addessen. In August, while the St Lawrence Fair was in session, Addessen, a yeoman of Chichester, became involved in an argument, killing another Chichester man, Henry Woodnet, with a rapier.

Of the other three inquests held during the reign of Elizabeth I, only one involved violence of one person against another. This was on 1 October 1597 when William Olliffe, a weaver, attacked and killed Henry Russell, a local tailor. Again, Olliffe was branded on the left hand. As for the other two inquests, one was a suicide of a prisoner held in the city gaol and the other was a suspected infanticide, later proved to be a death by natural causes.

5

Civil War

Chichester, throughout the seventeenth century, was a divided town. At the heart of this divide was a small group of strong-willed individuals who wished to influence the general direction and course of the city. Among them were William Cawley, Samuel Harsnett, William Speed, Guy Carleton and Henry Edes. Each, at the time, was a well-known city name. However, only one of them, William Cawley, is still recalled in the present-day city, through the attachment of his name to the former almshouse (now converted to housing) in the Broyle Road and the naming of Cawley Road (off Market Avenue). The others have no such memorials, other than that of their general contribution to a period of great bitterness.

Before being drawn into the story of those various individuals, mention needs to be made of a further demographic crisis. In 1608 plague once again struck the city and appears to have claimed several hundred lives. In normal circumstances, the number of deaths in the city should not have exceeded 50 but in the event there were 223 burials. The parish clerk of the subdeanery, in recording the names of Chichester's first plague victims, also desperately pleaded for an end to the pestilence: '[10 August 1608] Willoby and his wife, who were the first buried of the sickness, God for his son Christ Je[sus] sake cease it and take away this heavy punishment from us. Lord in mercy take it away.' So severe was the plague that it forced one parish church, St Andrew Oxmarket, to close for a total of twenty-two weeks. Among those whose lives were claimed in 1608 were William and Elizabeth Bullacker. They were the two Catholic parishioners of St Andrew's who had frequently been brought before the dean during the reign of Queen Elizabeth. While William had died in March, suggesting that he was not a plague victim, his wife probably was. Her burial took place on 9 September when the disease was at its peak.

Despite the deaths of William and Elizabeth, the Bullacker family were still to play an important role within Chichester's Catholic community. Their only son, John Bullacker, together with his son, Thomas, held the same views and were, themselves, to be presented to the dean's court as recusants. John Bullacker, who like his father also lived in the parish of St Andrew, came to be accepted as the leader of a small group of similarly minded individuals.

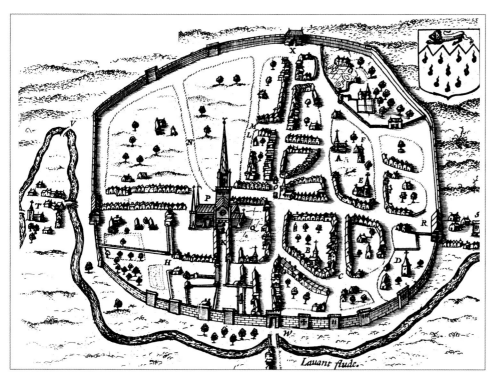

Chichester, 1610. Drawn by John Speed, this map shows the city of Chichester as it appeared immediately prior to the Civil War siege. Two thriving communities outside the city wall are shown, both destroyed at the time of the siege. (*West Sussex Record Office*)

Thomas, on the other hand, showed his commitment in another way, entering the Catholic seminary of Valladolid in 1621. Here he trained as a Catholic priest, secretly returning to England in 1630. Appointed Catholic guardian of Chichester in 1637, he was eventually arrested by the authorities and executed at Tyburn. Perhaps, indeed, John and Thomas Bullacker should be counted as the first of those strong-willed individuals who so dominated Chichester during this period. Certainly, as leader of the recusants, John Bullacker was pitted in ideology against William Cawley, a man who was of Puritan persuasion.

That William Cawley, a former pupil of the Prebendal School, should have a name that so outlived his contemporaries was only partly a result of the almshouse he founded. He was also involved in national affairs. Siding with Parliament during the Civil War, he was one of an elite number who later determined the fate of the king. As one of fifty-nine signatories to the death warrant, he was to gain the enduring epithet of 'regicide'. For this, upon the return of the monarchy in 1660, he was forced to leave the kingdom. Furthermore, he was to be frequently reviled in later centuries, many writers failing to forgive this act for which they could conceive no good reason. Even his son appeared to turn against him, calling the action of his father 'a wicked thing'.

The almshouse that he founded is more properly titled St Bartholomew's Hospital. It was established in 1626 as a charity for the purpose of housing 'twelve decayed [elderly] tradesmen' and in many respects was similar to St Mary's Hospital, but without a connection to the established Church. It was financed through a permanent endowment of adjoining land, and its trustees were the mayor and corporation of the city. Its establishment clearly marks William Cawley as a man who wished to serve the community rather than to profit from its needs. Already his father, John Cawley (who had died in May 1621), had paved the way, serving the city on three separate occasions as mayor. It was from his father's wealth, the product of a large city-based brewery, that William had financed the building of the almshouse. A few years later, in 1628, Cawley became an MP, elected by the freemen and members of the corporation to represent the city of Chichester.

At the heart of Cawley's beliefs was a commitment to Puritanism. This set him completely apart from recusants such as John Bullacker, who were opposed to the established Church because of its rejection of all things Catholic. As a Puritan, Cawley was also opposed to the established Church, but from an opposite standpoint. He viewed the reforms of the previous century as not having gone far enough. For him, and other Puritans, the clergy were still embroiled in too much pomp and ceremony, while the need for bishops and cathedrals was seriously questioned. It was for this reason that the new almshouse had few connections with the established Church and the trusteeship was placed firmly in the hands of the corporation, at that time normally dominated by those of Puritan persuasion.

That the corporation had such sympathies meant that it was completely at odds with those resident in the Bishop's Palace and Cathedral Close. This was made worse by the appointment of Samuel Harsnett (1609–19) as bishop, and not improved by that of his two immediate successors, George Carleton (1619–28) and Richard Montagu (1628–38). All three were 'Arminians', a new school of Anglican divines who vigorously opposed Puritan thought and proceeded to root out signs of its influence in both the cathedral and parish churches of the city. For this reason, penalties were introduced for those leaving services early (corporation members often leaving during the midst of a sermon they disliked). Also, city churches were not to be laid out in a fashion more appealing to Puritan tradition, while vestments and ceremony became a full feature of religious services.

Regardless of the increasing hostility that was developing between the two sides of the city, some of those living in the Close did little to help their own cause. In a series of inspections (or visitations) carried out by Bishop Harsnett, a man most noted for his bullying and hectoring, both the canons and vicars choral were shown to have a strong addiction to alcohol. Some appear to have spent more of their hours drunk than sober. Fuelling this addiction were a number of alehouses within the Close, some of them owned by members of the clergy. It was this prevalence of drink that created a further problem: there was frequent fighting within the area, also involving churchmen. Relatively insignificant by comparison was the revelation that many of the canons who were paid to be resident spent most of their time elsewhere. Those who did remain, when sober, spent considerable portions of their time in honing their bowling skills rather than in the important work of the Church.

As well as the religious differences that existed between the cathedral and corporation, the two bodies were also at odds over more general affairs of the city. Changes in the city charter, which had once restricted corporation power, now seemed to extend their authority into the Close. In particular, the issue of taxation was raised, with the corporation making impositions upon the residents. This was fiercely resisted, with the matter, when brought before the Privy Council, resolved in favour of the Church. At the same time, the corporation was attempting to restrict the power of the clergy within the city, refusing to allow them to act as justices of the peace. In 1635, when these quarrels reached a peak, the two bodies were refusing to talk. It was a situation brought to the attention of Samuel Brent, a representative of the Archbishop of Canterbury, during a visit he made to the city: 'the mayor and his brethren came not to visit me, because I lodged in the Close, there being some difference between them and the dean and prebendaries.' Of the corporation, Brent confirmed, 'they are puritanically addicted'. It appears that Brent even went so far as to clash with an alderman of the corporation who insisted on wearing a hat during church service.

Another player in the complexities of Chichester's city politics was William Speed, the rector of St Pancras' Church. Each Sunday he would preach to a packed church, his style of service and sermon popular among the Puritans of the city. To accommodate the increased numbers, it became necessary to add a special gallery. This was not to the liking of those in the Close, especially as it affected the attendance of other churches. Eventually, in 1635, William Speed was brought to task. Not only was he forced to have the gallery removed but he had also to confess 'his error in being too popular in the pulpit'.

Overshadowing these local differences was a series of national events in which Parliament clashed with King Charles I (1625–49) over finance and his use of the royal prerogative. Adding fuel to this dispute were the 'Arminian' bishops, such as Montagu of Chichester, who in supporting the king, laid emphasis upon the divine right of both bishops and kings. Given that the lines of demarcation in Chichester were similarly drawn, it is no surprise that, within the city of Chichester, those from the corporation sided with Parliament. A marked exception, however, was Robert Exon, the city's mayor. Having attempted to get the city to side with the king, he promptly fled from the area, joining the king's forces in York.

It is at this point that William Cawley needs to be reintroduced. A staunch Parliamentarian and member of the corporation, he had been elected MP for Midhurst upon the recall of Parliament in 1640. To prevent Chichester falling into Royalist hands, he was ordered to the city in August 1642 where he assumed the office of military governor. While Cawley oversaw the training of militia for the support of Parliament, others were training in the Close for the purpose of supporting the king.

Among the tasks Cawley attempted was that of reinforcing the defences of the city. This task had barely started when, on 15 November, the supporters of the king within the city took action. At the time Cawley was addressing a meeting of citizens at the town hall, concerned that he should have their support if a Royalist army should attack the city. According to Cawley, in a letter he later wrote to the Speaker of the House of Commons,

When we came into the street we perceived some swords drawn at the Northgate of the city – where one of the guns we had from Portsmouth was placed – which swords were drawn against the gunner. We endeavoured to pacify the rage of the people, but we could not, but they then overthrew the gun off from its carriage and possessed themselves of it, and from thence they went to the other parts of the city where the other guns were placed and possessed themselves of them also.

Having also gained the keys to the magazine, together with a total of seven pieces of ordnance, the supporters of the king had taken control of the city. On the following day the Royalist position was strengthened with the arrival of one hundred cavalry under Sir Edward Ford, High Sheriff of Sussex. He also brought with him one thousand infantry, but they were clearly not to be trusted: upon entering the city all of them were immediately disarmed. It was Sir Edward Ford who now replaced Cawley as governor.

High-profile Parliamentarians within the city, including Cawley, took flight, removing themselves to the more friendly city of Portsmouth. When Parliament received news of the changed situation, orders were sent to William Waller, commander of the nearest field army, to move south from Winchester to clear the area of Royalists. This became even more urgent when Sir Edward Ford, using Chichester as a base, mounted an unsuccessful attack upon Lewes.

Damage to the medieval church of St Pancras was so severe that the building was eventually demolished and replaced by the present-day nineteenth-century structure that stands on the same site.

With a Parliamentary army soon to be moving towards Chichester, further efforts were made to improve the defences of the city. Over the years the walls had continued to decay, with a good deal of emergency repair work undertaken by Cawley. Sir Edward Ford must have carried out further improvements; there is a suggestion that he also created (or rebuilt) a north-west bastion using stone from the churches of St Pancras and St Bartholomew. This would certainly account for the destruction of the two churches during this period, although the loss of the two buildings could equally have been the result of fighting that took place over the next few weeks.

Waller himself arrived before the gates of the city on Wednesday 21 December, his forces having first captured Arundel. The defenders must have been shocked by his strength, Waller having a force of over 6,000 men. According to a pamphlet, printed in 1643 by Henry Twyford of Fleet Street, terms of surrender were immediately offered, but were rejected by those holding the city. The pamphlet, assuming it to be accurate, is supposedly a copy of Waller's own account of the action, this having been submitted to Parliament early the following year. The terms offered were:

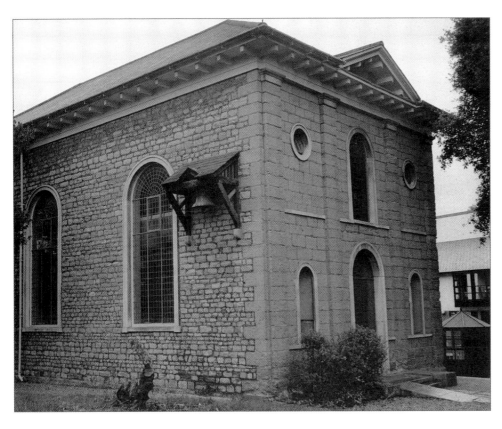

St Bartholomew's Church, Mount Lane. The original medieval church was also destroyed during the Civil War siege with the present building, although classical in design, dating to 1832.

An absolute surrender of the town.

A delivery of the sheriff, and other delinquents voted in parliament, and all papists.

A permission to the common soldiers to pass out without any arms: to the officers to ride out with their swords, and one horse a-piece to be allowed them for their journey.

An oath to be taken by them never to serve against parliament.

While these negotiations were under way, Waller ordered his troops to occupy the Broyle. Although a woodland area, it had the advantage of a shallow rise, allowing the Parliamentary troops to look into the city. It was also a good area for the positioning of their ordnance, which was positioned on land later occupied by the Royal West Sussex Hospital. Once in place, and over the next few days, these guns were fired indiscriminately into the city. Despite the size of the target, it took some time to find the range. Apparently, some of the earliest shots flew straight across, falling outside the south gate and close to where further Parliamentary troops were engaged in reconnaissance. Most of the later shots, however, were very definitely on target and caused considerable damage within the city. The Cathedral Close appears to have suffered quite severely, with the deanery heavily damaged and the chancellor's house completely destroyed. Also damaged by cannon fire were the Bishop's Palace together with several roofs and two of the larger windows of the cathedral. In reply, the seven pieces of ordnance defending the city also opened fire, their targets being the newly established gun batteries on the Broyle.

The fourteenth-century gateway to the Bishop's Palace. Much of the surrounding area, including the cathedral, was heavily damaged by the Parliamentary troops who besieged the city in 1642.

According to Twyford's printed account, a concerted attack upon the city was not undertaken until Christmas Eve. Initial efforts were directed to the area around the west gate, this resulting in some of Waller's infantry occupying the houses that made up the suburb. To remove them, the defenders deliberately set fire to these houses, possibly including the Church of St Bartholomew. Shortly after, and to prevent a similar attack on the east gate, the defenders also set fire to the buildings of this suburb. Most of the houses here belonged to the industrious needle-makers of the city, although the fire may also have engulfed St Pancras' Church.

Following their retreat from the suburbs to the west, Waller's troops proceeded to take possession of the almshouses established by William Cawley. Situated 'within half musket shot' of the north gate, it was an ideal location for ordnance. Once positioned, these guns 'played through the gate up into the very marketplace of the city'. That same evening, attention was also given to the south gate where two companies of foot and two troops of horse held their position following a 'warm skirmish'. At the same time, or shortly after, other troops took up position outside the west gate while the now partially demolished east-gate suburbs were reoccupied.

Now completely surrounded, and unable to break free through any of the gates, those within the city had to endure one final indignity. Overlooking the wall on the east side was the partially demolished Church of St Pancras. It provided ideal cover for the troops, while its tower was converted into a gun platform for Parliamentary ordnance that was now able to fire directly into the city. With the defenders unable to occupy even the wall walk on the east side, there was little they could do to prevent further movement of artillery: a number of guns were placed close to the east gate, ready to batter it down. Doubtless, these guns would have opened fire in unison with those close to

The Vicars Close as seen in an early engraving. Here, damage from the siege was less extensive with post-war repairs more quickly undertaken.

the north gate, while a further set of guns were to have been brought into position on the west side. However, it did not require a military genius to predict the outcome: the defenders of the city soon began seeking out terms for submission.

Initially, the Royalists had hoped to submit under the terms offered on 21 December. However, Waller was in such a position of strength that he simply refused anything less than unconditional surrender. To allow them the opportunity to consider their situation more fully, Waller did permit just one concession, 'which was touching a cessation of arms during the treaty'. On the morning of 28 December, a formal surrender was made, but it appears that not all within the city were in agreement. According to Waller's published account, 'Some of the Scottish officers of my Lord Crawford's troops grew into a rage at the strictness of the article concerning the yielding of the horse and arms, and they had vowed rather to die than submit to it; but they seeing our troops ready to receive them without, upon a second thought yielded quietly, whereupon we took possession of the town.'

Chichester was now under occupation, with Waller taking up residence in the Friary, a substantial sixteenth-century house built on the lands of the Franciscan monks (modern-day Priory Park). At the same time, he also took care 'to release and fully set at liberty, all the honest men of the town who had been imprisoned'. They were now the ones who took up positions of authority within the town. As a result of this dramatic change in the fortunes of the city, many of those in the northern two quadrants of the city had much to celebrate. Openly hostile to the occupation were the residents of the Close and others attached to the cathedral and Prebendal School. It was these Royalist sympathisers who appear, on the evening of the occupation, to have laid barrels of gunpowder under Waller's rooms in the Friary. Fortunately for the Parliamentary commander, the plot was discovered. A gunner was suspected, 'but he would confess nothing, and all the gentlemen (noble prisoners) being questioned about it, utterly disclaimed it'.

Some of the troops who had entered the city seem to have been either of the Puritan or Presbyterian persuasion, for they appear to have had an intense dislike of the established Church and its episcopal base. While most of their animosity was directed to the fineries of the cathedral, they may first have fallen upon the market cross in the city centre. Within its eight niches were figures assumed to be those of past bishops. This would not have been to their liking and it seems probable that it was Waller's troops, on their first arrival in the city, who were responsible for the removal and breaking-up of these figures.

Whether it was before or after the attack upon the market cross is not clear, but we are also informed that a number of Waller's troops also entered the cathedral for not-dissimilar reasons. The informant on this occasion is a singularly biased supporter of the Royalist cause, Bruno Reeves (alternatively spelt Ryves), a future dean. He makes a number of claims that may (or may not) be exaggerated, accusing the Parliamentary colonel of taking on the role of spectator as his troops set about desecrating the building. These troops, according to Reeves, not only seized vestments and ornaments but also attacked and destroyed the altar rails and communion table while defiling books and breaking a number of windows. The organ of the cathedral was given special attention, the keys smashed and the pipes pulled down by poleaxes. A further treasure damaged at the time was the painting by Lambert Barnard that had been commissioned by Bishop Sherburne. Depicting many of the cathedral's former bishops, it was an obvious target for an anti-episcopalian mob. Of this particular episode, Reeves gives a full description:

Detail of the lantern at the top of the cross. This was added some time after the end of the Civil War as the original (possibly with statues of past bishops within the niches) was destroyed by Parliamentary soldiers.

These monuments they deface and mangle with their hands and swords, as high as they could reach; and to show their love, and zeal to the protestant religion established in the Church of England, one of those miscreants picked out the eyes of King Edward the Sixth's picture, saying, that all this mischief came from him, when he established the Book of Common Prayer.

The attack was also extended to the altar of the subdeanery:

There they tear the common prayer books, both those belonging to the church, and likewise those, which were left there by devout persons, which did usually frequent divine service . . . they stole the minister's surplice and hood and all the linen serving for the communion; and finding no more plate but the chalice, they stole that too, which they broke in pieces to make a just and equal dividend amongst themselves.

Nor does this appear to have been the end of the affair. Some five or six days later, Sir Arthur Haselrig, one of the five members of parliament whom Charles I attempted to arrest, appeared in Chichester to claim the cathedral's silver plate. Apparently he had learnt of its hiding place, the information passed to him by an 'officer of the church'. Entering the chapter house, he proceeded to tap the

Although drawn in about 1650, this engraving of the cathedral by Daniel King gives little impression of the damage it sustained. The destruction of the north-west tower is unrelated to the siege, this having collapsed in about 1630, with no funds available for its repair.

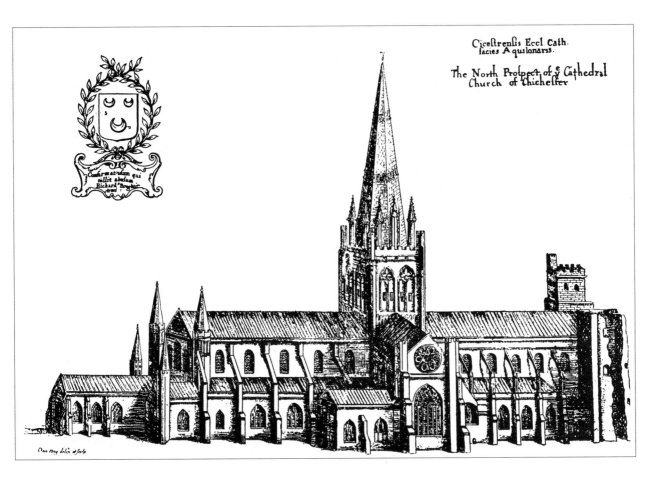

surrounding wooden panels for signs of hollowness. After a short while he cried out, 'There boys! There boys! It rattles.' From a small, hidden cubbyhole were removed a number of highly valuable pieces of plate.

Alexander Hay made suggestions of further damage to Church property. His account, however, dates to 1803 and may well have even less veracity than that of Reeves. To begin with, and ignoring Reeves' given chronology, Hay claims that removal of church plate from the chapter house did not take place until either 1647 or 1648. Hay also draws in the name of Cawley, claiming that it was 'by the procurement of Mr Cawley' that Oliver Cromwell sent Haselrig 'to finish the work of demolition'. In continuing, and not making it clear whether he is referring to events immediately after the siege or the supposed return visit of Haselrig, Hay adds, 'Though the cathedral was the principal object of their fury, the other churches in the city and neighbourhood felt the weight of their zeal.'

Apart from Hay, no other authority appears to claim damage to the various parish churches of the city and it may be necessary to put this assertion down as an exaggeration of likely events.

More significant, and having already progressed considerably by 1647, were both the abolition of Chichester as an episcopal see and the redistribution of cathedral property. This was all initiated in 1646 and part of a national programme that had seen the Church of England adopting a presbyterian style of governance. In other words, all bishops were removed from office and replaced by a form of government at parish level, with provincial and national assemblies subordinate to Parliament. As for income derived from property of the cathedral, much of this between 1646 and 1649 was distributed among sixteen nearby towns and villages. Out of this same income, an annual sum of £150 was also to be set aside to support 'three learned and orthodox divines appointed to officiate within the city of Chichester'. These same individuals, Thomas Hall, John Corbett and William Martin, were also assigned 'convenient places of habitation in dean, chapter's and prebend's houses'.

Outside the Close, a number of changes were made to ecclesiastical arrangements within the city. In particular, the number of parishes was reduced to two, with St Andrew and the subdeanery dividing the city between them. This immediately reduced the necessity of having so many clerics in Chichester, a move also helped by the placing of St Mary's Hospital under the authority of the corporation. At the same time, recognition was given to those who claimed themselves to be Presbyterians or Baptists, with both sects having preachers within the city during this period.

Further changes affected the gentry who had supported the king during the Civil War, many finding themselves divested of their lands and property. Overseeing this particular task was William Cawley, appointed commissioner and sequestrator for the county of Sussex. In carrying out the work he attempted to use it for the better securing of his charity hospital. Originally it had been endowed with lands adjoining, but these were now exchanged for better lands taken from Royalists. In the long term, this proved a less than satisfactory arrangement as, upon the restoration of the monarchy in 1660, these properties were returned to their original owners. At the same time, the originally donated estates could not be retrieved, which meant that the hospital had to be funded by the city corporation.

The Civil War and its aftermath had effectively shattered the social and economic fabric of the city. Among the losers were the gentry and any merchants of the city who had supported the king. In most cases, these individuals had their properties sequestered by William Cawley. Similarly, in the Close, many, particularly those of high office, were summarily dismissed. Some were the holders of prebendaries, the lands that supported these no longer available to those formerly connected with the cathedral. In addition, the canons who made up the chapter also lost office. As for Bruno Reeves, nominated dean in 1646, his office was abolished even before his arrival. Nevertheless, because of his support for the king, he was fined £150. Finally the bishop, Henry King, a rather ineffectual character, having also been dismissed, resided outside the county until invited to return in 1660.

Perhaps the most unwitting sufferers were the inhabitants of the suburbs, many of whom saw their homes completely destroyed during the siege. These included the needle-makers of the east gate suburb. Virtually every house in the area was destroyed and the local needle-making industry never recovered. Instead, needle-makers in Birmingham, Sheffield and Studley benefited. Because of the destruction of this area, the whole system of poor relief broke down, with nineteen nearby parishes contributing to the support of St Pancras.

In their different ways, the dramatic changes in the Close and the loss of the needle-making industry, seriously impacted on the rest of the city. For one thing, there was considerably less money entering the city and far fewer jobs available for the skilled and learned. For this reason it was to take Chichester more than fifty years to recover. In fact, it is not until the eighteenth century that it is possible to detect a return to an earlier level of prosperity.

6

Restoration

The eleven years of republican government (1649–60) that followed the execution of Charles I had one immediate impact upon Chichester. The well-entrenched divisions that had so characterised the city temporarily disappeared. The leaders of the corporation, who had once argued and disputed with the residents of the Close, now found themselves unopposed. The removal of the bishop, dean and chapter meant that they had few outspoken opponents.

This removal of clerical opposition even extended to the churches of the city. Not only were they fewer in number, but also those who led the services had to be approved by the newly empowered county committee that was made up of local gentry who had supported Parliament. Within the committee, the corporation of Chichester had some influence and could therefore successfully lobby for the removal of clergy of whom they disapproved. In 1657 this was the fate of Durrant Hunt, replaced at St Andrew's by the more amenable William Martin.

It would, however, have been most remarkable if the Common Council of the Corporation had remained in unanimity on all issues during these strange and unusual times. Among themselves there was always an element of disagreement, these frequently coming to the fore during elections. The year 1660 was a case in point. Important decisions were about to be made in Parliament, with two contending groups having emerged within the city. At the head of one of these was William Burry, the mayor. As their candidate for Parliament, this group had chosen William Cawley. Opposed to them was a group of citizens who wished to see the election of John Farrington, an important merchant who lived in South Street. As much as anything, the dispute was one of personality; there was no marked difference between Cawley and Farrington in terms of their overall outlook.

In the event, it was William Cawley who won the election, but the method by which he gained victory was singularly flawed. William Burry, in overseeing the election arrangements, had restricted voting only to those who were either on the common council or had been appointed by the corporation as freemen of the city. In other words, most of those allowed to vote were part of the corporation clique, while those not allowed to vote were the outsiders. However, the rigging of the ballot was to do the city little good. The Convention Parliament, as it was known, in voting for the return of the monarchy, also sealed the fate of William Cawley. As a 'regicide', he now had little future in a land shortly to witness the crowning of Charles II. Immediately, he fled to Switzerland where he died six years later. Supposedly he was buried in the city of Vevey but a strong local tradition holds that his body was returned to Chichester. In an act apparently overseen by his son, William, the body was finally laid to rest under the floor of the Cawley almshouse chapel. Confirmation of this was claimed in 1816 when a tomb was discovered during the installation of a water pipe. The remains of three people were found, one wrapped in a sheet of lead and supposed to be William Cawley.

With the return of the monarchy came also a reinvigorated Close. For the past decade it had been without its traditional residents and the buildings of the area either rented out or allowed to decay. Within a few months, however, the old administrative structure headed by the bishop had been re-established. The two-parish system was abolished and all the standing churches provided with a clergyman. At St Andrew's this included the removal of William Martin and the return of Durrant Hunt, the new order requiring men whose belief in the episcopacy was unquestioning.

The bust of Charles I. Following the destruction of the figures within the larger niches of the cross, a bust of Charles I was placed in the remodelled niche that faces East Street. The current occupant of this same niche is not the original bust but a fibreglass replica.

Among those who now took up residence in the Close was Henry King, reinstalled as bishop. He had a huge task ahead of him. Not only had he to re-establish the authority of his office but he had also to attend to a cathedral much in need of repair. Since the Reformation, there was little money available for the general upkeep of the building, and the crisis of the Civil War had only added to the problem. Demanding particular attention were the great east window and the large window in the south transept, both of which had been shattered at the time of the siege. In addition, the roof of the sub-deanery was so decayed as to be dangerous for those attending parish service, and the north-west tower required rebuilding following a partial collapse some time around the mid-1630s.

To bring about some improvement to the cathedral, King initiated a fund-raising campaign that had only limited success. Even with the sale of a substantial amount of cathedral plate, less than £2,000 was eventually raised. It was insufficient, resulting in only the most urgent repairs being undertaken. This undoubtedly included the subdeanery roof but it could include neither a full repair of the north-west tower nor restoration of the two great windows. Instead, the tower was reduced in height and capped, and the east window was provided with wood rather than stone mullions; the weakened mullions of the south transept window were secured through judicial use of wooden props.

As well as for the cathedral, additional expenditure was needed on repair of buildings in the Close. Among them was the palace, still not repaired since the damage it had sustained during the siege. It is generally assumed that the south-east wing was built during this period. A second building, the deanery, had been much more seriously damaged and no immediate funds could be found for its repair, so that the dean had to be found alternative accommodation. As for the chancellor's house, having been completely destroyed, it was never rebuilt, the site being left untouched for many years.

In failing to achieve any real improvement in the state of the cathedral and many houses of the Close, King was also fighting a losing battle in his attempt at re-establishing the former authority of the Church within the city. Leading members of the corporation were as much opposed to the established Church as they had ever been. Furthermore, a number were prepared to demonstrate their opposition by encouraging the growth of non-conformist sects. Among them was John Farrington, the failed candidate during the election for the Convention Parliament. Residing in South Street, his family had thrown their doors open to those non-conformists who believed in spiritual regeneration through adult baptism. Known, therefore, as Baptists, they were to erect a chapel in Eastgate Square in 1671 at a cost of £14 5s.

Less appealing to the richer merchants of the city (but favoured by the artisans) was a second non-conformist sect, that of the Quakers. Founded by George Fox in 1650, it quickly became established in Chichester. At the time of Fox's visit to the city in 1652, he was able to recall in his journal that 'there were many professors [believers]'. As with the Baptists, early meetings were held in private houses, among them John Smith's 'high red house' in St Pancras and Margaret Wilkinson's in North Street. From 1673, however, the Quakers acquired a separate meeting-house, attached to a burial ground in the Hornet. This land was acquired from Rumboldswyke yeoman, William Cooper, on a thousand-year lease at an annual rent of 4d.

The existence of a vibrant Quaker community in Chichester was one further thorn in the side of the established Church. Frequent confrontations would occur, with attacks on Quaker meeting-houses not unusual. At the same time, Quakers themselves also entered Anglican churches during service and attempted a discourse. On one such occasion, it led to the imprisonment and death of James Larbec, one of their number. He appears to have entered the cathedral and tackled one of the priests on matters of 'false doctrine'. Subsequently committed to prison, he was beaten and bruised 'and dyed within a few days' of being set free.

Further placing the Quakers in direct opposition to many of those in the established Church was the support they gave freely to the Duke of

Monmouth in a campaign of opposition to the king. Many of the issues revolved around the position of Catholicism in the country with Parliament having taken a strong stand against those who claimed sympathy with its ideals. In February 1679, the Duke of Monmouth, in building up support for a recall of Parliament, made a visit to Chichester. Among those he met was a representative of the local Quaker community. A description of this meeting was sent to the Archbishop of Canterbury:

> A tobacco-pipe maker here in Chichester came to visit the Duke, and was introduced by the Lord Grey under the character of a very honest man – this noble tradesman was a Quaker. The Duke graciously received him and talked to him with his hat off, the Quaker with his hat on. The Duke asked him what their numbers were that frequented their meetings. The Quaker answered about 100, but we are all for thee, said the Quaker. Are you disturbed at your meetings, said the Duke. No, said the Quaker, we are not molested.

The archbishop's informant was the newly appointed bishop, Guy Carleton (1678–85). He was one of the more intransigent holders of that office and was in marked contrast to Henry King, who had died in 1670. The latter expected his clergy to 'lay controversy asleep' whereas Carleton would never forget the slightest insult against him. Such was his temper that he even came to blows with one of his own legal officers, the chancellor. This was in the cathedral during an important hearing, the bishop using his crozier as if it were a club. However, Carleton's real enemy while at Chichester was the cathedral precentor, Dr Henry Edes. He was another whom the bishop informed upon as a dangerous Monmouth supporter. Edes, at the time of Monmouth's visit in 1679, had not only dined with the Duke but had also acted as his chaplain. Because of these activities, the bishop claimed of Edes that he was neither 'towards the king' nor 'really a cordial son of the Church of England'.

In an earlier attempt to undermine Edes' position, Carleton attempted to discover more about his general activities, appointing his most loyal supporter, Oliver Whitby, to act as a spy. This, at least, appears to be the view of those who supported Edes, considering Whitby to be particularly favoured by the bishop. On one occasion Whitby, who was both archdeacon and *custos* of St Mary's Hospital, was not pressed for a £20 donation to the fund for restoring the cathedral. On all other clerics this payment had been mandatory and Whitby's non-payment was put down to the bishop having found Whitby 'so serviceable in furthering his designs upon us'.

As it happens, Edes was to take his revenge on Whitby, but not until Whitby's death during the summer of 1679. With the hospital needing a new *custos*, Edes himself was appointed to the position and immediately set about examining the work of his predecessor. In doing so, he claimed to have discovered that Whitby deliberately neglected the upkeep of the building and that he had misappropriated to himself money that might otherwise have been spent on these repairs. An action in the Court of Chancery was brought against the executors of Whitby's will, with judgment given against the former *custos*. At this point, Carleton attempted to intervene, writing to the Archbishop of Canterbury in support of 'widow Whitby's claims'. This proved of little avail, for although the Archbishop rejected many of Ede's claims, he still required Ann Whitby, the widow, to pay over to St Mary's Hospital the sum of £171 14s 8d. This was duly undertaken 'in the chappell of the hospital' on 2 April 1682. Going some way to support the supposition that this action was a product of revenge was the fact that the court case cost the much higher sum of £277 12s 5d. This amount had to be paid by the hospital and not by Henry Edes himself.

While the hospital suffered in one way, it also gained from the appointment of the new *custos*. Having noted that the building was in much need of repair, he then did something about it. While claims were being made against the Whitby family, work was also going ahead on improving conditions within the hospital. Most important was construction of the four brick chimney stacks over the fireplaces in each of the living areas. One of these stacks bears not only the date 1680 but also the initials 'HE'. It may also have been at this time that the eight separate living areas were created, the residents previously living in the open aisle of the hallway.

It was another of Carleton's spies who provided information against the city's leading non-conformist, Richard Farrington. In 1681 Farrington was accused of being one of many citizens of Chichester who were 'in great readiness for rebellion'. As supposed evidence of this, Carleton was informed that Farrington's house in South Street was being used as an arms store. Carleton authorised a raid upon the house but no weapons were found. For this, Carleton had a ready excuse, claiming that the man leading the search was also a dissenter and had been responsible for warning Farrington of the impending raid.

Interior of St Mary's Hospital. Improvements to the hospital were undertaken during the time that Henry Edes was *custos*. Among these alterations was the introduction of brick chimneystacks over the fireplaces, with the one in the foreground bearing the monogram 'HE'.

Carleton's informant on that occasion may well have been Richard Habin. He was one of several informants against dissenters, frequently bringing information to the bishop. Another of his activities was that of forcing his way into both Quaker and Baptist meetings for the purpose of breaking them up. The Quakers' own records for Chichester show that such occurrences were quite frequent. As for Richard Habin, his activities were brought to a sudden end in August 1682 when he was attacked in South Street. Possibly he was engaged in spying on the Farrington household, for it was John Davies, Farrington's coachman, who carried out the attack. By all accounts, the affair was extremely bloody, with Habin seeking refuge in the Bishop's Palace where he was to die of his injuries. The bishop immediately assumed that Farrington had orchestrated the attack and attempted to bring sufficient evidence to ensure a successful prosecution. Although brought to trial, Farrington was acquitted.

Interestingly enough, despite Carleton's fears, the support for Monmouth rapidly dissipated in 1685 when the Duke turned from parliamentary opposition to full-blooded uprising. Monmouth's failed attempt to capture the throne seems to have generated little sympathy in Chichester, with only one local man even remotely connected with the affair. This was John Sherer who, following imprisonment at Portsmouth, was examined by agents employed by the notorious Judge Jeffreys. No hard evidence was found against him and Sherer escaped the 'Bloody Assizes' that later committed 600 to the gallows.

For his part, Carleton had quite simply confused a genuine upsurge of popular feeling against the Catholic heir to the throne with a belief in the nation being on the verge of another civil war. In Parliament, the emergent Whig party represented these quite legitimate feelings. For them, a violent overthrow of the accepted monarch was not part of their creed. Matters obviously changed in 1688 when James II's unconstitutional rule led to an invitation to the Duke of Orange to land an army in England. The instant collapse of the old order was a contest without bloodshed, leading to a ready acceptance of the new situation. To mark the event in Chichester, a proclamation was read at the city cross, celebrations went on throughout the night and members of the corporation formed a club to celebrate the event permanently. On the other hand, Bishop Carleton, who had died in 1685, probably turned in his grave.

For the city as a whole, the foreshortened reign of James II did produce one small advantage. This was the granting of a further charter, that of 1685, which clarified the authority of the corporation within the city and the continued independence of the Close. Earlier in the century the clergy of the Close and the burgesses of the remainder of the city had clashed over this particular issue. The problem had been created in 1618 by an earlier charter, in which the corporation had been given the authority it sought, only to have it revoked by the Privy Council decision of 1635. While the new charter of 1685 confirmed that the common council of the corporation should have power to make laws and statutes, dispose of lands, impose fines and imprison offenders, it did affirm the independence of the Close. It specifically declared that the mayor, aldermen, justice and officers of the council should in no way exercise any authority within the cathedral church or Close. While it must be accepted that this was a blow to the council, it did ensure that, after fifty years of confusion, the matter was now laid to rest. The charter, which was the most detailed of all charters given to the city, also named the various officers of the city (including the high sheriff, port reeve, coroner, constable, chamberlain, recorder and town clerk), and ordered that a mayor and bailiff be annually elected by the common council assembled at the Guildhall on the Monday before the feast of St Michael.

In contrast to the trials and tribulations of those living in the Close, the merchants and traders of the city were beginning to witness an upturn in their fortunes. At the heart of this was the existence of the nearby harbour and the plentiful supply of locally grown wheat and barley. The harbour, of course, is that expanse of water whose name still confuses the occasional visitor. In contrast with other harbours, the city for which it is named lies some miles beyond its perimeter. Specifically, as set out in 1680, the perimeters of that harbour were,

> from the Hermitage-bridge (near Emsworth) on the further confines of Sussex, westward from thence down the whole channel or river running southward to the harbour's mouth, called Hormouth – from thence in a line eastward to Selsea hill – thence eastward to Pagham-point, at the mouth of Undering harbour – thence to the most eastern part of the parish of Felpham, in the county of Sussex aforesaid – so back again to Hormouth, and so by the river north-east to the key commonly known and called by the name of Dell-key, situated within the parish of Appledram.

Despite its distance from the city, all vessels using its constituent quays and jetties were recorded in the port and customs books of the city. More importantly, merchants using these facilities, particularly Dell Quay, frequently centred their activities upon the city. It was this that was bringing most of the additional wealth into Chichester.

The value of Chichester Harbour clearly pre-dates the mid-seventeenth century, but in earlier years it had served as a poor rival to Rye and other nearby ports. The development of the corn trade reversed the situation, with Chichester taking on the role of regional entrepôt, large quantities of local produce being stored here and then exported to a variety of foreign and domestic locations. A significant landmark in the growth of this trade was the provisioning of Cromwell's army in Ireland. Between 1650 and 1652, vessels using Chichester Harbour were placed on government con-tracts, conveying considerable quantities of malt and wheat. Putting exports to Ireland aside, the average number of ships using the port of Chichester during the third quarter of the seventeenth century was approximately two per week. It was a number that was to double by the beginning of the following century.

Two small blips in the surge towards renewed prosperity seem to have occurred both in 1659 and the mid-1660s. These were years of epidemic disease with that of 1659 known as 'the little plague'. It was not, as it happens, of the bubonic or pneumonic variety, but more likely a serious outbreak of influenza. Across the city of Chichester it claimed over a hundred lives, a conclusion based on the burial register of the subdeanery. In that year there were 144 burials, this figure three times the norm.

Potentially more serious was the arrival of plague in 1665. This was the year in which thousands died in London, the disease also attacking many towns and villages in the south of England. For a short time, for instance, Portsmouth was recording some fifteen plague victims every day. As for its effect on Chichester, this is open to question. One apocryphal account claims that in this particular year the mayor, following a number of deaths, ordered the city into quarantine. A cordon was drawn around the walls while nearby villagers were asked to leave fresh provisions outside the cordoned area for later collection. Although it is a good story, there is no conclusive evidence that the city succumbed to the plague on that occasion. The most likely source of evidence, the parish burial registers, is less than conclusive. Some fail to record any burials while others only a very small number. Even the subdeanery records a mere fifteen burials, a surprisingly low number. A large gap on the page for that year might suggest space having been set aside for a number of subsequently unrecorded burials – but this is mere conjecture. Another possibility is that plague struck in the following year. Some eighty-six burials are recorded in the subdeanery register for that year. Even this seems a low number and it may well be that Chichester was one of the few towns in the south that remained free of the disease.

Regardless of the effects of plague, the growth of the city economy continued. Daniel Defoe, who visited the city in 1722, tells of how the wheat trade was by then being developed into something much more sophisticated than mere trans-shipment: '. . . some money'd men of Chichester, Emsworth and other places adjacent, have join'd their stocks together, built large granaries near the Crook, where the vessels come up, and here they buy and lay up all the corn which the country on that side can spare; and having good mills in the neighbourhood, they grind and dress the corn, and send it to London in the meal about by Long Sea, as they call it.' In other words, the merchants of the city were increasing their profits through the employment of a number of mills for the purpose of processing corn and wheat.

The outward signs of Chichester's increasing prosperity are easy to detect. A number of the city's finer houses were built during this period, in particular Westgate (since renamed Edes' House), Pallant and a new house in South Street for the Farrington family. Of these three houses, only the one for the Farrington family no longer exists; it was an extremely large building on the site once occupied by the Odeon cinema and subsequently Iceland food store.

John Edes, the nephew of the Monmouth sympathiser, built Westgate House. It appears that he built it with his wife, Hannah, and it is for this reason that the house displays the monogram 'JHE' next to the completion date of 1696. A further clue to its original ownership is the lead drainpipes, which simply carry the initials 'HE'. That John Edes was able to finance such a substantial building was a result of his owning lands in Chidham and possibly a malting in Chichester. Westgate House is a fine, five-bayed, two-storey building, once (wrongly) attributed to Christopher Wren. Among those impressed with its style was Celia Fiennes, who visited the city in 1696. From the top of the cathedral tower, of which she confides there were '260 old steps', she declares, 'You may see the whole town, there are three or four good new houses (one is the Dean's, Mr Edds, a very good man).' Unfortunately she is incorrect as to the ownership of the house, but she does confirm its completion by the time of her visit together with the existence of a number of other newly built houses.

As for Pallant House, Henry Peckham, a wine merchant and active Tory politician, completed this in 1713. Given that he was known as 'Lisbon' Peckham, it is usually assumed that his wealth was garnered from the Portuguese wine trade. The area in which the new house was situated was an ideal location for Peckham, there being several maltings and small breweries located nearby. Every-thing associated with the house was of the highest standard and Peckham stamped his affinities on the building with the inclusion of royal arms on the keystones.

Serving the needs of Chichester's expanding community of affluence were a number of skilled artisans who were moving into the town during this same period. Several groups of these artisans became so numerous as to be able to form guilds that gave them legal protection against unskilled interlopers. Of particular note were the free tailors (incorporated as a guild in 1685); barbers and glaziers (1685); cutlers and blacksmiths (1686); saddlers, rope-makers, stationers and bookbinders (1686), glovers (1687) and white tawers (1687). The latter were leather-makers who used a process of soaking hides in a solution of alum and salt. Among tradesmen issuing

Pallant House, one of a small group of brick houses built in the city during the early years of the eighteenth century. Today it contributes to the city as an art gallery with frequently changing exhibitions.

trade tokens during this period were grocers, butchers, mercers and cordwainers.

A final product of these increasing signs of affluence was the founding of the Oliver Whitby School in West Street. A charity school established 'for the maintenance of a master and 12 poor boys' it was the outcome of a bequest made by Oliver Whitby (1664–1702) in his will. This was signed on 16 February 1702, just three days before his death. This particular Oliver was the son of the Oliver Whitby who had clashed with Henry Edes some twenty years earlier. Having entered into the legal profession, the younger Oliver Whitby acquired land in West Wittering, which was used to provide a permanent endowment for the school.

It was not until 1712 that the trustees were able to embark on the great project as, before that date, insufficient capital had been accumulated. By that particular year, however, some £1,000 was available and it was this sum that was used to acquire the necessary equipment and materials. To begin with, the school building was merely leased, with an eventual purchase made in 1721. Shortly after the purchase, a roof tablet was added, facing towards the street and proclaiming, 'charity school founded by Oliver Whitby, Esq., AD 1702'. The institution was to survive over two hundred years, eventually moving into the much larger premises that are currently occupied by the Army and Navy stores.

Another early eighteenth-century addition to the city was the Oliver Whitby School, established in West Street. However the school building seen here was constructed in 1904. Nowadays, it is the Army and Navy Stores.

7

Transformation

Despite the evident signs of progress, Chichester was not exactly among the nation's wealthiest cities during the early part of the eighteenth century. While a few grand houses had certainly been constructed, most of the city's housing stock was aged and decayed. As for the streets, they were in an appalling condition, quagmires in winter and heavily rutted during summer. Matters were made no better by the absence of adequate lighting, the lack of street cleaners and a system of policing based on each parish appointing one luckless individual to take on this task each year. With the exception of improved policing, these were the aspects of the city that were to undergo considerable improvement during the early Georgian years.

Financing this transformation of the city was the continuing success of Chichester-based merchants. The harbour had become the busiest port in the county and was one of the largest in England for the export of grain and flour. A visible statement of the increased importance of the area for the purpose of processing corn and wheat was the number of windmills that were soon littering the landscape. Some encroached virtually into the city, such as those located at St James and Portfield (rebuilt 1721) while there were two on the Broyle. Other newly built or refurbished mills were at Dell Quay and Westhampnett.

The weekly markets were a further important factor in generating money for the transformation of the city. Increasing numbers of cattle, sheep and horses were brought into the city for sale, this also creating a need for a number of slaughterhouses. By about 1750, there were at least seven tucked away from the central area of the city, with three in Chapel Street and others in the Pallants and St Martin's. As well as the cattle market, the fish shambles in South Street and the Saturday corn market in North Street were also busy.

In trying to understand the poor and backward state of the city at the beginning of the century, there is no better starting point than the recorded memories of James Spershott. Born in 1710, the son of Charles and Mary Spershott of Shopwyke Manor Farm, he became a member of the local Baptist community and was appointed pastor in 1756. Towards the end of his life, he chose to write down his thoughts on the changes taking place,

giving particular attention to the state of the city when he was in his early teenage years:

> When I was young the city had a very mean appearance in comparison of what it has since arrived to. The buildings were in general very low, very old, and their fronts framed with timber which lay bare to the weather, and had a step down from the street to the ground floor, and many of them over the first floor projected further into the street. The shops in general had shutters to let up and down, and no other enclosure, but were quite open in daytime, and the penthouse so low that a man could hang up the upper shutters with his hands.

These were the opening remarks of his observations, Spershott contrasting what he had seen as a teenager with the city of the 1780s. By then, it had banished open-fronted shops and had seen many of its buildings refaced and improved. Referring back to his earlier years, Spershott remarked,

> There were very few houses even in the main streets that had solid brick fronts except such as appeared to have been built within a few years back. For a specimen, I note this to be at the Cross: the house at the southeast corner was new, built AD 1709. The other three corners were of the old, low, timber built sort.

An eighteenth-century print of Chichester that gives a clear impression of the tremendous building resurgence that took place during that particular century. A great number of new brick buildings are to be noted. Earliest of these, and pre-dating the start of the eighteenth century, is Westgate House (the tall building to the left). Still in need of considerable attention is the cathedral, its partially collapsed west tower an obvious scar on the city's skyline.

Turning his attention to the four main streets, he went into more detail as to the generally unmodernised condition of most buildings:

> In the North Street there were two or three houses with sash windows. The West Street had none.

As for South Street, he drew attention to one particular building, the house of the Farrington family. Lady Farrington, the widow of Sir Richard, occupied this at the time. Spershott described it as,

> Lady Farrington's large new house nearly opposite the Canon Gate which, some years after her decease, Mr Baker and Mr Bennet purchased, at a low rate, intending to pull it down and get money by selling the materials, but having taken down one room in width at the north end and finding their mistake in it closed it up again which was the cause of the front being so disfigured.

Lady Farrington, as a memorial to her husband, had given the city a clock with three faces, which was placed on the market cross. This was in 1723 and was seen by many as a disfigurement to a fine medieval building. Spershott was among them:

> The Cross clock, the gift of Lady Farrington, was set up upon the top of the centre pillar of the Cross in a large four-square case with three dial plates, close under where the bell now hangs, which had a very heavy awkward appearance and greatly disfigured the Cross, yet stood so for more than twenty years.

If buildings and other features in the city's main streets were poor, things were even worse in the minor roads and sidewalks. Spershott continued,

> The back lanes had a very mean appearance, but few houses and bad ones. The Little London in particular, which now appears so gay, had only a few old houses as it were under ground, the street not pitched but very dirty with deep cart ruts.

Of the Pallants, this

> . . . had a few houses of the better sort but in general were very old and consisted much of malt houses. There was formerly, as I have been informed, a leather market kept, and in the centre a market house for that purpose.

As for the streets in general, they

> . . . had no paved foot-walks, only a broad stone or two at most of the doors.

A key building in Chichester's eighteenth-century resurgence was the Deanery of 1725.

Elsewhere,

> The North walls were in a very broken, ragged condition, some places high, some low and over run with ivy like as the southeast wall now is, and the walk very rough and uneven.
>
> The road from the Northgate to the new Broyle was deep, dirty, narrow and crooked; great part of it not wide enough for two carriages to pass each other and foot people went over styles into the fields.

One particular building that marks the beginning of Chichester's renaissance was the rebuilt deanery. The earlier building, despite some half-hearted attempts at repair and restoration, had served as a stark reminder of the darkest days of the Civil War. It had never been returned to its former glory and should have been demolished many years earlier. In 1725, however, under Dean Thomas Sherlock, it was completely rebuilt. Of brick construction, it was described by Ian Nairn in the Buildings of England series, as 'cheerfully rustic'. In parallel with the rebuilding of the deanery, work was also in hand upon the palace, Bishop Edward Waddington (1724–31) overseeing a complete renewal of the central block.

Of considerably greater significance was the construction of a new council-house, undertaken between 1729 and 1733. A fine baroque building designed by the London architect Roger Morris, it was to become one of the city's showpieces. It was here that the common council was to hold its future meetings, a simple council chamber incorporated into the first floor. Soon after completion of the new building, the earlier council-house was demolished, this described by Spershott in his litany of ageing buildings that

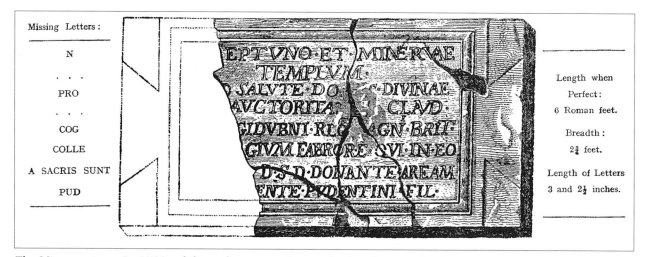

Missing Letters:

N

. . .

PRO

. . .

COG

COLLE

A SACRIS SUNT

PUD

Length when
Perfect:
6 Roman feet.

Breadth:
2¾ feet.

Length of Letters
3 and 2½ inches.

The Minerva stone. In 1723, while workmen were laying the foundations of a house at the corner of North Street and Lion Street, they uncovered a slab of stone that provides an interesting insight into Roman Chichester. Unfortunately, only part of the stone was recovered, this taken to Goodwood where it was restored by the Duke of Richmond. Assuming that the correct missing letters were added at this time, then the inscription reads: To Neptune and Minerva, for the welfare of the divine house by the authority of Tiberius Claudius Cogidubnus, King Imperial Legate in Britain, the guild of smiths [or shipwrights] and those therein gave this temple from their own resources . . . the son of Pudentinus giving this site. Cogidubnus is normally associated with the palace at Fishbourne while the reference to a temple would suggest that this particular building, dedicated to Neptune and Minerva, stood in this same area of the city. Following the restoration of the stone, it was eventually returned to Chichester and is now mounted on the wall outside the Council House in North Street.

had so characterised the city on the eve of its eighteenth century renaissance. Standing on North Street, close to the site of the new building,

> It was pretty long from south to north, one side of it was close to the gutter in the middle of the street and the other within about six or seven feet of the houses. It stood upon posts or framed timbers, panelled up about breast high. It had an entrance on each side, but its chief entrance was at the south end about half its width next the houses, the other half being the cage which was boarded up breast high and wood bars perpendicular above. Behind the cage was the stairs up into the council chamber, which was low and had low old windows. It was a very old building. The north end was nearly opposite the south end of the new market house.

A major contributor to the financing of the new council-house was Charles, 2nd Duke of Richmond (1701–50) whose family had acquired Goodwood Mansion in 1692. Throughout the eighteenth century the dukes of Richmond were closely associated with the city, the 2nd Duke briefly serving as MP for Chichester and, on two later occasions, mayor. In 1746, as a further gift to the city, he was to underwrite all costs connected with a restoration of the market cross. This included the removal of Lady Farrington's clock and its replacement by a four-faced timepiece that was more in keeping with its surroundings.

In 1783 the council-house itself was extended by the provision of an east wing. Designed by James Wyatt (1746–1813), this was the assembly room, by which title the building is more commonly known. An assembly room was an important feature of eighteenth-century fashionable life for it was here that society gathered. The room itself was of oblong shape, measuring 60ft by 38ft, and was well lit, with a raised platform to the east. The new room replaced the old assembly room that had been situated in North Pallant and it was here that regular programmes of evening concerts were organised. So successful did these become that an organ was added to the room, the first organ concert, featuring concertos by Handel and Corelli, taking place on 4 November 1791.

Another landmark building was the city's first purpose-built theatre. Erected in 1791 at an approximate cost of £1,000, it replaced an earlier theatre that had existed within a converted malt-house. Situated on the corner of South Street and Theatre Lane, the new theatre had its official opening in May 1792 with a performance of *The Siege of Belgrade*.

The Council House, another particularly important building dating from the eighteenth century. Constructed between 1731 and 1733, it had the Assembly Rooms added to it some fifty years later.

Two further eighteenth-century buildings that should not go unrecorded were meeting-houses built by two of the city's dissenting sects. The first of these, built in 1721, was a Presbyterian chapel in Baffin's Lane, on the site of their earlier chapel. Similarly, the General Baptists also built a new chapel, on the site of their previous chapel in Eastgate. The Presbyterian chapel appears to have gained much of its congregation from those visiting the city, particularly locally billeted soldiers from Scottish regiments.

Paralleling construction of both public buildings and larger residences were a number of medium-sized town houses. These replaced a good many more of the ageing and decaying structures that Spershott had highlighted. Of particular note, and still surviving from the mid-eighteenth century, are Mariott House (West Street), Friary Gate (Priory Road) and East Pallant House. To this list, and from slightly later in the century, can be added Richmond House (South Street), the Ship Hotel (North Street) and 15 West Street. Finally, and part of a constant programme of building and rebuilding, were groups of smaller houses that were often built in terrace form. Among the finest of these are those of East Pallant, with others to be found in Little London and Northgate.

Situated at the corner of South Street and Theatre Lane is Chichester's first purpose-built theatre, which was completed in 1791. The building is currently occupied by a pasta and pizza restaurant called Zizzi.

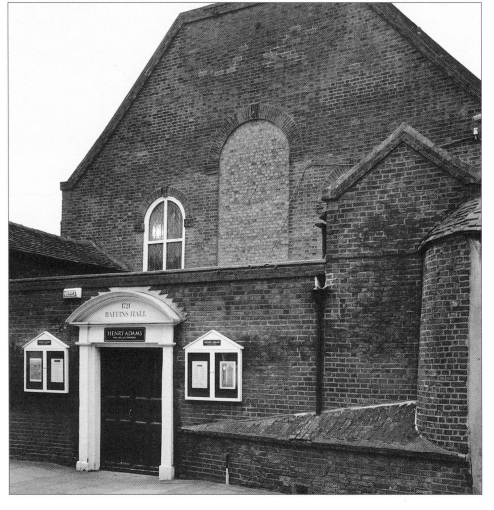

The Presbyterian chapel in Baffin's Lane, completed in 1721.

Apart from the complete replacement of earlier buildings others remained standing but were given either an entirely new façade or a series of alterations to the street frontage. In East Street, the Old Punch House (Royal Arms) is a substantial sixteenth-century building with the exterior offering no clues as to such a date. This was because it was completely refaced in the eighteenth century with only a finely decorated plaster ceiling and wood panelling on the inside proving the building to be of a much earlier provenance. On the other hand, the late-seventeenth-century North Walls House (43 North Street) has simply been given a series of external additions, including a fine porch and door, together with a first-floor bow-window.

A small improvement to the state of the streets had been undertaken in 1774 but this work was limited, financed solely by the city's two Members of Parliament. Indeed, the corporation depended heavily on individual householders maintaining and cleaning the pavements and roads immediately adjacent to the properties they owned. Anything more ambitious would require a considerable increase in the rates, something that the corporation was keen to avoid. For this reason, some members of the corporation favoured the imposition of tolls to be collected from those passing through the city gates.

It seems likely, however, that the continuing decline in the state of the streets and constant misuse to which they were being put, forced a sufficient number of corporation members to rethink their position. This led to the establishment of a new body, the Board of Paving Commissioners, with powers dedicated to the improvement of streets and which would finally terminate a blight that had long overshadowed the character of the city.

Two examples of the many fine Georgian period entrances that are to be found throughout the city.

Established in 1791, it assumed responsibility for a wide range of matters relating to the streets of Chichester, a role it continued to perform until 1872.

The parliamentary act that created the new board gives a number of clues as to the state of the streets at this time. Apart from a general need to maintain and repair the footways, pave the roads and remove considerable amounts of accumulated filth, the act referred to a number of nuisances. Many house owners, for instance, appear to have extended their property rights on to the streets through the construction of bow-windows and sheds and the planting of inappropriately placed trees. As for the footpaths, these were unsafe at night, being both uneven and lacking in permanent lighting. During the daytime, matters were no better, with sledges, sedan chairs and carriages often pushing pedestrians to one side, and tradesmen creating further hazards by slaughtering beasts and shoeing horses on these same thoroughfares. For these, and a number of other offences, the new act permitted the commissioners to impose fines.

Membership of the new Chichester board was restricted to those citizens with property to the value of at least £20. This, in itself, had created a degree of controversy, with the Duke of Richmond supporting a proposition that 'property does not imply fitness' to be a commissioner. Surprisingly for a man of wealth, Richmond was a noted radical who firmly believed in a widened suffrage and the election of annual parliaments. Given the opportunity to address members of the corporation, he declared that all members, regardless of the property that they owned, should automatically be members of the board, their election to the corporation being, in his view, a sufficient qualification. While he gained some support from those who made up the common council of the corporation, his proposal was, nevertheless, defeated.

The first meeting of the new board took place on the morning of 1 July 1791 at the 'Swan' in East Street. Over eighty citizens were present, each one taking an oath that would allow him to act officially in the capacity of commissioner. Once these formalities were complete, a chairman was appointed. The chosen individual was Loftus Nunn, mayor of the corporation. This was an obvious choice, as the commissioners would have to work closely with the corporation. Furthermore, upon the retirement of each mayor, the new mayor was to be promptly elected to chair the board. Thus, in 1792, Robert Quennal replaced Loftus Nunn. Three other items of business were transacted at this first meeting: the appointment of Thomas Rhoades as clerk; the appointment of the bankers Messrs Griffiths, Chaldecott and Drew as treasurers and the agreement to raise a loan of not more than £3,000. The loan was to be secured against future sums of money to be raised through the rates while allowing the commissioners to begin the task of improving the city.

A second meeting was held only four days later, in which the commissioners agreed to employ a scavenger, whose task was regularly to sweep the streets clean of all dirt and other nuisances. At the same time John Murray of Portsmouth was appointed Surveyor of Pavements. Indeed, he might be regarded as Chichester's first civil engineer, given that his remit was to oversee the laying down of new pavements and drains throughout the city. He was to be allowed a salary set at 5 per cent of all money expended on repairing and paving.

Further meetings soon followed, the commissioners demonstrating a level of dynamism rarely equalled in Chichester's constitutional history. In these following meetings, several of their number agreed to make the necessary loans at an interest rate of 4 per cent, with the sum of £3,000 available within two weeks. Those responsible for the loans were Mary Frankland (£2,000), Joseph Baker (£500), Capt Henry Chadds (£300), George Tufnell (£100), Elizabeth Ferth (£100). The availability of this money meant that a few immediate debts could be paid, most pressing the sum of £542 which had to paid to William Fowler, the solicitor employed in overseeing the passing of the act. As for the collection of rates that would ensure repayment to lenders, this was finalised in November. The amount to be collected was set at 9*d* in the pound, with George Broadbridge the appointed collector.

The next task was that of employing builders who would carry out the work overseen by John Murray. It appears that, despite a series of newspaper advertisements, only William Ellis and James Bailey of Portsmouth came forward. As a result, their tender was accepted and contracts were signed at the end of September. The terms were quite simple: Ellis and Bailey were to be responsible 'for paving the city of Chichester and farming the dung soils &c in the streets, lanes &c of the same'. The first task given them was that of repairing the public water pump situated in St Martin's Square, which had been out of action for several months.

Ellis and Bailey started work on repairing the pavements in April, beginning in West Street. The commissioners determined that the highest standards should be adopted, with Aberdeen stone used for the pavements, while the curbs were to be edged with Purbeck marble. At the same time, new steps were built at the entrance to each house fronting West Street, with each individual owner expected to meet the cost (or the new steps would be removed). However, in carrying out this work, Ellis and Bailey may have fallen below the standards expected of them: it appears that they attempted to replace some of the Aberdeen and Purbeck stone with material of a lesser value. But the matter appears to have been quickly resolved, and Ellis and Bailey were employed upon the repairing of East Street throughout May and much of June before moving on to South Street. By the autumn of 1793, all four main streets had been completed, together with St Martin's Square and Street, Friar Lane, Little London and Shamble Alley.

A further controversy arose over the removal of various street obstructions. In June 1792 the board 'ordered that all signs, sign posts and sign irons projecting into or standing or being in any one of the Streets, Lanes and Public Way or Passages within the walls of this city be taken down on or before 15th July next'. A number of innkeepers challenged this instruction, which led to the board's seeking legal advice. The board's solicitor had no doubt as to the legality of their order, with notices served in September 1792 on the owners of the Swan (where the earliest meetings of the board had taken place) and the Dolphin. These were followed in December by a further set of notices served on the owners and occupiers of the Bell, the Bell and

White Hart, the King's Arms, the Little Anchor, the Wheat Sheaf, the George, the Sun, the Royal Oak and the Great Anchor. Those that had still failed to comply by March 1793 had their signs forcibly taken down, the board employing a carpenter, smith and bricklayer for this purpose.

Another contentious issue was that of property owners who had extended their property on to the streets about to be paved; to address this problem, it was required that a number of the newly fashionable bow-windows and other abutments be removed. In order to clarify the matter it was specifically declared, by order of 13 April 1793, that

> No Pent House shall be suffered to remain that projects more than 2 feet over the footways and that no cantilever shall be suffered to remain that projects further than 18 inches where the footway is 7 feet wide or upwards, and that no Bow window shall project more than 14 inches where the footway is less than 7 feet wide and of the width of 6 feet and that no Bow window shall project more than the sixth part of the footway where the same is less than 6 feet wide . . .

The Royal Arms, one of numerous buildings refronted in the eighteenth century. Its exterior now gives few clues as to its much earlier origins.

Not surprisingly there was considerable opposition but, once again, through the force of law, the board was able to ensure that house owners were brought into line.

To further aid the growth and improvement of the city it had also become increasingly important to ensure improved communication with other towns, especially London. Any long-distance traveller at this time was still dependent upon the original Roman roads, which provided little more than direction. Supposedly, each parish through which they ran was responsible for their upkeep. This rarely worked, with the roads from Chichester to Portsmouth, London and Brighton frequently impassable. The eventual solution was the establishment of turnpike trusts, bodies authorised by act of parliament to levy tolls for the upkeep of highways. The first Chichester turnpike was the road to Midhurst, authorised by an act of 1749 while the road to Portsmouth was turnpiked in 1762. For the purpose of laying this second improved road, a gravel pit was dug on the south-east corner of the New Broyle. Finally, a two-mile stretch of turnpike road to Dell Quay was completed in 1779.

Not that the new improved roads were to everyone's taste. In later years, Member of Parliament and idealist of pre-industrial England, William Cobbett, preferred to avoid using the turnpike road out of Chichester when journeying from Petworth to Lavant:

> In cases like mine, you are pestered to death to find out the way to get from place to place. The people you have to deal with are inn keepers, ostlers and post boys; and they think you mad if you express your wish to avoid turnpike roads, and a great deal more than half mad if you talk of going even from necessity by any other road. They think you a strange fellow if you will not ride six miles on a turnpike road rather than two on any other road.

However, despite their detractors, the turnpikes did much to further the growth and prosperity of Chichester, with a number of coach companies beginning to offer both regular and faster services to the capital and other major towns. From the 1760s onwards, newspaper adverts abounded, with a journey to London able to be completed in less than ten hours and at a cost of either 18s for an inside seat or 10s outside. The normal places of departure were from either the Dolphin in West Street (for London-bound coaches) or the Swan in East Street (for those bound for Portsmouth).

To facilitate the greater movement of traffic in and out of Chichester, it became necessary to remove a serious bottleneck caused by the medieval gateways situated at each of the city's entry points. Three of the gates, the north, west and south, were demolished in 1773, while the east gate was demolished ten years later. The reason for delaying demolition of this last gateway was that the upper part of this building was being used as the city gaol. Sufficient funds, therefore, had to be available for building a new prison; this was eventually constructed close to the old gateway on the south side of East Street. Spershott, in recording the events that took place in the city during his lifetime, names Mary Beadle as the first to be held in the new prison. She was a young woman, also pregnant at the time, who had been in service with Lady Franklin and brought to trial for stealing a quantity of linen:

> After her sentence to seven years' transportation she was immediately put into it, 12 January 1784, before it was quite finished and when the water ran down the walls and a great snow and extreme cold winter followed upon it. And no bed or fire allowed her, nor friend to visit her, so that she was nearly perished and her husband, a civil man, almost distracted.

Following these various improvements to the city, those who now wrote about Chichester were much more favourable about its state and condition. Spershott goes so far as to suggest that the eighteenth century was its 'golden age' but suggested pessimistically,

> But being in this, elevated to its meridian height, it may be greatly declined again by the end of the next, for Divine Providence generally brings pride to a fall.

The Dolphin Inn, an eighteenth-century coaching inn that was rebuilt in 1768. From here 'The New Post Coach' left for London at 6 a.m., taking the newly completed turnpike to Midhurst. Next door stood the Anchor.

Concurring with Spershott in his overall views on the progress of the city was Alexander Hay. In his *History of Chichester*, published in 1804, he declared that it had seen more improvements than virtually any other city in the kingdom. Another commentator of this period was G.S. Carey, who fittingly declared that it was 'one of the most desirable cities in England' and that 'every stranger should repeatedly see Chichester.'

Mirroring the growth of affluence within the city were developments taking place outside the city gates. With a general improvement in the state of the roads, the suburbs also witnessed a growth in the numbers choosing to live outside the walls. These developments had been slow in coming, however. It had taken the suburbs a good deal longer to recover from the Civil War, with few quality buildings constructed in the St Pancras area until the late seventeenth century. Earliest of these was the Unicorn Inn, Eastgate Square (the same site later acquired for the Minerva Studios, subsequently the *Observer* newspaper office), probably built in the late 1670s. The majority of houses built at this time were small artisan cottages. The real change for St Pancras came in 1750 with reconstruction of the church. This had lain in ruins for over a century but was replaced in that year by a Gothic-style building designed by William Ride.

Among the first to be buried in the grounds of the new St Pancras' Church were the celebrated portrait and landscape painters John (d. 1764), William (d. 1764) and George (d. 1776) Smith. They were the sons of William Smith who, between 1714 and 1719, had been minister of the General Baptist chapel in Eastgate Square. Once they had proven their general talents, the Duke of Richmond offered them his patronage while encouraging each, at the appropriate moment, to move to London. Here, they clearly established themselves, with two of the brothers, George and John, exhibiting under the auspices of the Society of Arts, and George also at the Royal Academy. Among the subjects painted by William was the Duke of Richmond himself who subsequently presented the portrait to the city. From about 1750 onwards, the brothers returned to Chichester, with George and John establishing a studio in North Street. Buried alongside the three brothers in the churchyard of St Pancras was Ruth Smith, wife of George.

Further out, Shopwyke was also undergoing transformation. This was where James Spershott had spent his childhood and, for this reason, he took great delight in its description. At the beginning of the century, when Spershott was a child,

> This village consisted only of five old dwelling houses and was often spoke of by the name of the five houses. Nor was there then any house at the end of the lane opening into Portfield where there are now several. In the farmhouse connected with Portfield standing farthest north by the lane leading to Maudlin lived my father, Charles Spershott.

Countryside near Chichester, 1767 engraving by George and John Smith. Outside the growing city of Chichester farming and husbandry were the prevailing industries, but a strong link existed between town and country. Chichester provided the necessary markets for the sale of livestock and produce. More pertinent, with regard to this picture, is that the artists George and John Smith were long-term residents of the city, their father being the minister of Eastgate Baptist Chapel.

The city's rapidly improving position did not mean that everyone was automatically benefiting. As in all cities at this time, there were a substantial number of poor. Fortunately, they were not ignored. During times of poor harvest, the Duke of Richmond would ensure that bread was available at a reasonable price for the poor to purchase, while other affluent citizens would often leave special bequests in their will. The Oliver Whitby School was still going strong, its emphasis upon the teaching of navigation and the apprenticing of boys to the sea. In 1729, to support this aspect of the school's work, Henry May, recorder of the city, willed that £50 from his estate be given to the school. Alongside the Oliver Whitby School, there were also the Grey Coat Charity School for Boys (which shared the Oliver Whitby building) and the Girls' Blue Coat School, both established in 1710. These two institutions were well supported, receiving regular donations from both the bishop and Duke of Richmond.

Holding an even more secure position was St Mary's Hospital, which possessed a large amount of property from which to draw revenue. Within Chichester alone, the hospital possessed about 100 houses, together with two gardens in the Pallants. In 1728 the orders of the charity were revised, increasing the salary of the *custos* to £26 a year, equal to the salary of the five inmates. For their part, each inmate was to receive *2s* per week, paid out from rents collected by the hospital. In addition, they were to have a new gown every two years. It was also ordered (or reaffirmed) that the *custos* should provide a minister of the Church of England who should read prayers in the chapel every morning (except Sundays and holidays), which the poor of St Mary's were 'diligently' to attend. The minister was to be paid £10 annually and was also to visit the poor when they were sick. In return for their accommodation, 'The poor of the Hospital shall keep themselves and their several apartments in the said Hospital sweet and clean, and if they neglect to do so after twice admonished by the *custos*, they shall, upon complaint made to the dean and chapter, be by them (if there be just cause for such complaint) expelled and removed from the said hospital.'

East Pallant House.

Independent of any of the earlier-established charities was a public dispensary that was created in 1784. Housed within some cottages situated alongside the road to Midhurst, it was subsequently to develop into a much larger infirmary, the Royal West Sussex Hospital. The founders of this dispensary were Dr T. Standen and the Revd William Walker, rector of St Pancras, Chichester and Rumboldswyke (1774–1827). With its first patient admitted on 1 October 1784, it was eventually to treat a total of 160 patients in its first twelve months. Of these, 91 (57 per cent) were completely cured and 65 (41 per cent) relieved. In a further 4 (2 per cent) cases, the treatment was unsuccessful and the patient died.

While these various charitable institutions played their part, ultimate responsibility for the relief of impoverishment was in the hands of Chichester's eight parishes. To allow them to undertake this task, a poor-relief rate was levied upon all property owners, with the amounts raised subsequently disbursed either in the form of cash sums or in supporting a parish poorhouse. It was an arrangement that operated independently of the corporation, which had no direct authority to interfere in the workings of the parishes. Nevertheless, the corporation did play a significant role in the care of the poor through its responsibility for the Cawley almshouse. Although, to begin with, it had been run on the lines originally conceived, offering relief to 'twelve decayed tradesmen', this had not continued. Instead, the corporation attempted to develop something much more imaginative and generally more useful. In 1681 Henry Peckham, the then mayor, had expressed his intention of turning the almshouse into a manufactory for the poor. Unfortunately few documents survive, and little is known about how the arrangement worked. Possibly, each of the parishes selected some able-bodied unemployed from within their numbers to work at the almshouse on the manufacture of woollen garments. Any profit from their work would have been used to offset the overall poor rate.

The entire arrangement for maintaining the poor of the city dramatically changed in 1753 as a result of the city's acquiring the right to unify the then existing nine parishes (including those of St Pancras and St Bartholomew) for the purpose of maintaining the poor. The legal tool that permitted this was a privately sponsored act of incorporation which allowed for the annual election of thirty Guardians. They were drawn from the parishes as follows:

St Peter the Great (alias subdeanery)	13
The Close	2
St Andrew	3
St Olave	2
St Peter the Less	2
St Martin	2
All Saints (alias the Pallant)	2
St Pancras	2
St Bartholomew	2

Edward Gilbert, appointed clerk to the guardians in 1816, later described the mode of election:

The elected Guardians are chosen by the major part of the inhabitants of the several parishes who are rated to the relief of the poor of such of the same parishes wherein they inhabit and go out of office annually on the Tuesday in Easter week, when others are elected in their room. Public notice is given of the time of election on the Sunday next preceding the

Long established as a wine merchant in Chichester, Arthur Purchase boasts this elegant eighteenth-century bay window and door case.

day of election; and in case of the death or removal of any such Guardians, others are elected to fill up the vacancies so occasioned. Should the inhabitants refuse, or neglect to choose the Guardians at the time, and in the manner specified, the Magistrates of the city of Chichester are empowered to appoint the requisite number.

Once elected, the thirty guardians joined the High Steward, mayor, recorder and magistrates of the city to form a Board of Guardians that now had responsibility for the overall management of poor relief. To assist them in this work, each newly elected board elected a president and treasurer from among their own number. In addition, they either appointed, or confirmed, the appointment of a number of officers, including collectors of the poor rate, a master and mistress of the poorhouse and a medical officer.

Under the new arrangement, the Cawley almshouse was now to play a much more central role in matters connected with the poor. Instead of providing employment for limited numbers, it was now converted into a workhouse that would accommodate all who were homeless. In preparation for this new role, the building was generally renovated and provided with two new wings at a total cost of £680 9s 11¼d.

Generally, life in the renovated and enlarged workhouse was harsh but not unbearable. All those brought into the building were provided with a bed, regular meals and the 'common parish dress' that replaced the clothes they normally wore. To occupy them during the day, most were expected to undertake some form of useful work while children were taught to read and write. The time of rising was 5.30 a.m. in summer and 7 a.m. in winter, with prayers immediately following. Some work was expected before breakfast with much of the rest of the day seeing most of the inmates occupied in the manufacture of woollen clothing. In 1784 a spinning-shop was added to the house, in connection with which it was 'ordered that the people employed in the Manufactory be taken off for the spin for the use of the House at the discretion of the committee.'

In overall authority were the master and mistress, the Guardians specifically charging them with the following duties: 'care and management of the poor, keep[ing] the accounts, learn [sic] the family to read, card, knit and spin, and all other branches relating to the woollen manufactory as the Guardians should direct'. In return for the performing of these duties, the Guardians 'did agree to allow them after the rate of five and twenty pounds a year'. Overall, the inmates were expected to behave as if they were part of a large family group, treating each other with respect. The workhouse instructions specifically ordered 'That every person endeavour to preserve good harmony and look upon themselves as one family and to prevent disputes and differences among themselves . . .'. Mealtimes, as with any family group, were communal, a high standard of behaviour once again being expected: 'that great care be taken that the whole family do sit and behave decently at meals, that Grace be said by one of the house before meals, that all persons who are not in their proper place before Grace is said are to lose that meal and that none remove from the table till thanks are returned, that no provision be carried out of the room.'

For infractions against various rules a whole range of penalties existed, these ranging from a loss of various privileges through to solitary confinement and the lash. Failure to return to the workhouse at an agreed time following the granting of permission to go out in the evening would simply result in being unable to leave the building for two weeks. Something more serious, such as theft or the use of violence, was dealt with far more severely, with fifty lashes on 'the bare back' not unusual. Another infringement that was dealt with harshly was that of idleness: 'that if any person through idleness pretend themselves sick, lame or injured in order to be excused from working, such impostors when discovered either by their stomachs or by the apothecary shall be put into the stocks or wear the pillory for two hours and shall be kept on bread and water till they are willing to work.'

In 1768 a room in the south wing was set aside for the idle, named the 'Room of Infamy'. Within the room only a mat on the floor and a blanket were provided for sleeping while nobody was allowed to visit those incarcerated there. At the same time, a strict diet was enforced: 'For breakfast they are to have bread, the usual allowance with water instead of beer and the same for supper; for dinner they are to have the same as the rest of the family but they are to eat their meat cold after all the rest of the family have dined.'

RULE BY FEAR: THE LOCAL SMUGGLING GANGS OF CHICHESTER

Chichester, throughout the eighteenth century and earlier, had been a centre of the smuggling trade. In the Middle Ages the emphasis had been on the smuggling abroad of wool, the government having placed a high tax upon the export of this commodity. Those involved in wool-smuggling had created a massive infrastructure that brought considerable advantage to local farmers, merchants and ship owners while ensuring that vast amounts of money freely circulated within the city. It was this local infrastructure that readily turned itself into the even more lucrative import trade that emerged in the eighteenth century.

Import smuggling was based on the tea and brandy trades, both commodities taxed at extremely high rates. So extensive was this trade that little of the tea or brandy consumed in Chichester was actually legal. Most of it was clandestinely brought to the city, having been quietly offloaded at one of several remote landing places that existed around Chichester Harbour. A great many local citizens were involved in this

The murder of William Chater. Chater was first thrown down a well in Lady Holt Park before being stoned to death.

The interior of Guildhall. It was here that the trial of the seven smugglers took place. Located within the grounds of Priory Park, the Guildhall was formerly the church of the Franciscan Friars.

activity, either financing it or providing the necessary muscle to sail the boats or secure the smuggled cargoes once they had been run ashore.

To bring this illegal trade to an end, the government, at the end of the seventeenth century, established a much enlarged customs service that was responsible for patrolling the coastline and seizing smuggled goods. Unfortunately, those carrying out these patrols, known as riding officers, frequently acted alone, and consequently stood little chance against a well-organised gang. Admittedly these officers could always call upon a troop of dragoons to provide assistance, but the chances of such a body arriving in time were fairly remote. For this reason, most riding officers, recognising that their task was little better than hopeless, undertook the minimum work necessary to retain their posts.

As for Chichester's locally based smuggling gangs, they were primarily composed of vicious thugs who freely used violence against all who stood in their way. The Mafia-like quality of these gangs was clearly demonstrated in January 1749, when a group of seven smugglers was brought before a special assize that assembled in Chichester. They were all members of a gang that seems to have been based on Chichester and some of the surrounding villages.

The enquiry, which sat in the Guildhall, quickly revealed a shocking tale of cruelty and murder. It had all started in September 1748 when a revenue cutter from Poole had captured one of the gang's boats on a return voyage from Guernsey, carrying a large quantity of tea and brandy, all of it to be sold in the Chichester area. Among those on board the captured vessel was John Perrin, a native of Chichester. He had begun his working life as a carpenter but had become incapacitated through illness. Joining the local gang, he had been usefully employed as a purchaser, making all the arrangements for the cargo to be shipped back from Guernsey.

Surprisingly, the smugglers themselves were able to avoid capture, apparently escaping in a boat. It is at this point that Perrin takes a leading role. Seeing the loss of the tea as a severe blow, he urged that the entire gang should descend on the custom house at Poole and repossess themselves of the smuggled tea that was being held there. It was an amazing operation that involved about thirty men drawn from across Sussex and Kent. Having established guards on the roads leading into the town, the remainder approached the custom house and smashed down the doors before removing all that it contained.

It was, for the smugglers, shortly after the attack on Poole that things began to go wrong. One of those involved, John Diamond, was identified and placed in the gatehouse gaol at Chichester. To ensure his successful prosecution, a second witness was also to be brought to Chichester to confirm Diamond's involvement. This was Daniel Chater, an acquaintance of Diamond, who had seen him with the gang upon their escape from Poole. Escorting Chater was a single revenue officer, William Galley from Southampton.

Smuggling & Smugglers in Sussex.

THE GENUINE HISTORY

OF THE INHUMAN AND

UNPARALLELED MURDERS

OF

Mr. WILLIAM GALLEY,

A CUSTOM-HOUSE OFFICER, AND

Mr. DANIEL CHATER,

A SHOEMAKER,

BY FOURTEEN NOTORIOUS SMUGGLERS,

WITH THE

TRIALS AND EXECUTION OF

SEVEN OF THE CRIMINALS AT CHICHESTER,

1748-9.

Illustrated with Seven Plates, Descriptive of the Barbarous Cruelties.

A full account of the two murders was later published. The author, whose name was never revealed, was described as 'a gentleman of Chichester'. It is usually assumed that the writer was the Duke of Richmond.

Galley's main object was to ensure that Chater was taken to the East Marden home of William Battine, Surveyor General of Customs for Sussex, where he was to be interviewed. This decision seems to have been nothing less than crass stupidity. Despite Chater being a key government witness in a major criminal investigation, he was to be escorted by one elderly individual. Furthermore, the course of the journey, which had as its starting point Chater's home village of Fordingbridge, would take the pair through the heart of gangland Hampshire and Sussex. The inevitable happened. Upon reaching Rowland's Castle, where they stopped at the White Hart for a drink, they were recognised. Immediately word went out and, within a few hours, the fate of the two travellers was sealed. Over the next few days, both men were severely beaten and eventually murdered. Galley appears to have been killed first, buried alive at Harting Coombe. As for Chater, after being thrown down a dry well in Lady Holt Park, he was brutally stoned to death.

It was an anonymous letter to the Duke of Richmond, a man noted for his opposition to the smuggling gangs, that first alerted the authorities to the two ruthless murders. The letter told of a body 'buried in the sands in a certain place near Rake'. In digging up the body, they found it to be the missing customs officer, 'standing almost upright, with his hands covering his eyes'. Soon after, a further letter was sent to the Duke, this giving more specific information that directly led to the arrest of several of the murderers. Among them was Benjamin Tapner, a shoemaker who had once been employed in Chichester. Also with Chichester connections was Thomas Stringer. He was a cordwainer, still employed in the city, but he managed to escape arrest and was not brought to justice at this time.

The seven members of the gang who were brought before the special assize that sat in the Guildhall at Chichester were all convicted of either murdering, or being an accessory in the murders of, Chater and Galley. It was a brief trial, lasting no longer than two days, with all seven executed the following afternoon. For them, a gallows was erected on the Broyle, with a strong escort of dragoons and foot-soldiers employed to escort them from the city gaol to the point of execution. To mark the event and deter others from being drawn into the smuggling trade, several of the murderers were left to hang in chains. This included Benjamin Tapner, whose body was taken to St Roche's Hill (beside the Trundle) where it could long be seen from a great distance. At the execution site, where an inscribed stone was eventually laid, two of the gang were buried: Richard Mills and his son John. Both were from Trotton and both were convicted of being accessories in the murder of Chater.

8

War and Peace

Between 1793 and 1814, Britain and France opposed each other in an intercontinental struggle that, in all but name, was a world war. First breaking out in February 1793, it began as a war against Revolutionary France. Following a short period of peace, governed by a treaty signed at Amiens in March 1802, fighting once again broke out in April 1803. This time, revolutionaries determined on liberty, fraternity and equality no longer governed France. Instead, there was a new leader: the Emperor Napoleon, a masterful tactician who seemed determined upon a degree of domination previously equalled only by the Romans.

The extent and nature of the French Revolutionary and Napoleonic Wars ensured that every inhabitant throughout the length and breadth of the British Isles was drawn into the conflict. Chichester was no exception. A likely point of invasion through its proximity to the south coast, it was a front-line city. Large numbers of its inhabitants volunteered or were forced into military service, and numerous regiments were frequently billeted in the town. As a result, the entire social and political infrastructure of the city gradually changed. In particular, the young men of the area were drawn into the army and navy, with women undertaking much of the work that these able-bodied men had once performed.

Previous historians of Chichester have tended to see this wartime period as one of great unity. Emlyn Thomas, in his excellent and detailed study of the Georgian city, emphasizes a rush to join the colours, the many fine banquets and balls that celebrated every British victory and the huge crowds that attended the various military reviews. All this most certainly took place. But who, exactly, attended the lavish banquets and had time to cheer on the British army as it exercised? Quite simply, it was the rich and well situated: the town's nobility, gentry and merchant class. But they were not the majority. A much larger group, the poor and labouring classes, were far less supportive. They had little to gain from the war, especially if they lost family members to a regime of military expansion while spending increased amounts of their meagre resources on basic foods that were rapidly escalating in price.

The streets of Chichester, as an important garrison town, were frequently filled with men in uniform. Infantry and cavalry regiments were always present, their main task to be on hand to counter the expected invasion. The calibre of these troops varied considerably: some were full-time recruits and others no more than part-time amateurs. Among the most efficient were the regulars and fencibles; locally these included the 35th Sussex regiment and the Sussex Fencibles. Both were full-time, although the latter were restricted to home service only. A further addition to the fighting force was the militia, which was under the general control of the Home Office. At a more local level, it was commanded by the Lord Lieutenant of the county, Charles Lennox, the 3rd Duke of Richmond (1735–1806). Although it consisted of volunteers, the majority were conscripts chosen by ballot from each parish. At the beginning of the war, and in common with the fencibles, it could only be called upon to fight at home. It differed, however, in that it could be mustered only during periods of hostility. At other times it merely assembled periodically for drill and manoeuvres. Finally there were the volunteers. Composed primarily of local gentry and having much in common with a private club, they were often characterised as play-soldiers. Normally, they undertook a few hours of training each week and spent much of the rest of their time strutting around in their expensive uniforms. Within the county of Sussex, the Duke of Richmond raised a volunteer yeomanry cavalry, which included a few of Chichester's most influential residents. It was a particularly elitist body: those joining were required to provide both their own horse and accoutrements. A second volunteer regiment, and one much more confined to the city, was the Chichester volunteer infantry. Although composed of some of the most affluent merchants of the area, it was considerably less exclusive than the countywide volunteer yeomanry.

With regard to the regular troops, these regiments had often a secondary role in preventing civil disturbances. For this reason it was often an advantage for those quartered in Chichester to belong to regiments recruited some distance from Sussex. This made sense: a local regiment would have local attachments and be more likely to support any expressed grievances. As a further aspect of this same policy, no regiment remained in one area for an extended period of time – so preventing the establishment of local roots.

The billeting of a large number of troops in Chichester caused problems. Apart from anything else, it helped ensure high food prices in the area, the food consumed by these soldiers having to be purchased locally. Furthermore, it was difficult to procure accommodation. At the beginning of the war there were no barracks in Chichester, with troops having to be billeted in the various inns of the town. This left no room for ordinary guests; furthermore, innkeepers were only reimbursed after a considerable lapse of time. For this reason, and as early as November 1793, some of the innkeepers and leading inhabitants of the town petitioned the Home Secretary, Henry Dundas:

> Your petitioners have suffered exceedingly by the experiences attending thereon and the very insufficient allowance established for the supply of forage, they therefore most earnestly entreat, that the very heavy burden

they are subject to may be taken into consideration of His Majesty's ministers and they may be indulged with barracks sufficient for the accommodation of cavalry and such other of the forces of the kingdoms which may be thought necessary to be stationed in this part of the county of Sussex.

Dundas, himself, was not unsympathetic:

I have perused the petitions from the innkeepers of the city of Chichester together with the address of its inhabitants on the subject of barracks. So many applications of a similar nature have of late come before me, that I am sensible the subject must undergo the consideration of government in a general point of view and I shall not on that occasion fail to give due attention paid to the circumstances of the city of Chichester.

In fact, something was already being done. The government had recently appointed a barrack-master, his task either to rent or oversee building of new barracks. At Chichester, in 1795, this resulted in construction of a small barrack-block alongside the Broyle Road. Although it did not completely solve the problem, housing no more than 500 men, it did help alleviate the situation.

The problems associated with the need to accommodate troops were as nothing when compared to the food shortages that occurred in 1794 and 1795. In part, the shortages were created by two consecutive poor harvests.

Chichester Barracks, Broyle Road. Initially constructed in 1795, the barracks were greatly enlarged both during the Napoleonic Wars and then again during the reign of Queen Victoria.

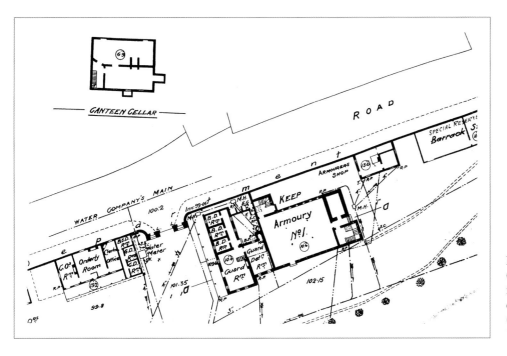

Detail of the entrance to
Chichester Barracks
from a nineteenth-
century War Office map.
(*National Archives,*
WO40/25)

However, the war was an important contributory factor. Previous shortfalls in
the supply of cereal crops had usually been made good through foreign
imports. The war had made this difficult, with merchants less willing (and
sometimes unable) to enter into overseas contracts. In consequence, the price
of wheat soared, leading to a similar increase in the price of bread. In
September 1794, before the crisis had taken effect, wheat on the Chichester
market sold at approximately 42*s* a quarter. Twelve months later it had
reached 80*s*. Furthermore, it was to remain at this high level until March
1796. By that time, the government had determined on direct action,
securing large imports of wheat and other cereals from both Canada and the
Baltic.

For the poor, of whom there were a great many in Chichester during this
period, bread was the staple diet, a major item of any meal. As a result of the
disastrous harvest and the consequent effect upon the price of bread, the very
poorest in the city came close to starvation. Desperate to survive, many took
matters into their own hands, demanding of the city bakers that they lower
their prices.

Signs of discontent appear to have first manifested themselves among the
locally billeted Herefordshire Militia. They too were grievously unhappy at the
high price of bread, with a number of militiamen taking several loaves from a
baker's shop. To the baker they proffered no more than 6*d*, a normal amount
in earlier years, instead of the much higher sum now requested. In
consequence, the soldiers were arrested and placed in confinement.

This appears to have been the catalyst for a major riot that broke out on
Monday 13 April 1795. Various leaflets had been distributed throughout
Chichester and neighbouring villages, calling for some sort of action to be
taken against high prices. In consequence, a huge crowd assembled in the

city, their number augmented by soldiers of the Herefordshire Militia. For the authorities, this was viewed as a very dangerous situation, since the Herefordshires were the only troops available to quell such disturbances. Having now assembled, the combined mob marched upon the gaol, where they 'effected the release of the imprisoned militia men'.

A report of the 'riot' that appeared in the *Sussex Weekly Advertiser* (20 April edition) portrayed the event in the poorest light possible. Yet, the evidence is of a well-controlled situation in which the poor were merely seeking the moral right to acquire food at an affordable price. Although accused of 'committing several acts of riot' they did little more than dispose of market produce, such as meat and bread, 'at the prices they themselves thought proper'. Only when a stallholder or shopkeeper refused to cooperate was money withheld and the product distributed more freely. Thus, it must have been with some glee that the newspaper reporter was able to latch on to some real evidence of lawbreaking, the rioters apparently breaking 'most of the windows of the Dolphin Inn'.

In an effort to prevent further disturbances, corporation members were among the first to respond. On the following day Thomas Jones, the mayor of the city, 'called a meeting of the inhabitants at which a number of resolutions were passed for the security of the city against further depredations of the insurgents'. In a more practical vein, those attending the meeting agreed to subscribe a total of £300 to be used 'for the purpose of retailing to the soldiery, and other necessitous persons, at 6*d* the quartern loaf, and meat at 4*d* per pound'. At the same time, a committee was formed to oversee the working of this arrangement.

Elsewhere in the city, the Duke of Richmond was organising a second meeting, for the discontented members of the militia. It was fortunate that he was resident at Goodwood House at this time, as he was one of the few individuals in the area with sufficient authority to lead such a meeting. As Lord Lieutenant of the county and therefore responsible for the militia, he was able to make them an important promise. He would guarantee restoration of a temporary additional payment that was known as 'bread money'. On this condition, the troops promised a return to duty.

A few days later, the Duke of Richmond was undertaking a very different role when he attended the city gaol. Here, he was present at an examination of soldiers who had been arrested during the demonstration of 13 April. They were not to be treated lightly, and were committed to Horsham gaol. Even then, the authorities could not draw a veil over the affair, as it was feared that there might be an attempt to release these prisoners once they had reached Horsham. Rumours certainly abounded. Within Chichester it was suggested that 800 men from the Herefordshire Militia were ready to attack the arms store in Chichester, remove the weapons held there and march on Horsham. The only evidence supporting the existence of such a plan was the appearance of a cannon on Spital Hill (south of present-day St Richard's Hospital); it had apparently been dragged there by a large force of mutinous militia. Subsequently abandoned, but threateningly pointing into the city, it was quickly retrieved by a troop of Royal Artillery.

Although the following summer was relatively peaceful, the failure of that second harvest caused a further outbreak of protest. On Wednesday 30 October, a large number of women assembled at the market. Their object was to dictate the sale price of essential food items not covered by the subscription raised earlier in the year. In particular, marketers were forced to sell butter at 8*d* per pound instead of 14*d*. The women also made it clear that if these prices were not held, they would return in force.

Further disturbances were recorded in May 1796 when a large number of people assembled outside the residences of Messrs Reynolds and Hayler, two of the largest millers and bakers in the city, who had recently raised their prices. Following the breaking of several windows, some of the demonstrators were arrested, leading to further scenes outside the city gaol.

The more affluent citizens of the area were inclined to believe that these various acts of protest were rather less than spontaneous. Instead, they looked for a hidden hand, believing it to be the result of an outside influence. One Chichester clergyman claimed that there were 'seditious people of the lower class' who were 'going about from place to place to excite soldiers'. To support these assertions, he produced no actual evidence, only a supposition that this was how things were.

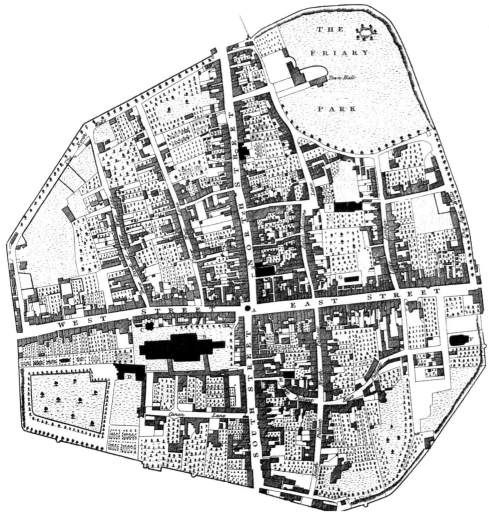

A plan of Chichester based on a survey undertaken by George Loader in April 1812. (*West Sussex Record Office*)

In the north of England, as a result of what had taken place in Chichester, a contributor to the *Blackburn Mail* feared the country to be on the brink of revolution:

The cap of liberty was not exhibited on pikes at Chichester, but the French trick of inflaming the populace in exposing the things cried was practised; by holding up beef and loaves on sticks . . . conducted by similar worthy characters to those who had first the honour to lead the revolutionists in France – a raw indisciplined militia and a rabble of women.

If there was a potential leader, it was Joseph Richards. A tallow-chandler, he was also a key figure in a locally formed radical society. Consisting of a mere handful of individuals, it had once regularly met in one of the inns of the town. However, this was not to the liking of the local magistrates, who, in an effort to bring an end to the society, told the publican that his licence would be revoked if he continued to permit these meetings. As a result, the society moved to Richards' workshop, described by the *Sussex Weekly Advertiser* as being situated in 'one of the bye-ways of Chichester'.

The October disturbances had taken the radicals by surprise as much as it had the authorities. All that Richards' group could do was watch the unfolding events and pass a few resolutions of their own. In particular, they called for punishments to be meted out to dealers who attempted to profit from the food shortages, particularly those who hoarded wheat and resold later at a higher price.

Also watching the passing events in Chichester was a more distant figure. Possibly located in Portsmouth or London, and likely to have had connections with the much-feared London Corresponding Society (a group that unified many disparate local radical societies) this individual was aware of the activities of Joseph Richards. Possibly he gained his information from various snippets that had appeared in the *Sussex Weekly Advertiser*. Either way, he (or she) chose the moment carefully. In May 1797, coinciding with a series of naval mutinies at Portsmouth, Joseph Richards received a mysterious package. It contained a large number 'of inflammatory hand bills' directed towards the military. The sender was clearly hoping that the recipient would distribute these across the town. However, Richards was no revolutionary. He sought parliamentary reform but only through peaceful means. Instead of distributing them, he brought them to the attention of the Duke of Richmond.

A series of more abundant harvests ensured that the Chichester market witnessed a temporary return to normality between 1796 and 1798. Yet, throughout that period the price of wheat was never to return to its pre-war level. Furthermore, the harvests of 1799 and 1800 also failed, leading to further discontent. On these occasions, there was no replication of the earlier protests in Chichester, possibly because of the continuing work of a reformed emergency relief committee. The *Sussex Weekly Advertiser* says little about the attitude of the Chichester market crowds during this period but does hint at the committee's having set up a soup kitchen for those most in need.

The fear of further crowd violence is very apparent, especially as there were a number of violent episodes at Lewes during this period. For this reason, the local press gives considerable attention to the state of each new harvest and carefully notes any fall of food prices. In November 1801 the *Sussex Weekly Advertiser* enthusiastically reported that the butchers of the city were retailing mutton at the much-reduced price of 6*d* per pound and beef was 'cried at 3*s* 6*d* per bone'. To underline the point, it was further noted,

> A wager was offered at the market on Wednesday, to receive 10 guineas to return fifty if wheat was not currently sold in this market under 10 guineas a load before Christmas.

As well as this keenly awaited fall in food prices, the end of 1801 saw an important government announcement: a peace treaty was about to be signed. The war with France would soon be brought to an end and the bitterness of the past few years could be firmly cast aside. By February of the following year, it was even possible to buy French hogs at the Chichester market, there now being a return of open trade. However, attitudes had changed little: the *Sussex Weekly Advertiser*'s local correspondent described them 'as very inferior to those bred in England'.

A further benefit of peace, following the signing of the treaty in March, was the standing-down of the Sussex Militia. A final parade took place at the Broyle Road barracks, attended by the Duke of Richmond. At the same time, the Duke's own volunteer cavalry was mustered, passing him by on horseback.

The return of peace also ensured that Chichester's latest attraction, horse racing on the open grounds of Goodwood Park, would be well attended. The previous year, 1801, had seen the first-ever meeting, the course specially laid out by the Duke's own groundsmen. Although hundreds of racegoers had attended, with many staying for a ball held at the assembly rooms on the second evening, the occasion was more muted than it might have been. This was in part because of the continuing war. However, the organiser of the event, the Duke of Richmond, was unable to attend, suffering from a recurrence of gout. Things were very different in 1802, with a three-day event spanning the period 28 to 30 April. Not only was the Duke fully recovered but also this was the first major Sussex sporting occasion since the signing of the peace treaty. The local correspondent of the *Advertiser* noted,

> The turf was in excellent order and the course, by good management, kept free of those dangerous obstructions, which have long been complained of by the proprietors of horses, and their jockeys, at other race courses.

Unfortunately, the peace proved short-lived. In 1803 Britain and France were once again at war. On this occasion, Chichester was more prepared for the expected influx of troops. In particular, the barracks had been greatly enlarged, able to accommodate approximately 1,400 men and having stabling

for at least 400 horses. As well as heading off the complaints of local innkeepers, this enlargement of the barracks also ensured that there would be less fraternisation between the town's people and the soldiers, so reducing the chances of an alliance during times of poor harvest. The work on the barracks extension had been undertaken between August 1802 and November 1803 at a cost of £76,000. Since 1958 it has been known as the Roussillion Barracks, the name commemorating the defeat of the French Roussillion regiment during the capture of Quebec. The victor, on that occasion, was the local 35th Sussex.

With the return of war, an immediate step was that of mobilising the militia, this governed by proclamation of 11 March. Each area of Sussex had to provide a minimum number of militiamen, with the precise details for recruitment established by a meeting of the lord-lieutenancy (a council that governed military matters relating to Sussex). Held at the beginning of June, it was determined that the names of all men aged between 17 and 55 years should be listed and a ballot held for those who would be enrolled into the militia. The city and its immediate area (the Rape of Chichester) would be responsible for drawing 772 names.

At a further meeting of the lord-lieutenancy it was also decided that a new level of soldiery would be created and to be known as the 'county volunteers'. Again, 772 names would be required from the Rape of Chichester, with these men, less onerously, expected to be called out only 'in

Horses and riders preparing for a race at Goodwood. Although racing had been a regular feature of Goodwood for a number of years, the first official meet was not until 1801. The impressive stand, providing a focal point for each occasion, was added in 1804.

case of actual invasion or appearance of the enemy in force'. To prepare them for this eventuality, they were also expected to muster on two occasions in every week between April and December, for purposes of training:

That they are liable to be called out to exercise on every Sunday from the 25th of March to the 25th of December, or if they have any religious scruples concerning being exercised on a Sunday, then they are to be exercised on some other day, to be fixed upon by their commanding officer but are not to receive any allowance for such Sunday or other days exercise, and that they are to be exercised at least one other day in each week to the amount of twenty days at least, and for such additional days not being more than twenty in a year, they are to be allowed one shilling per day provided they have been exercised on the previous Sunday or other day in lieu thereof.

In most respects, other than that of their method of recruitment, they can be seen as a nascent Home Guard, the genesis of the body that came into existence in 1940. Balloting for both the militia and the new 'county volunteers' was undertaken, on two separate occasions, at the Swan in East Street. Those drawn, who could afford it, might relinquish themselves from service by payment of £10 or £15, which exempted them from service for five years.

The title page of Alexander Hay's *History of Chichester*. Published in 1804, it provides an interesting contemporary account of the city. Hay, at the time of publication, was chaplain of St Mary's Hospital and occupied a house in Upper West Lane (now Chapel Street).

THE

History of Chichester;

INTERSPERSED WITH

Various Notes and Observations

ON THE

EARLY and PRESENT STATE of the CITY,

The most Remarkable Places in its Vicinity,

And the COUNTY of SUSSEX in GENERAL:

WITH AN

APPENDIX,

Containing the CHARTERS of the CITY, at three different Times;

ALSO AN

Account of all the Parishes in the County,

THEIR NAMES, PATRONAGE, APPROPRIATIONS, VALUE IN THE KING'S BOOKS, FIRST-FRUITS, &c.

DEDICATED, BY PERMISSION,

To *WILLIAM HAYLEY,* Esqr.

" Non de Villis, domibusque alienis;
————————Sed quod magis ad nos
Pertinet, et nescire malum est, agitamus."—HORACE.

" Art must to other works a lustre lend,
But History pleases, howsoe'er 'tis penn'd."
HAYLEY'S Essay on Hist. p. 71.

By ALEXANDER HAY, A. M.

Vicar of Wisborough-Green, and Chaplain of St. Mary's Chapel in this City.

Chichester :

Printed and sold by J. Seagrave ; the Booksellers in the County, and by Longman and Co. Paternoster-Row, London.
1804.

The renewal of war also brought with it a heightened fear of sedition. In January 1804 the multitalented poet and artist William Blake was placed on trial at the Chichester Guildhall, accused of this crime. A dragoon, Private Schofield, had stated that, during a heated argument, Blake had 'damned his soldiery'. It was further claimed that Blake had also insulted the king while welcoming the threatened invaders. All this took place at Felpham where the poet was in temporary lodgings. The dragoon, it appears, had been invited by Blake's gardener to assist him, but the poet had taken exception to this arrangement. It was at this point that the argument had broken out, with the two men virtually coming to blows.

Blake's first appearance in court was in August 1803 when he was brought before the city magistrates. Released on bail, he returned for a full trial at the beginning of the following year. On that occasion the hearing was overseen by seven of the city's magistrates, including the Duke of Richmond and one of the Members of Parliament for the city, George White Thomas. Given that Schofield could produce no corroborating evidence, and Blake was adamant as to his innocence, the bench had little choice but to find for the defendant. At the same time, it must be added, Blake had a very strong case. At the Fox Inn, where the argument finally ended, none of those present heard anything that touched on sedition. Furthermore, Blake's counsel suggested the accusation had been made out of revenge, while drawing attention to Schofield's reputation for drunkenness.

In 1807 the Market House in North Street was built to a design by the famous London architect John Nash (1752–1835). The top storey, however, was added in 1900. The purpose of the Market House was to provide more room for enclosed trading and replaced the market cross.

Putting the Blake trial aside, in all other respects, Chichester was now a more unified city than it had been during the earlier years of conflict. The knowledge that Napoleon had assembled thousands of troops across the Channel for the purpose of invasion was bound to assume an overriding importance. Both the Sussex Yeomanry and Chichester volunteer infantry were reformed in these years, with the latter quickly oversubscribed. By 1804, several more companies had been added to its ranks. Helping ensure the success of this particular rush to arms was new government legislation that required all able-bodied men to volunteer for some form of military duty.

The presence of so many men in uniform continued to create many problems for the town. On 1 March 1807, St David's Day, celebrations at the Wheatsheaf got out of hand. Members of the Monmouth and Brecon Militia refused to return to barracks, and a local constable was bayoneted. In 1812, the West Sussex Militia were involved in further scenes of rowdiness. Following a dance at the Anchor Inn, several members of the militia continued to mill around West Street late into the night. An officer, having ordered them to return to barracks, received in return a torrent of abuse. A number of arrests were subsequently made, resulting in a good deal of local sympathy for the imprisoned soldiers. On the following day, Sussex militiamen and local townspeople joined together and began abusing both officers of the militia and members of the corporation. With the situation unchanged by the end of the day, the magistrates agreed to call on the 89th Regiment for support. Arriving in the city with fixed bayonets, they apparently dispersed the assembled crowd without injury.

The volunteer yeomanry, on the other hand, were undoubtedly much better at expressing themselves. As fine strutting peacocks, they expected their uniforms to reflect their social status. Some of those from Chichester who had joined the Duke of Richmond's light horse artillery at its re-embodiment in June 1803 were aghast at the quality of their new uniforms. Made of the same coarse material as that worn by those in the regular army, it was not seen as acceptable. Several resigned, with the *Sussex Weekly Advertiser* not unsympathetic to their grievances.

Doubtless, this entire wartime period must have seen many similar disturbances played out on the streets of the city, albeit on a smaller scale. The problem for the troops was boredom and inactivity. There were too many troops billeted in the city, with the enlarged barracks unable to contain the greatly increased numbers. By 1808 even the Guildhall had been given over to the military, while in 1811 a thousand troops were recorded as being accommodated in less than forty houses.

On the upside, the war was now beginning to provide plenty of opportunities for celebration. Several outstanding victories had brought an end to earlier invasion fears, chief of these being Nelson's defeat of the combined French and Spanish fleets at Trafalgar (1805). This, together with other national battle honours, was duly marked. A thanksgiving service at the cathedral and parish churches was the usual starting point, with formal balls and huge banquets also arranged. Among the normal venues for these occasions were the assembly rooms and council chambers, although the White Horse and the Swan proved equally popular.

The real centrepiece of each and every one of these events was the city cross. It was here that the town crier officially announced the event that was to be celebrated, the cross itself frequently being illuminated. In 1814, following Napoleon's exile to Elba, the corporation spent £50 on lanterns, these placed decorously around the cross. On previous occasions, the cross had been decked with candles to mark victories gained at Vittoria (1812) and Leipzig (1813), and in 1815 the cross was once more illuminated for the final victory at Waterloo.

The eventual conclusion to the wars failed, unfortunately, to herald a new age of prosperity. A series of poor harvests, combined with massive local unemployment, ensured that Chichester had little to celebrate in the long term. The year 1814, noted for its particularly poor harvest, once again saw the establishment of an emergency relief committee. Working tirelessly, its members eventually provided 3,000 loaves at a much-reduced price. The committee was again at work in 1816, this time its starting point being a

meeting in December that successfully raised £1,000 in promised
subscriptions.

Through a combination of poor
harvests and high unemployment,
the relief committee was now a
semi-permanent feature of the city,
its members regularly canvassing
for fresh contributions. Again in
1817, bread was provided at 6d a
loaf and a soup kitchen was also
established. Admittedly, periods of
temporary prosperity did bring
about an occasional reduction in
the number of those requiring support. Overall, however, the number
of impoverished remained at a
much higher level than previously
recorded. At the beginning of 1820,
a total of 400 were receiving support, leading to the allocation of
tickets to ensure that only the most
needy benefited from the committee's rapidly diminishing resources.

Eventually, Chichester was to
fight its way out of this era of depression. In part, this was through
a determination on the part of
some of the city's leading citizens
to bring certain improvements to
the city. In so doing, they also ensured that many of those without
an income would soon be gainfully

The Ship Hotel. Built by
Admiral Sir George
Murray (1759–1819),
who fought alongside
Nelson at the Battle of
Copenhagen (1801),
this is a fine Georgian
house dating from about
1790. Of particular
note within this
building is an iron
staircase in the Adam
style.

EDUCATIONAL PROGRESS

Towards the end of the Napoleonic Wars, two important educational
initiatives were witnessed in Chichester, with the establishment of the
Lancastrian and Central schools. Effectively they differed little: both aimed
to educate the children of the poor, were financed through subscriptions
and used the same teaching processes. Only philosophically was there a
real difference. The Lancastrian schools were founded by the dissenters of
the city, using proposals laid down by the Quaker educationalist Joseph
Lancaster. On the other hand, the Central Schools were a product of the

Church of England and adhered to the ideas of Dr Andrew Bell, a member of the Anglican clergy.

First on the Chichester scene were the Lancastrian schools, with a boys' school founded in 1810 followed by a girls' school in 1811. Following rapid growth in its first year, the boys' school settled into a new school building in Tower Street. Similarly, the girls' school was located from March 1812 in a new building alongside East Walls (moving to Little London in 1849 and Orchard Street in 1910). Concern that many children with Anglican parents were being drawn into schools founded by dissenters led the Bishop of Chichester, John Buckner, to take a leading role in the establishment of the Sussex Central Schools, with two founded in Chichester in 1812. The first, a boys' school, was located in New Park Road (now the New Park Cinema) while a girls' school, after an early move, took up residence in the Vicar's Hall. The creation of the two Central Schools brought an immediate end to the declining Blue Coat and Grey Coat Schools, whose pupils transferred to the two new establishments.

The system of teaching adopted by the National and Central Schools was dissemination of information through monitors. These were senior pupils who, having received instruction from the teacher, proceeded to teach the same material to small groups of younger pupils. Normally this took place in one large room, with the teacher overseeing and looking on for the purpose of maintaining discipline.

Aerial view of the two Lancastrian schools. The girls' school, first opened in 1958 and completed in 1959, is to be seen on the right. (*West Sussex Record Office*)

employed. The first of these improvement schemes was the canal basin together with the cut that ran from the edge of the city to Hunston. Here, a junction was formed with the newly constructed Portsmouth–Arundel Canal, which itself, through the use of the Arun and Wey rivers, made a direct waterway link with London. For the merchants of Chichester this provided an undoubted advantage, allowing heavy cargoes of coal and general building materials to be brought close to the very centre of the city. Work on the new cut began in September 1818, helping to bring much-needed employment to the area. The advantage of this work was underlined during the winter of 1819, when a section of the canal was cut by only those on poor relief.

A second major project that brought employment to the city was the installation of gas lighting. Overseen by the Board of Paving Commissioners, this was undertaken in 1823. It first required a gas production unit, which

A view of Canon Gate, 1822.

was built alongside Southgate, close to the newly constructed basin. At the same time, a team of labourers was employed on the task of laying the pipes and erecting the new lamps. By the end of that year, the new system of lighting had been extended to each of the city's main thoroughfares, with individual householders also allowed to buy into the scheme.

Such improvements as the new canal and the arrival of gas ensured that the city was beginning to be seen as a more attractive place, both for residence and the setting-up of new businesses. Hence, more houses began to be built. Some were directly associated with the canal, a number of small houses being built close to the basin. In addition, the Richmond Arms was also built at this time. Other developments saw a general expansion of Somerstown and the continuation of house-building in the south-east quadrant of the city.

The house-building project to the south-east was New Town. Centred upon St John's Street and including buildings that faced on to East Street, this was some of the land that had once been occupied by the dissolved friary of the Dominican Order. In 1809, for the purpose of creating attractive and

A map of Chichester published by Longmant & Company in 1822. (*West Sussex Record Office*)

The West Sussex Hospital shortly after completion in 1826. The hospital was renamed the Royal West Sussex in 1913, following a visit to the hospital by King George V.

affordable housing, some of the land in this area had been divided into small individual plots. As the development went ahead, attention was given to the spiritual needs of the community, with St John's Church being constructed between 1812 and 1813. Although representing the nation's established religion, the building has more in common with a non-conformist chapel than an Anglican church at the centre of its community. The product of a private act of parliament and financed through subscription, the building of a church in this situation outwardly offered the wider city little additional value. After all, it was within close proximity to at least two other churches while the immediate community it drew upon appears to have numbered less than 150. Yet it did fulfil a need: through its low-church style, characterised by its high altar that virtually hides the communion table, it drew a congregation that, in future years, frequently outnumbered any other single church in the area.

Another area of development was the Broyle Road. Here, several houses were constructed between the city and the barracks. It was also in this vicinity that a new infirmary was built. Eventually to become the Royal West Sussex Hospital, it was constructed at a cost of £8,985. The site chosen adjoined the original public dispensary, with the new hospital extending the work of that particular institution. It was financed through a subscription scheme, of which Charles Gordon Lennox, the 5th Duke of Richmond (1791–1860) was the largest single subscriber. The foundation stone was laid on 10 June 1825 and after taking just over a year to complete, the new building was ready for occupation on 31 October 1826. At that time it offered bed-space for approximately fifty patients.

Not surprisingly, all this new construction work had a considerable impact upon the size of the population. The nation's first official census, taken in

1801, declared the city population to number 4,774. However, this assessment was not particularly accurate, for those making the count, the parish clergy, were specifically instructed to exclude all 'men actually serving in HM regular Forces or Militia'. It is this that explains an apparent anomaly, the census recording considerably more females than males living in the city; the reason for this was that regiments posted to Chichester attracted large numbers of women who, as non-military personnel, were included by the census enumerators. (As it happens, inclusion of the military in the census would have added at least 1,500 male soldiers.) In April 1795, for instance, when two divisions of the Montgomery Militia left Chichester, the *Sussex Weekly Advertiser* recorded that it was 'augmented by 100 females' who marched with them.

In 1811, the population of Chichester was given as 6,425; in 1821 it stood at 7,362. These two figures are considerably more accurate than that of the first census and provide a more realistic estimate of the city's rate of expansion. During that second ten-year period, Chichester seems to have witnessed a 14.5 per cent population increase. In reality, it could have been higher. While the 1811 population count was swollen by a large number of soldiers (who were now to be included), the subsequent census of 1821 was looking at a town that was no longer in uniform. In other words, there were fewer soldiers to count and proportionately more civilians.

9

An Age of Reform

In Chichester, on 16 November 1830, a massive protest meeting was held in the marketplace. Approximately a thousand farm labourers entered the city during the early part of the day, all of them intending to make their views known. A series of poor harvests, as bad as those of 1814 and 1816–17, had dramatically raised the cost of living. As a result, the poorly paid farm labourers could no longer afford to feed their families. It was for this reason that they had come into Chichester, intent upon persuading the principal farmers of the county that a general rise in agricultural wages was absolutely essential.

In addition to their vast numbers, the labourers had one other very persuasive weapon in their armoury. Throughout the previous few nights there had been a number of attacks on nearby farms. Those carrying out these raids were part of a much wider movement, some people mistakenly believing them to be led by the mysterious Captain Swing. Among farms recently attacked, with hayricks burnt and threshing machines destroyed, were those in the parishes of Bognor, Felpham and Yapton. Nor did these attacks cease with the meeting at Chichester. Instead, they merely shifted to the west, with further attacks over the next few days at Emsworth, Funtington and Westbourne while at Bosham and Fishbourne money was also forcibly levied.

To counter these attacks, the magistrates of Chichester formed an emergency force of special constables who began scouring the local villages in search of the protesters. Following the incident at Bosham, eight were arrested and brought to the city for examination. According to a report in the *Hampshire Telegraph* (22 November 1830):

Their names were Burgh, Budden, Triggs, Snow, Boxall, Jenman, Smith and Binstead. It appears that these individuals were leaders of a mob, amounting to about 200, who on Thursday night visited nearly all the farmhouses in the parish of Bosham, compelling all they saw or met to join them, and destroyed a great many thrashing machines, and collected money to the value of £10 or £12.

At this time, because of the large number of arrests made, the Chichester magistracy were meeting virtually every day. On 29 November 1830, the *Hampshire Telegraph* carried a further report on these proceedings:

> Evans of Nutborne, who was apprehended, and underwent an examination at Chichester, on Saturday last, on a charge, we understand, of purchasing of Mr White, a Chemist at Chichester, and concealing combustible matters, for the purpose of adding incendiaries.

With much of southern England fearing further attacks, a new government was being formed in London. The Tories, who had been in power for twenty-three years, were in the process of being replaced by a Whig-led coalition under the 2nd Earl Grey. Furthermore, this newly elected government was determined upon seeking a long-term solution to the agricultural crisis. In particular, the leaders of the new administration turned their attention to poor relief, aware of its inability to meet the needs of the unemployed and impoverished. For Chichester, these failings had been frequently witnessed, with money levied through the poor rate quite inadequate during times of poor harvest or high unemployment. While a temporary crisis committee might help ease the situation, a much longer-term solution was clearly necessary.

Initially the new government had no real idea as to how the system should be changed. In fact, the House of Commons was completely split, with some favouring an overall increase in the amount of rates being levied while others preferred subsidised emigration. However, the issue was to be finally resolved by a Royal Commission that set about examining the workings of the Poor Law. It was to present its final report to the House of Commons in February 1833. In this report a more efficient system was proposed, with groups of geographically linked parishes (known as unions) sharing the burden of poor relief. Much more important, it was required of these unions that they be far less liberal in their approach, terminating outdoor relief to all able-bodied poor. Instead, those falling into this category were only to be given relief if they entered the workhouse. Following receipt of that final report, the government not only accepted these recommendations but also had them placed on the statute books within the space of six months.

For Chichester, the new arrangements were not only to have an impact but were to take effect considerably earlier than in many other parts of the country. For this, there were two main reasons. First and foremost, the parishes of Chichester had been united since 1753, so it was unnecessary to expend time and effort in this direction. Instead, the Board of Guardians, aware of some of the other proposals made by the Royal Commission, decided to act upon them. As a result, the restrictions upon outdoor relief for able-bodied poor were introduced at the beginning of 1833. So as not to exceed available accommodation, it was also decided that the workhouse should be made considerably less welcoming by reducing the scale of food allowances for those who were considered 'refractory'. Accordingly, it was 'directed that such persons thus sent into the House should be allowed only bread and butter and water'. According to Edward Gilbert, Clerk to the Guardians, who

Abstract of the Receipts and Expenditure of the Guardians of the Poor of the United Parishes of the City of Chichester, from Easter, 1833, to Easter 1834, being 51 weeks.

RECEIVED.	£	s.	d.	EXPENDED.	£	s.	d
Balance from last year	545	5	9	Paid to weekly Out Pensioners	1912	12	0
Arrears of Rates	86	3	1	By occasional Aid	943	0	10
Reimbursements from Sundry Parishes and Persons	82	10	6	Provisions	688	8	8
Repayments for Bastard Children	97	14	6	Clothing	151	12	0
Earnings of the Inmates of the Poor House	72	7	7	Leather and Shoe Nails	62	8	5
Amount of Pensions assigned	111	6	9	Repairs	31	9	3½
Yeast and Coal Ashes sold	2	0	11	Removals	53	0	3½
Hogs sold	10	14	3	Burials	38	1	2½
Gravel sold	12	3	6	Stationary, Postage, Printing, Stamps, and Parish Clerks giving Notice of Poor Rates	34	15	5
Registering Freeholders and Lists sold	1	7	0	Bastardy	1	10	0
Amount received on 10 rates, including three from Hardham's Dividend (£728 12s. 3d.)	4181	11	5	Rates by Order of Sessions	353	2	10
				Paid to Vagrants passing through to January, 1834	11	13	4½
				Ditto since opening the Watch House	0	13	6
				Vagrant Passes	1	6	5½
				Coals and Wood	46	8	8
				Insurance of Poor House	3	12	0
				Salary to Clerk, Master and Mistress	100	0	0
				House Expences, including Soap, Candles, Domestic Utensils, &c.	66	7	3½
				Law Expences, including Appeals, Summonses, Warrants, apprehending Offenders, appointment of Overseers, and Town Clerk's Fees on Magistrates allowance of Poor Rates	72	13	2
				Board and Clothing of Lunatics	151	16	2
				Mrs. Penfold's Annuity one year	7	0	0
				Surgeon's Salary and Bill	93	11	6
				Carriage of Gravel	0	5	0
				Registering & Printing Lists of Voters	34	0	10
				Subscription to Dr. Bell's School	5	0	0
				Coroner's Inquests	2	13	6
					4867	2	0
				Balance to next year	336	3	3
	£ 5203	5	3		£ 5203	5	3

STOCK IN HAND.

EASTER, 1833.				EASTER, 1834.			
Provisions and Clothing	121	1	9½	Provisions and Clothing	109	18	4

GAS AND WATCH ACCOUNT,
From Easter, 1833, to Easter, 1834.

	£	s.	d.		£	s.	d
Balance from last year	49	7	2	Mess. Ainger & Co. Lighting Lamps, &c.	464	1	6
Arrears of Rates	95	11	6	Watchmens' Wages	125	6	0
Amount received on two 6d. Rates	553	3	9	New Coats and Hats for Watchmen	17	4	0
				Straw for Watch House	0	11	8
				Bedding and various Articles for ditto	6	10	10
				Law Expences attending Lease of ditto	9	2	4
				Advertising new Vagrant System in various Papers and Printing Bills	8	10	6
					631	12	10
				Balance to next year	66	9	7
	£ 698	2	5		£ 698	2	5

Average number in the House daily 126.

E. GILBERT Clerk

A page from an account book of the Guardians of the Poor showing expenditure for the year 1833–4. (*National Archives, MH 12/12813*) wrote a report of the changes introduced at this time, the result was highly satisfactory, with 'many casual, as well as permanent paupers, having found that work was not so unobtainable as they supposed it to be whilst they were receiving relief. In fact, the lounging places and corners of the streets formerly occupied by the idlers are now very nearly deserted.'

At the same time, the Guardians also directed attention to a further aspect of the local system: the provision of pensions for the impoverished elderly and those with large families. A committee was established to review these arrangements, with every recipient asked to appear before them. Each was then examined as to the amount of their earnings and the amounts they expended: 'In all the cases thus examined the amount of expenditure so ascertained exceeded considerably the admitted amount of the paupers' earnings. Very many persons were struck off this list, they not appearing to be proper objects of permanent relief, and the amount paid to others was reduced.'

Finally, attention was also turned to other minor abuses 'such as suppers for the Guardians' and the supplying of the workhouse 'other than by [regulated] contract'.

The workhouse, which was now far more central to the administration of poor relief, was essentially that same building that had been donated to the city by William Cawley. Over the years a number of improvements and additions had been made, such that the building was now able to accommodate a maximum of 200. However, at the time of the introduction of these reforms the building rarely contained more than 130. Within the institution there was a rigorous separation of the sexes although young boys were normally allowed to remain with their mothers. Meals, which were served three times a day, lacked both variety and vitamin content. Instead, there was a heavy reliance on bread and potatoes, with meat and split peas served occasionally.

The education of children in the workhouse was not neglected but differed considerably according to gender. All young boys were automatically sent to the Central School in New Park Road, the Guardians annually subscribing £5 for this purpose. Girls, on the other hand, were educated within the workhouse, receiving lessons in reading and needlework from Mary Gilbert, the daughter of the clerk. Ultimately, it was the intention that all children should become usefully employed; the boys sometimes found apprenticeships and the girls usually entered into service. On finding work that allowed them to leave the house, each was given a new set of clothes together with a pair of shoes. It is interesting to note that the shoes were usually made within the house, the Guardians having a contract for the regular supply of leather.

Among the Guardians, as well as within the wider community, there was considerable opposition to the new regime of harshness. Edward Gilbert went so far as to express his fear that, in a future election, many of those in favour of these reforms might well be removed. For this reason he favoured a change to the electoral procedure that would make it more difficult for this opposition group to achieve power. Fundamentally, he suggested that the qualification to hold office, which was based on the amount of rate levied on individuals, should be raised. According to Gilbert, this would have the effect of 'excluding

At a Meeting convened at the Fountain Inn, April 22nd, 1836, by public Handbill to consider the tendency of the **POOR LAW AMENDMENT ACT**, and the consequent propriety of petitioning Parliament either for its Immediate Repeal, or for great Modifications in its Provisions.

Mr. JAMES GRAY in the Chair.

The following Petition to Parliament was proposed by the Rev J. FULLAGAR, *seconded by* R. H. LACEY, Esq. *and* UNANIMOUSLY *adopted.*

THAT your Petitioners are fully aware of the clamour, that was raised against what was deemed the excessive increase of Poor Rates, before the passing of the *Poor Law Amendment Act*, a clamour which in the estimation of your Petitioners was hardly called for : since, notwithstanding their increase, arising from causes, which your Petitioners will not here discuss, they did not bear a greater proportion to the revenue of the Country raised by direct taxes and duties, than they had done in former years : besides its being incontestibly true, that *since the admission, by the legislature in the reign of Elizabeth, that the nation was under a solemn obligation to support all its distressed subjects, the Country has prospered in power and in wealth beyond all expectation and example.*

That your Petitioners have however no objection to any of the pecuniary burthens of the Community being lessened, provided it can be done without injustice : but they have seen with horror and disgust the machinery and working of the POOR LAW AMENDMENT ACT, which, with the exception of the alteration effected by it relative to settlements, whereby much trouble and expence will be saved to parishes, and the means of employment facilitated to the poor, they cannot but consider as holding out the expectation of moral advantages to the poor, which is manifestly deceptive, while in its principle the Act is not only unjust, but oppressive, and opposed at once not merely to the *spirit* of the *British Constitution*, but to *that* of *Christianity.*

Copy of a poster that appeared on the walls of Chichester advertising a meeting to protest against changes that were taking place in the treatment of the poor. (*National Archives, MH 12/12813*)

persons too immediately connected with the lower classes' and therefore most opposed to the reforms.

A more concerted campaign of opposition emerged at the beginning of 1836 with a public meeting at the Fountain Inn. At the meeting a petition was organised for a modification of government policy. In particular, the organisers were concerned that an unsympathetic approach was being taken towards the needs of the poor, contrasting sharply with the old Poor Law, which had been administered with greater kindness and understanding. Organised by the Revd John Fullager, an active radical, the meeting was well attended, with nearly 600 signatures added to the petition. Duly presented to parliament, the petition was one of many being sent at that time, all of them having little effect on the new law.

A further piece of government legislation had considerably less impact on the city than might be expected. This was the Great Reform Act of 1832, normally credited with providing middle class property holders with the vote for the first time. This was achieved through a simple ruling that all males over the age of 21 owning or occupying property of more than £10 in value, would now be eligible to vote. In Chichester, where the right to vote had previously been held by those who paid the poor rate (a low-level property qualification), the increase in the number of voters was relatively small. In the subsequent general election of 1832, the first in which the newly enfranchised could vote, a total of 852 voters were registered in the city. Prior to this, in 1831, the last of the elections using the old system, there had been 716 voters in Chichester.

Nevertheless, the campaign to ensure the passing of the Reform Bill had been widely supported throughout the city and its passing was received by a public demonstration of 'joy and satisfaction'. The *Hampshire Telegraph*, on 19 June 1832, described how the news was received, referring to the ringing of bells, an outburst of banners 'and smiles that lighted every countenance'. At midday, a huge crowd of 500 assembled in St John's Street. Accompanied by the band of the Royal Sussex Militia, they all marched in unison to the 'Great Oak Field' (now Oaklands Park), just outside Northgate, where booths and marquees had been erected. Here was the real party. The local committee that had been established to support the passing of the Reform Bill had purchased huge quantities of food. All those present were invited to eat, with plum cake and 'strong beer' widely distributed. In the evening, further organised gatherings were held at the Assembly Rooms and Fountain Inn while fireworks were set off throughout the city and the cross was once more illuminated.

An engraving of the city and cathedral as seen from the west.

Of course, it should not be forgotten that, for every one of those eligible to vote in Chichester, there were another six adults who were denied the vote. As it happens, this was not something that particularly concerned the Whig-led coalition government that actually introduced the Reform Bill. In themselves, the Whigs were an aristocratic force that was doing its best to maintain the status quo through the principle of watering down a widespread universal demand for a more equitable electoral system. Among those who had made far more radical demands was the late 3rd Duke of Richmond who had once placed before parliament a bill that sought to enfranchise all adult males. Despite such beliefs, which were not in fact shared by his successors, the Richmonds were generally viewed as an autocratic and undemocratic force within the city. When it came to elections – even those of the post-1832 period – the family had little difficulty in determining who was elected. A petition containing 180 signatures and presented to the House of Commons in 1835 expressed the concerns of a number of Chichester voters. They indicated the Richmonds to have an 'undue influence', the result of their control over the corporation:

> That your Petitioners hailed with joy the passing of the Reform Act; by which direct Borough influence in the returning of Members to your Honourable House was destroyed; but from want of a summary and decisive enactment against bribery and treating, from the continued undue influence of Corporate Bodies, from these municipal corporate bodies being self elective, from their generally being under the control of a principal neighbouring peer or landowner . . . your petitioners feared that the elective franchise was still likely to be prostituted to the very worst of purposes.

A flavour of how elections were conducted during these years can be gained from the recorded memories of William Hoare. A native of Chichester in these years, he set down his recollections, these now deposited in the West Sussex Archives Office. Referring, specifically, to elections that took place during the 1830s:

> Now I will tell you the colour of the ribbons. Conservative, purple. Liberal, blue. Radical, pink and purple. The parties paraded through town from morning till evening and as it lasted some days, it was a great expense to the candidates for the parties were well paid and there was a dinner provided every evening and there were open houses for anyone who liked to have a drink. I have also seen barrels of ale rolled out into the

To feed an increasing thirst for knowledge, a Literary and Philosophical Society was established in Chichester in 1831. Later combining with the Mechanics Institute, a society dedicated to the learning aspirations of the working class, it held regular meetings in this delightful seaside-style town house, dating from about 1820.

street and placed on a stand for anyone to help themselves that liked to do so. There were also ribbons thrown about the street for anyone to pick up and show their colour. It was a very common thing for people at that time to wear an orange, blue, pink or a purple waistcoat and necktie to show their colours.

THE CORN EXCHANGE

An extremely impressive building that was added to the city during this age of reform was the Corn Exchange in East Street. Designed as a public market, its central enclosed area was used to display various pitchers that contained samples of locally harvested corn. These samples were then used to extract bids from dealers, with local farmers accepting the most favourable. Construction of the Corn Exchange was financed by seventy shareholders and building work was overseen by a committee of twenty-five agriculturalists and millers. The appointed builder, Messrs Mellew of Brighton, started work on the building in mid-1832, with progress remarkably rapid. Indeed, the building was actually in use shortly after Christmas, although at that time its now-familiar frontage was still incomplete. In part, this was because deliveries of the six iron colonnades together with the stones that make up the architrave were not to arrive in Chichester until February 1833. The columns, each weighing in excess of three tons, together with the architrave stones (weighing a further three tons) were finally placed in position towards the end of April. Originally the architrave, which was completed in cement, showed four emblems of agriculture: a plough, a harrow, a rake and a scythe.

A view of the Corn Exchange as it appeared shortly after completion.

Policing was another aspect of social life to which attention had to be given. This was an area that at one time was jointly overseen by the corporation and the Guardians of the Poor. Prior to the involvement of the Guardians, the city had been dependent on a number of constables, financed only by the corporation, who could be called upon by day or night. The Guardians of the Poor introduced a small number of nightwatchmen, the number eventually reaching seven. Each evening these watchmen reported to a specially built watch-house, newly erected in 1821, where they were each issued with a rattle, lantern and truncheon. From here they proceeded to their area of patrol, having to walk the length of their beat every thirty minutes. Providing limited comfort were watch-boxes, used by the watchmen when they were not walking their beat. Should a wrongdoer be apprehended, then he or she could be taken to the watch-house where the superintendent was usually to be found. The 'Gas and Watch Account' of the Guardians for the period Easter 1833 to Easter 1834 shows that £125 was paid for watchmen's wages while a further £17 was expended on coats and hats. The linking of gas into this same account was another aspect of night-time security in the city, the Guardians paying Messrs Ainger & Co. the sum of £464 for gas used in lighting the street lamps.

Further improvements to the policing system in Chichester were brought about in 1836. By that time, municipal corporations were required to improve law enforcement provision. In order to comply, the corporation not only took over all responsibilities for policing but also formed a watch committee to oversee the workings of a newly created police force. At the time of its inception, the force consisted of a superintendent, a senior policeman and six constables. The superintendent received a salary of £40 a year, the senior policeman 15s per week and the constables 14s per week. This body, exclusive to Chichester, continued to act on matters of law enforcement until 1889 when it was disbanded and absorbed into the county force.

The political and social unrest that had prompted so many changes to the city also affected a further facet of Chichester life, that of the Church. Nationally there was increasing concern that the Church was playing an inadequate role in maintaining social order among poorer sections of society. To correct this, it was considered that more churches were necessary, these to be located in areas of most need. While such a policy was primarily directed at the new industrial towns, it was also to influence developments in Chichester, with three new Anglican churches built during the middle years of the century. First of these was St Bartholomew's, Mount Lane. To the west of the city, where the ruins of the old Church of St Bartholomew were still discernible, a new area of housing was being developed. To meet this particular need, the new church was built on the site of the old, and consecrated in 1832. Financed through local subscription, it was built in the classical style. Another church that was to meet the needs of a newly developing community was that of St Paul. Built between 1836 and 1837, it was designed to serve Somerstown. Later writers have not considered it an architectural success, with Ian Nairn describing it as 'a really horrible lancet Gothic church'.

A final Anglican church of this period was that of St Peter the Great, the subdeanery. Although St Peter's was the largest of all the city parishes, there was no separate church prior to 1852. Instead, services had always been held in the cathedral, a parish altar having been established in the north aisle. Among the regular congregation during the early years of the century was William Hoare. His recollections of the city include a description of the subdeanery within the cathedral:

> The aisle of the church was straight for about sixty feet and then it turned to the right for about the same distance. When I was a boy I used to go with my mother and we used to sit in one of these high pews, aside as the pulpit was round the turn in the aisle, we could not hear either parson or clerk. I used to say it was a first rate place to go to sleep on a hot Sunday afternoon.

As can well be appreciated, the existence of the subdeanery within the confines of the cathedral was far from satisfactory, especially with the continued growth of the parish throughout the early years of the nineteenth century. For this reason, at the beginning of 1847, the dean and chapter launched an appeal to raise money for a new building. The appeal circular went to great lengths in describing a number of additional problems that confronted the holding of regular services:

> This church [the subdeanery in the cathedral] is not unsightly and sordid in its actual condition, but it is incapable under any circumstance of being made a suitable place of worship for the large parish. As it is close adjoining the choir of the cathedral it can have no performance of divine service except during the time when the services of the cathedral are not going on, and thus there are and there can only be prayers and a sermon only once on Sundays and those at an inconvenient hour for a population of more than 2000 souls.

A prospective site, on the corner of West Street and Tower Street, had already been found, and purchased at a cost of £1,200. In the meantime, the large number of donations being received made it clear that the project was more than viable. As a result, Richard Carpenter, the resident architect at the cathedral, was engaged to draw up plans, and the first stone of the new church was laid by the bishop in August 1848.

At once the builders began to encounter the traditional problem that beset all new large-scale constructions in this area. Immediately below the newly acquired land, various ancient walls, later determined as Roman, criss-crossed much of the site. This made the laying of the foundations difficult, so adding to the original estimated costs while lengthening the completion date to mid-1852. As originally planned, the church was to have had a west tower but this was never constructed. Primarily this was a result of cost, since the construction of the tower would have necessitated the purchase of two cottages that immediately adjoined the site of the church.

Two other Anglican churches should be mentioned: All Saints and St George's. That of All Saints, in Church Road, Portfield, was completed in 1869. It was set in a strangely remote location, surrounded by fields, allotments and the city cemetery. In 1902, St George's in Cleveland Road was added, serving the expanding Whyke community. Built at a cost of £4,000 it was consecrated by the Bishop of Chichester in September of that year.

A further Anglican initiative in Chichester was the establishment of a teachers' training college. This was the Bishop Otter Memorial Training College for Schoolmasters, established shortly after the death of that particular bishop in 1840. The college was thought a fitting memorial to a man who had devoted much of his life to bringing about improvements in education. The college itself began life in St Martin's Lane before moving to dedicated premises in College Lane. In these early years, the future of the college was not a clear-cut certainty and it was temporarily closed in 1867. Up to that point, it had only been involved in the training of male teachers, with insufficient numbers of students coming forward. Eventually, in 1873, it was reopened for the purpose of training women, a role it continued to perform until 1960 when it became co-educational.

Outside the Anglican community, a number of new churches and chapels were also built, to meet the needs of a variety of non-conformist sects. Briefly, these included the Ebenezer Independent Congregational chapel, St Martin's Square (c. 1830); the Methodist chapel, East Walls (1840); the United Methodist church, the Hornet (1865); the Methodist chapel, Broyle Road (1875); and the Methodist Church, South Street (1876). To these, in later years, were added the Congregational church, South Street (1892) and the Dependent chapel, Adelaide Road (1891).

The Bishop Otter College as it appeared towards the end of the nineteenth century. At that time, the number of students attending the college was usually no more than forty.

The reading room at Bishop Otter College.

In 1851 a national census on church attendance was carried out to establish whether England was fundamentally a churchgoing nation that was committed to the established religion. Nationally, the outcome was not as had been expected: the numbers of committed Anglicans and those attending any form of church service were both considerably less than supposed. In Chichester, however, the situation was very different. Here, out of a population of 8,647, approximately 4,300 (49.7 per cent) regularly attended church services. Of these, a clear majority, 3,144 (74 per cent), regularly attended Church of England services. Both figures were, statistically, much higher than for the rest of the country.

The mid-century period also saw the beginnings of a revolution in transport. On 8 June 1846 the London, Brighton & South Coast Railway (LBSCR) opened Chichester's first railway, creating a link, via Ford, to Brighton. Inevitably there was considerable local celebration, with these events captured by local newspaper reporters. This account appeared in the *Sussex Agricultural Express*:

This long anticipated event took place on Monday, June 8, and on no occasion have we seen the excitement of the public so high as on this. Large booths and stalls were erected near to the station, and at an early hour hundreds of persons were assembled to witness the departure of the first train for London. Eight trains left here during the day, and as many arrived. The shops were closed and all business suspended, and the city and villages adjacent were drained of their inhabitants. Several bands of music poured forth their enlivening strains, and all was gaiety and animation. During the day, hundreds went by the trains, some to Brighton, some to Shoreham, and others shorter distances, and although many thousands were present, we are happy to say that not the slightest accident occurred.

A particularly fine addition to Bishop Otter College was the chapel, which was built in the Decorated style and completed in 1850.

A view of Chichester railway station showing the original booking office that was first constructed during the mid-nineteenth century. (*Photo courtesy of the late Dave Turner*)

Soon after, continuing work on the line saw the opening of the westward-running section, connecting the city to Havant (15 March 1847) and Portsmouth (14 June 1847). Upon completion of the entire Portsmouth to Brighton route, Victorian Chichester was soon enjoying a regular service of eight trains a day in both directions. The journey time varied according to the number of stops involved, with a journey to Brighton now possible in 1 hour 15 minutes. Connections could also be made with trains to London but this was only possible through the link with Brighton. It was not until 1859 that the London and South West Railway (LSWR) opened a rival route, which made a connection to London via Havant and Guildford.

The ease and frequency of modern-day transport makes it easy to forget that a relatively simple journey in the early nineteenth century was often a painfully slow event. Prior to the arrival of the railway, the fastest way of getting to Brighton was the stagecoach. These ran four services a day and each took approximately four hours. The earliest to leave was the *Royal Sussex*, which left from the Dolphin Hotel at 9 a.m, arriving in Brighton at approximately 1 p.m.; there was no return coach until the following morning. With the railway offering a cheaper, faster and more frequent service, it was not surprising that coach services were rapidly superseded. Upon the opening of the Havant section of the line, the *Sussex Agricultural Express* underlined the situation when it stated,

> We almost bid farewell to stagecoaches; the Southampton and Portsmouth coaches have left us, and the only remaining coach starts every other day to Guildford, there taking the rail for London.

A further extension to the Chichester rail network took place in July 1881 with the opening of the Chichester to Midhurst line. This never proved particularly profitable, being very much a rural line. It survived into the late twentieth century, but lost its passenger service (with the exception of a special school run) from 7 July 1935, although freight services continued until final closure of the line in 1972.

A few years after the arrival of the railway, the city was headline news when the crossing tower and spire of the cathedral collapsed into a heap of

The interior of the cathedral following the collapse of the tower. (*West Sussex Record Office*)

rubble. This was not unconnected with the earlier decision to remove the parish altar to the new subdeanery. The move had allowed the dean and chapter to sanction a number of alterations to the cathedral, which played a part in the eventual collapse. Such works, concentrating upon the north transept and central body of the church, were for the purpose of creating an aesthetic and unified interior that would allow services to flow through the entire building.

As it then stood, the cathedral lacked any form of unity. In part, this had been a product of the north transept having been used as a parish church. An uninviting adjunct, its 'miserable collection of pews and galleries' was not to be removed until 1852. At about this same time several windows were restored and the roofs of both the north and south transepts were raised. To complement this work on the inside, a number of buildings were demolished on the outside. These were a series of shops and houses on the south side of West Street that effectively crowded the cathedral and destroyed its visible dominance.

It is not impossible that vibrations created by these works may have hastened the later collapse. However, irrespective of this, it was a series of further attempted improvements that were more directly connected with the event. Since the construction of the Arundel screen in the mid-fifteenth century, the choir had been effectively separated from the nave. The consequence for the cathedral was that most religious services centred upon the choir, with the nave remaining deserted. To correct this, and return the nave to its original significance, it was decided to remove the screen and place it elsewhere. At the same time, new seating was to be introduced into the choir, for use by the clergy and those officiating.

An artist from the *Illustrated London News* captures the exterior of the cathedral following the collapse of the tower.

In the process of removing the screen, huge fissures in the supporting piers of the central tower became apparent. In essence, they were considered to be of some age but indicative of an underlying problem. The cathedral, but most particularly the central crossing point, had not only been built in an age of limited engineering awareness but had not been designed to sustain the weight of the heightened thirteenth-century tower and spire. Unfortunately, those who examined the fissures underestimated their significance, considering the building to have stabilised. Instead, only a limited amount of remedial repairs were undertaken. These, in the event, proved quite inadequate.

Following the collapse of the spire in February 1861, various attempts were made to deny a connection with the removal of the Arundel screen. It seems unlikely that the timing of the collapse was just a coincidence. Furthermore, there was evidence of a rapid deterioration having taken place around the time of the screen's removal. The event that precipitated the collapse was a severe storm. However, according to one contemporary commentator, George Rowden Burnell, a civil engineer with an interest in the preservation of large medieval buildings, the long-weakened structure had managed to survive a far more violent gale just one year earlier. For this reason, he searched for a cause over and above the hypothesis that the spire was on the verge of collapse and would have done so anyway. Instead, he suggested that the cause was that of the remedial works that had been designed to strengthen the building. Mortar poured into the fissures had not only failed to bond but had helped undermine the existing strength of the supporting piers. More recently, the present surveyor of the cathedral fabric at Chichester has concluded that the final straw was 'removal of the Arundel screen, which must have provided a little bracing on one side' together with 'disturbance caused by subsequent patching' to fill the revealed fissures.

While various enquiries into the cause of the collapse were instigated, much greater attention was given to the destroyed central portion of the cathedral. An immediate decision was taken to restore the central tower and spire to its original design. To undertake this work, the eminent church architect Sir Gilbert Scott was commissioned. His first task was to collect evidence of the original style and design of the collapsed area, his son George Gilbert Scott (1839–97) collecting and annotating much of the fallen debris. In the meantime, a restoration appeal had been set in motion, which received substantial contributions from Queen Victoria,

From collapse to completion of a new tower and spire took approximately five years. This contemporary illustration shows the crowning of the spire, which took place on 28 June 1866.

the Duke of Richmond and the Bishop of Chichester, together with the dean and many of the canons. Although it was a struggle to raise the necessary £48,000, it was eventually achieved, allowing the central tower and spire to be substantially completed by the summer of 1866. It differed from the original only in that it was 8ft higher overall and its windows lacked the partial walling of the original lancets.

Returning to the various social reforms that were affecting the city in these years, we can see that there was one particular issue that was beginning to take priority. This was the need to improve the city's appalling health record. Throughout the nineteenth century various preventable contagions continued to hit the city, including typhus, cholera and dysentery. In theory, there were two ways in which these various diseases could be tackled: better medical facilities and improved hygiene. Both were pursued within the city at this time but the latter was disgracefully long in being achieved.

As regards improved medical facilities, the establishment of the West Sussex Hospital had been an important stride forward. Among the proponents of the new hospital had been Dr John Forbes, originally physician to the dispensary, whose sound knowledge and experience were subsequently transferred to the hospital. Unlike many of his contemporaries, he favoured the use of physical examinations and was one of the first doctors in the country to use a stethoscope.

In terms of preventative medicine, inoculation was playing an increasingly important role. Primarily used in the fight against smallpox, it had been available in Chichester since 1740. In that year, prompted by an outbreak of disease, some 300 were inoculated. A more systematic approach was not to be developed until the beginning of the nineteenth century, a result of the pioneering work of Edward Jenner (1749–1823). In 1804, vaccination centres were established in the city, overseen by a number of local doctors. Supporting this official initiative were a number of amateurs who also offered their own forms of inoculation. Apparently a Bosham farmer, Pierce, was regularly undertaking such work and claimed to have vaccinated 'ten thousand people'. In 1821, following a further outbreak of smallpox in the city, Pierce suggested that Forbes might like to enter into a wager, based on the farmer's ability to generate a mild form of smallpox that could then be used on volunteer patients. It is doubtful whether Forbes accepted the wager but the farmer certainly proved his point, successfully vaccinating more than two hundred pauper children.

The success of the inoculation campaign became apparent in 1831 when the city suffered a further outbreak of smallpox. On that occasion, it was restricted to 130 cases. Much more important, the vast majority of those who had been inoculated through the official scheme were not among those who contracted the disease. Yet, smallpox aside, little impact was being made on the various other killer diseases. For this, there was a particularly good reason: the appalling environmental conditions that dominated city life.

Effectively, Chichester was a vast repository of disease. As yet there was no street drainage, with the street scavengers employed by the Board of Paving Commissioners only able to remove the worst excesses of accumulated filth.

On market days, with hundreds of cattle, sheep and other farm animals brought to the very centre of the city, the resulting accumulation of animal excrement defied description. In summer, with windows and doors open and food often left uncovered, the movement of many thousands of flies must have ensured an unbelievable frequency of diarrhoea and other more serious illnesses. For the city scavengers, the removal of excrement on market days could easily have proved overwhelming. However, they were not expected to take on the entire task. Instead, there was a separate tender, with the individual responsible paying for the right to undertake this work. In fact, it was quite profitable, the product being sold separately as manure.

Adding to the problems of the city's health was that of poor or non-existent domestic sanitation. Household sewage, although collected in cesspits, was usually allowed to drain into the gravel beds beneath the city. Alternatively, those families living near the Lavant simply allowed their household sewage to be deposited into the river. Either method was injurious to health.

Market day in Victorian Chichester prior to removal of the cattle market to Eastgate in 1871. (*Photo courtesy Chichester District Museum*)

The gravel beds, saturated by increasing amounts of sewage, were also a main source of drinking water; the Lavant was little more than an open sewer.

The failure to tackle the three main health issues of the town (the location of the market, drainage and water supply) meant that the health of the city was rated as among the worst in the country. While the national death rate for England and Wales was 22.6 per thousand, for Chichester it was 24.12. Furthermore, in 1888, with main drainage still only a distant dream, the city had more incidents of tuberculosis and typhoid than any other district in Sussex.

At the heart of this failure to come to terms with these serious health issues was the problem of money. It was not that the city was unable to afford the necessary improvements; it was simply that leading inhabitants did not wish to spend the money. Only through continual government pressure, combined with that of a number of more forward-thinking residents, was the problem to be finally addressed.

First to be tackled was the siting of the market. With as many as 15,000 sheep, oxen, pigs and horses brought into the city on market day, the cattle market not only occupied the entire length of East Street but also

The new cattle market alongside Market Avenue. The removal of the market, together with the hundreds of sheep and cattle that were regularly brought to the centre of the town, resulted in a dramatic improvement in the health of the town. (*Photo courtesy Chichester District Museum*)

An extremely rare photograph that shows the laying of the foundation stone of the waterworks engine house at Fishbourne, June 1874. Present at the event were a number of local dignitaries including Chichester's Member of Parliament, Lord Henry Lennox, the Bishop of Chichester, Richard Durnford and the Mayor, J. Caffin. (*Portsmouth Water*)

encroached into West and North Streets. On occasions, trading was undertaken within a few metres of the cathedral. Following a petition, delivered to the corporation in 1865, serious thought was given to removing the market from the centre of the city. A committee was established, which recommended a site close to Eastgate and adjacent to Snag Lane (now Market Avenue). It was, however, a rather controversial choice, with ownership of the land to be purchased in the hands of several members of the council. Notwithstanding suggestions of irregularity, the necessary properties were acquired, albeit at the rather inflated cost of £5,000. By the summer of 1870, work was underway upon the construction of a new roadway and walls, the laying-down of drainage and the ironwork for cattle stands. All this was completed by the following year, with the new market officially opening on 10 May.

The problem of the city's contaminated water supply was effectively highlighted in 1879 with an outbreak of typhoid. In all, there were about fifty cases on the western side of the city (many in the Orchard Street area), leading to a total of six deaths. Careful enquiries revealed that a clear connection could be made with milk delivered by Moore's dairy. It was concluded that there were two possible causes: it originated either from the River Lavant or from a contaminated well used by the dairy. If from the Lavant, it was assumed to be the result of dairymaids' practice of washing the udders of the cows, before milking, in water drawn from the river. In the absence of the ability to analyse microbiological organisms, an alternative possibility was also put forward, which suggested that the outbreak might have its origins in water drawn from a well within the dairy, situated only a few yards from a cesspool.

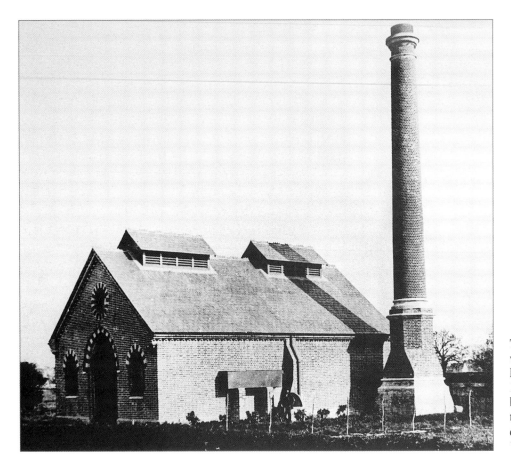

The original Fishbourne waterworks engine house as seen in the 1920s. Although the building still remains, the chimney has been demolished. (*Portsmouth Water*)

As it happens, efforts at improving the supply of drinking-water were already in hand. The Chichester Waterworks Company, since the passing of a private act in 1873, was in the process of providing domestic supplies, using water from works owned by the corporation. These works were at Fishbourne, where wells eventually pumped by three engines provided water for a reservoir that had a capacity of 230,000 gallons (1.04 million litres). Unfortunately, the process was painfully slow, with only 250 of 1,600 homes connected to the system during the first four years of pipe-laying. In 1897, Chichester Corporation, again through an Act of Parliament, acquired control of the Chichester Waterworks Company. This was to remain the situation until 1963, when Portsmouth Water took responsibility for the supply of fresh water.

It was only as a result of constant pressure, much of it by Dr John Freeland, Chichester's first Medical Officer of Health, that positive moves were made in the direction of domestic drainage. In November 1879 a start on this was made, with both drainage and piped water brought to Orchard Street and, in particular, Moore's dairy. However, little further progress was made, and insufficient attention was given to the worsening condition of the Lavant. By 1886 Freeland, who had hoped matters would now be much further forward, was in virtual despair. At that time, the city was in the throes of a further smallpox outbreak while tuberculosis was also taking a heavy toll.

The machinery housed within the pumphouse at the Fishbourne waterworks. Originally it was all steam powered, but has since been replaced by electrically operated machinery. (*Portsmouth Water*)

Unable to contain himself, Freeland declared that any recent improvements in the city's drainage were far too little and 'neutralised by filthings and carelessness. Slops and filth are thrown out not only into smaller streets and about the worst dwellings but also on the main thoroughfare into the gutters and the drain inlets of the chief streets and roads. . . .'

Matters eventually began to progress in 1889. By that time the corporation had formed a separate drainage committee, whose members took a close look at how other municipal bodies disposed of their sewage. In particular, visits were arranged to Southampton and Ealing, enabling the committee to see the chemical precipitation works that both of these boroughs employed. Subsequently, a recommendation was made that a similar system should be employed at Chichester, to be constructed south-west of the city on a site adjoining Apuldram Lane at a cost of £12,000. Once chemically treated, the sewage passed overland before being discharged on top of the tide into Chichester Harbour.

Although the population of Chichester continued to increase throughout the nineteenth century, its rate of growth from 1831 onwards was fairly insignificant. Between that year and 1881, the level of growth was no more than 3.3 per cent. Primarily this was because Chichester, or more particularly

Another glimpse of the steam-powered machinery at the pumphouse. (*Portsmouth Water*)

the original area of the city, had very little land available for housing. This is not to say that there were no open spaces: quite the reverse. Within the walls of the city, the Close retained its green swards, as did areas to the north-west and south-east, where a number of fairly substantial properties also existed within their own spacious grounds. However, the owners of these areas were ill-prepared to release their lands to property developers, which not only restricted population growth within the city but also allowed the areas to retain their characteristic 'genteelness'. In 1839 Pigot's *Royal National and Commercial Directory*, a listing of local tradespeople for the counties of Kent, Surrey and Sussex, described the town in terms that would have been equally applicable to 1889:

> The inns are very respectable, and the domestic and general retail trade of the place rarely experience depression; its prosperity is materially promoted by the circumstance of Chichester being one of those favoured towns which numerous genteel families, of moderate incomes and un-connected with trade, select for their residence; and consequently society here is of rather a select, but by no means of an unsocial character.

Because of the restrictions on further residential developments, those who wished to work in Chichester were increasingly forced to live in more distant suburbs. This, however, creates a statistical conundrum. At what point are such individuals to be regarded as residents of the city? Judging by the decennial census population count, this is only when the borders of the city are artificially extended to embrace these new areas of development. In Chichester this occurred in 1893, when the city was generally extended through the incorporation of various outlying areas. A few years later, because of this, the 1901 census was recording a population of 12,244, a figure that represented a 55 per cent increase since the previous census of 1891.

So, from where did these newly arrived contributors to the population of Chichester emanate? Well, to begin with, and to state the obvious, they were not necessarily newcomers to the area. The major part of the increase consisted of residents of the neighbouring parishes now drawn in to the new municipal borough. Furthermore, these were the same areas that had previously absorbed Chichester's nineteenth-century overflow population. While in earlier years they had not been included statistically as part of Chichester, they were, in reality, very much part of that original city. Among the areas now brought into Chichester were most of Rumboldswyke and Portfield together with part of the parish of Oving. A further administrative reorganisation also occurred a few years later, in 1896, when all of the parishes of the enlarged city were consolidated into the single parish of Chichester.

On its own, Rumboldswyke was the single most important contributor to this newly expanded population. At one time a completely separate community, Rumboldswyke had, during the nineteenth century, been linked to Chichester through housing that stretched the length of the Hornet. Within Rumboldswyke itself, however, a period of particularly rapid growth had occurred between 1851 and 1861. During those years, the population had expanded by 82.7 per cent, rising from 318 to 581. This was a considerable acceleration in the growth of an area that, during the previous fifty years, had witnessed only a 42 per cent increase. According to research carried out by Monica Maloney, the reason for that dramatic growth was the result of a land purchase scheme carried out by the National Freehold Land Society. In 1851, for the purpose of creating affordable housing, the society had secured a wedge of land (between Bognor and Wick (now Whyke) Roads and encompassing the subsequently named York Road), which was then divided into sixty-five separate plots. Upon each of these, with some further subdivided, were then constructed a variety of small houses.

It was the residents of those particular properties that accounted for that sharp rise in Rumboldswyke's population. Over the following decades, there was a continued increase in population, but at a much lower rate. Nevertheless, by 1901, following integration into the new municipality, Rumboldswyke and its offshoot of Whyke, represented 17 per cent of the borough's population.

The amalgamation of Whyke and Portfield into the expanded municipal borough had not been achieved without opposition. Some of the residents of the areas later to be absorbed fought the proposal fiercely, not wishing to pay the increased rates that would be the immediate result. Such an attitude was somewhat short-sighted as, once they had joined the enlarged borough, a number of general improvements could be effectively pursued. Most important of these were improvements to existing sanitary arrangements. In both Whyke and Portfield, these were particularly poor, with cesspools the only system of drainage. These were emptied, when full, by the occupiers of each individual house. Through integration into the municipal borough, residents would be connected to the city's new sewerage arrangements at an estimated cost of £4,830 and an annual rate of £359 thereafter. If their properties were drained separately, according to Baldwin Latham, the engineer of the sewerage scheme, the cost would be £11,130 and the subsequent annual expense £936.

A further predicted gain would be a general improvement in the state of the roads. While the highways and byways within the city area were now kept to a very high standard, this was not the situation immediately beyond. In approaching either Whyke or Portfield, the traveller passed from clean and well-lit streets into 'a desolation of filth'. Those who favoured integration, and there were a great many, did so because of exasperation with the situation. In March 1892, a number of Portfield parishioners approached the local vestry and urged the Way Wardens (those responsible for roads and pathways) to undertake some improvements. Apart from a small amount of kerbing and channelling work, their demands were totally ignored.

Following a full enquiry undertaken in March 1893, the decision to integrate Whyke and Portfield into the municipal borough was confirmed. Looking at the evidence presented by the two sides, there was simply no contest. Whereas one side showed concern only at the increase in rates, the other clearly looked to bring about considerable improvements to the local environment. Certainly, these two outer areas of Chichester could not continue without main drainage and clean water, except at considerable risk to health. Indeed, had they not been brought into the Chichester scheme, it is likely that they would have been subject to a government order to introduce their own schemes. This, of course, would have resulted in the parishioners of those areas having to pay the much greater costs, as estimated by Baldwin Latham during the enquiry.

10

The Era of the Selsey Tram

Complaints about the local rail service were as much a talking point in the Chichester of the 1890s as they were to be in the 1990s. Most certainly, late-Victorian Chichester had a problem with the reliability of its trains. On the line between Portsmouth and Brighton, it was not uncommon for trains to be running an hour late or to be cancelled altogether. Nor was the recently completed Midhurst line any better. Here, not only were delays just as serious, but the line was also subject to additional hazards. Shortly after Christmas 1886, the entire route was closed for several days, heavy falls of chalk blocking the line in two places. Nor did matters improve with the arrival of the new century. In September 1904 the Midhurst line was again in total disruption, a derailed locomotive responsible for tearing up a hundred yards of track just to the north of Cocking.

The official opening of the Selsey tram. In the foreground is the newly purchased locomotive *Chichester*. (*Photo courtesy Chichester District Museum*)

The cause of these problems was underinvestment, the London, Brighton & South Coast Railway having become financially overextended. Nevertheless, those who suffered, the residents of Chichester, were often able to make light of these problems. Alderman Ballard, mayor in 1897, made a point of recalling the despatches of one particular journalist, a man named Finegan. Having been asked by his editor to report on the problems of a particular train journey, he simply telegraphed, 'Down agen, up agen – Finegan'. That Alderman Ballard should choose to relate this particular gem was prompted by his being asked to address the assembled gathering that marked the opening of the Selsey tramway. It was an event that took place on 27 August.

Although known as a tramway, the new link to Selsey had more in common with the national rail system. Apart from anything else, its lightweight trains used the same gauge of rail as that commonly used throughout the rest of the country. Furthermore, an actual junction existed with the London, Brighton & South Coast Railway; this allowed the same trucks to be used on the two lines. Yet the decision to name it a tramway was no flight of fancy. Instead, it provided the operating company with the chance of exploiting a legal loop-hole. Normally a Light Railway Order would have been necessary, imposing upon the company a range of expensive safety measures, including, in partic-ular, crossing gates (when passing over a public highway) and a signalling system. On the other hand, if a Light Railway Order had been secured, this would have carried the right to undertake the compulsory purchase of land. Not having this, the Selsey tramway tended to meander across the country-side, using only land that was voluntarily sold for tramway use.

Only in two areas can it really be said that the Chichester to Selsey line reflected the operations of a normal tramway company. As already noted, operations were at a much reduced speed, with a normal journey time of about thirty minutes, suggesting an average speed of about 15 miles an hour. The second similarity was that of ticket distribution, with these sold on board by a conductor who also acted as the train guard.

The Selsey tram, or to give its full name, The Hundred of Manhood and Selsey Tramway, operated out of Chichester from a platform that was 150yd from the mainline train station. It was, in fact, just to the south of the coal yard, which necessitated a walk to secure a connection with trains to Portsmouth, Brighton and London. From its Chichester terminus, the line curved sharply to the south, using an ungated crossing to pass over Stock-bridge Road. The line's exit point from the city was via a shallow cutting that took it through farmland before running parallel to the canal. The rest of its 7½-mile journey took it through Hunston, Chalder and Sidlesham before terminating at Selsey Beach station.

To undertake its initial operation, the tramway company had purchased two engines, these appropriately named *Selsey* and *Chichester*. Unusually for a railway that seemed to look for economies in every direction, *Selsey* was a brand-new engine which had been purchased direct from the manufacturer. For the cognoscenti, this was a Peckett 2-4-2T and was to be the only new locomotive ever purchased by the tramway company. Much more in keeping with the style of the Selsey tramway was the *Chichester*, an engine built for the Great Western Railway Company in 1850. In future years, the Selsey tramway company was to purchase a number of ageing locomotives, these to replace earlier acquisitions that had reached a point of complete uselessness. Even the newly purchased Selsey was eventually run into the ground, good only for scrap on closure of the line in 1935.

At the time of the opening of the Selsey tramway, high hopes were held for a reliable and punctual service and that the line would not fall into the bad ways of the London, Brighton & South Coast Railway. Almost at once, such hopes were dispelled, the official opening delayed by the late arrival of the service from Selsey:

> A somewhat unpromising commencement was made to the new company's operations, inasmuch as the train was nearly an hour late in starting. Someone suggested that it had caught the complaint of unpunctuality from its big neighbour, whose trains have not been keeping the best times of late.

On this occasion, the reason was a change in the itinerary. At short notice an engine, *Chichester*, had been sent to Selsey to collect a number of residents who had expressed a desire to join in the celebrations at Chichester. Despite such an ominous start one local newspaper, the *Chichester Express*, fulsomely welcomed the new line. On 2 September an editorial proclaimed,

> The Selsey light railway has been opened with due rejoicing and Sussex possesses one more link between its enchanting inland district and its salubrious seaboard. The existing link is one of light iron; may the coming months forge links of solid gold.

As it happens, the lateness of the service on that opening day was not a singular event. Over the years, the Selsey tram acquired an unrivalled reputation for unreliability and lateness. Often this was a result of extreme economies, with its ageing locomotives frequently breaking down. Of greater concern, and also adding to these delays, were accidents at the ungated crossings. In theory, engine drivers were supposed to sound their whistles as they approached each crossing. While they undoubtedly did so, the encroaching hedgerows often muffled the sound, ensuring that motorists were often unaware of an impending collision.

The year 1897 also witnessed the opening of the West Sussex County Asylum at Graylingwell. Built to accommodate those with severe mental health problems, the building replaced an earlier arrangement that had centred upon the asylum at Hayward's Heath. East and West Sussex together with the County Borough of Brighton had jointly financed this particular building. However, the hospital at Hayward's Heath proved too small for their combined needs with West Sussex having to provide separate accommodation from its own resources. The new arrangement, which took effect from January 1894, was made more palatable by a severance payment of £37,920, which was put towards the construction of a new hospital. In the meantime,

A locomotive being lifted back on to the Selsey tramway. Derailments were a further and frequent cause of delays. (*Photo courtesy Chichester District Museum*)

Regarded as possibly Chichester's first car owner, Mr T.S. Adcock is seen in his chauffeur driven De Dion Bouton while touring the New Forest. An alternative to the train, motorcars were only an option for the most affluent at this time. (*Photo courtesy Chichester District Museum*)

however, it was necessary for the county council to make arrangements with any other nearby authority for available beds.

The situation as it stood was far from satisfactory. Fortunately, though, a site for the new hospital had already been identified, and a purchase price of £19,500 paid to the owners of the land, the Ecclesiastical Commissioners. This was for the 25-acre site at Graylingwell, which stood within the northern boundary of the city. Following preparation of the land for the new building, a contract was signed for its construction with Messrs James Langley & Co. of Crawley. This was in January 1895, the cost estimated at £114,669. Work commenced in May 1895, and the County Asylum finally opened for the reception of patients on 26 July 1897.

The newspaper-reading public, at the time of the hospital's completion, appear to have been fascinated by statistics. As a result, it is easy to find that the actual building covered 7¼ acres of ground, had 2 miles of ridges and hips, used 11 million bricks, required 21,000sq yd of slate and 120 tons of sheet iron. Furthermore, there was 4½ miles of piping, 9,000yd of pitch pine flooring, 722yd of corridor and . . . But need I say more?

To what extent such facts were absorbed is difficult to say. Fortunately, the *Bognor and West Sussex Recorder* provided an alternative and more human approach to the opening, going to great lengths to explain, in July 1897, how patients were to be treated. The article, based on an interview with Dr Kidd, the newly appointed medical superintendent, was slightly unusual in that it described 'the system as if already the Asylum were full of patients'. It was a

The Selsey tramway, as depicted in this postcard, was often overcrowded. On a weekend summer's evening the return journey from the seaside idéal was not to be envied.

situation that did not occur until the end of the year, the hospital not fully occupied until December. However, based on the interview, the reporter was able to make several observations. Referring to the clothing worn by patients:

> Care is taken to avoid anything like uniform or institution clothing. Tweed of different colour and patterns for the men, and varied, comfortable, and tasteful dress material for women, do away with any semblance of a distinctive badge. The shawls provided for the latter might be worn with pleasure by anyone.

For a newly arriving patient:

> He probably is not called upon to do anything for the first day or two, but he very soon spends his morning in work in the shops, the garden or in the farm, either at shoemaking, tailoring, plumbing, or in trimming the grounds or gardens, or assisting in field work. Again, there is no compulsion. If he objects he is allowed to remain in doors, but he very soon gets sick of doing nothing and is willing to join others.

As for the general course of the day:

> At 12.30 a good dinner is provided and after a quiet smoke (yes, actually a smoke!), at 2 o'clock they return to work. As they go to work each afternoon, the men are given a portion of tobacco, which is eagerly looked forward for. No work – no tobacco.

An aerial view of the sanatorium at Graylingwell Hospital. The addition of tennis courts and gardens was a special feature of the hospital, these being used to keep patients active. (*West Sussex Record Office*)

Finally, the entirety of the asylum was described as a small town:

> Lofty store rooms, huge kitchens and bakery, endless rooms and corridors, a splendid recreation room with a stage completely furnished in every way for theatrical performances, workshops for every trade, a dispensary fitted up with exquisite care and finish, these are some of the great features that compel attention.

Another landmark occasion during these final years of the nineteenth century was the arrival of public film shows. The first public showing of a film in Chichester was during a performance of the pantomime *Blue Beard* at the Corn Exchange. This was on Boxing Day 1896 when a series of short films was shown, including *The Arrival of the Czar in Paris* and the slightly less interesting *Gardeners Burning Weeds*.

The Corn Exchange, by that time, had taken on a more general role, having become a popular entertainment venue. Only a few years later, however, it was to be given over exclusively to the showing of films. In 1910, the clerk of the Corn Exchange, John Jacobs, acquired a cinematographic licence for the building, which underwent a number of internal alterations. Among them was the introduction of tip-up seats, electric ventilation and improved projection facilities. Undertaking the showing of films was J.W. Poole, an early pioneer of the cinema, who began a regular programme of film shows. Generally, these were in the evenings at 7.45, although matinees were held on Thursdays and Saturdays. At the end of the first year of regular screenings, the *Chichester Observer* reported,

> Messrs Poole continue to attract large crowds to the Corn Exchange where they are well maintaining their reputation as the leading exhibitors of electric pictures. Their films are carefully selected, and they have a happy knack of providing pictures exactly to the taste of

East Street, 1903.

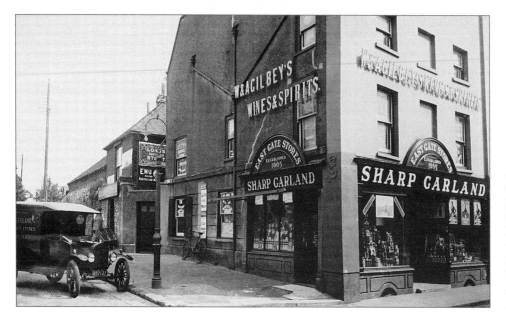

A Sharp Garland delivery van (note the precision parking) stands outside the Eastgate Stores. Motor vehicles quickly became indispensable for small businesses. (*Photo courtesy Chichester District Museum*)

the Chichester public. This is undoubtedly the most popular entertainment that has ever been presented to Cicestrians.

The organisation overseen by J.W. Poole continued to show films at the Corn Exchange for the next ten years. During that time it was known as Poole's Picture Palace and, somewhat briefly, as Poole's Electric Pictures. However, in the early 1920s, as a consequence of falling audiences, Poole gave up his interest in the Corn Exchange, with the showing of films continued by Stanley James.

Another film theatre to appear in Chichester immediately before the First World War was the Olympia Electric Theatre (usually known as 'the Electric'), situated in Northgate. Opened on 23 May 1910, it was owned by Chichester Olympic Ltd and counts as the city's first purpose-built cinema. Constructed by Vick and Son of Tower Street, it was given an impressive white façade in the modernistic style of the age. Inside, it had an auditorium and balcony that, between them, could comfortably accommodate 374 cinemagoers in standard tip-up seats. The local press, in reporting on the screening of its first major film, *Judas Maccabeus*, described its projection on to a plaster screen as 'very clear and with the minimum of vibration'. Immediately adjoining 'the Electric' was a roller-skating rink, also owned by Chichester Olympic Ltd.

Apart from the cinema, Chichester offered little else in the way of public performances. It had lost its theatre in 1847, and there were no music halls or dedicated sporting arenas. To make up for this, there was a heavy reliance on simpler forms of entertainment, with open-air concerts by the city band proving particularly popular. In addition, cycling, road running and tennis (the last of these in Priory Park) frequently drew large numbers of participants and spectators. Not to be missed was the annual visit of Alexandra, Anderton and Haslam's circus, which brought a rare glimpse of exotica to the city.

For the town's working folk, the annual Sloe Fair was particularly favoured. It was the sole surviving city fair, with St James's, Whit Monday and Michaelmas fairs having all disappeared during the early to mid-nineteenth century. Despite this, a concerted campaign to abolish the Sloe Fair was mounted in 1904. In that year, a number of prominent citizens petitioned the Home Office, claiming it to be the cause of numerous evils. If this could be proved, then closure of the event could be carried out in accordance with the Fairs Act of 1871. Specifically, it was claimed:

1. The Fair is the cause of a considerable increase of immorality and intemperance in the city.
2. The ill-effects upon young children, who are brought face-to-face with scenes of intemperance, immorality, dissipation and excess, which they would never see elsewhere, and hear language of the most revolting description.
3. The cases of crime and breaches of the peace brought before our magistrates at this period are much more numerous than other times, and are clearly traceable to this Fair.
4. The Fair is a nuisance and a cause of annoyance not only to those living near but also to the city generally.

However, this righteous group of individuals had no real proof upon which to base their assertions. The Home Office, in collecting evidence, wrote to Superintendent Ellis, Deputy Chief Constable of Chichester, seeking his opinion. While he admitted he neither liked nor disliked the fair, he could not support the claims of the petitioners. The one-day event, held at the end of October, was not, he indicated, a particular drain on police resources. If ever there was trouble, and here Ellis turned to his own deep-seated prejudices, it

The Chichester Sloe Fair. Still an annual event within the city, it came under considerable threat during the early years of the twentieth century. (*Photo courtesy Chichester District Museum*)

was through the presence of 'gypsies'. He went on to refer to this much-maligned group 'as a dirty and ill-behaved class'.

In fact, the debate over the continuance of the fair quickly transferred itself into a clash between two distinct classes. In his submission to the Home Office, Ellis referred to those wishing to abolish the fair as 'the ruling persons, the better class'. Those opposed to abolition, and whom he clearly did not support, he described as 'the working class'. In putting his own views forward, Ellis felt it would be better if money that they spent at the fair was used instead on 'food and clothing' for their families.

Not surprisingly, working class Cicestrians did not agree. One of their number, Joe Mills, a 62-year-old working cutler, took the trouble to write to the Home Office. Stating his credentials to be those of 'a Chichester man born and bred' he felt that 'doing away' with the fair would be 'a cruel shame'. He felt that those in favour of abolition were no more than a 'small clique' who simply 'didn't like people enjoying themselves'. As well as writing this letter, Joe Mills was one of a hundred working class signatories to a petition that was also submitted to the Home Office.

Throughout 1904 the battle raged. Increasingly it became clear that the 'ruling class' had an ulterior motive. Their reason for wishing the fair to be abolished was so that the land upon which it was held, Oaklands Park, could be used for the building of an enlarged workhouse. Since the expansion of Chichester, greater pressure had been placed on the Guardians, with the workhouse too small for current needs. Furthermore, matters had not been helped by a fire that had destroyed Westhampnett workhouse, which had accommodated some of the city's poor. Oaklands Park, which stood next to the existing building, was seen as the only available land upon which an extension could be constructed. However, in order to abolish the fair, under the terms of the Fairs Act, it had to be proved that the fair was a general public nuisance.

The 1904 Sloe Fair, held on Thursday 20 October, was viewed with great interest. Many expected it to be the last ever, especially if there was a general outbreak of disorderly behaviour. In the event, the fair saved itself. On that glorious occasion, there was very little that anyone could complain about. Admittedly, in the evening, a few people engaged in throwing confetti and squirting water, but even this did not prompt the involvement of the police. Anyway, such minor disturbances were overshadowed by the attendance of massive well-behaved crowds throughout the day. Each and every fair-goer was drawn by the good, wholesome fun provided by equestrian displays, shooting galleries, coconut shies, gingerbread stalls, a china emporium and fried-fish stalls. A major attraction was a mobile cinema, a temporary rival to the more frequent showing of films at the Corn Exchange. In the *West Sussex Observer*, it was noted,

> The cinematograph did a roaring trade. On the platform outside the booth a young girl, clad in cheap finery that makes so brave a show under the glare of naptha lights, was dancing to the tune of a popular song, blared from the pipes of a mechanical organ.

Apart from the mobile cinema, the other major attraction was the steam-driven switchback railway that was electrically illuminated after dark. Again, the local reporters were impressed, pointing out that the lighting system was well in advance of that used in Chichester, where the city lights were still dependent on gas, not changing to electricity until 1909.

The only real critics of the fair on this occasion were members of the Salvation Army. Throughout the day, their speakers proclaimed the fair a moral danger, but their efforts were largely ignored. Furthermore, with the day passing off so successfully, there was little that the 'ruling class' could do to bring about its demise. Not only was there a further Sloe Fair in 1905 but the event has continued into the twenty-first century. Its site, although no longer a grass field, has also remained fundamentally unchanged.

Less successful in the achievement of survival was St Martin's Church. Since the amalgamation of the parishes in 1896, it had been clear that there were too many churches in the city, and that some sort of reduction was necessary. The two most likely contenders were St Martin's and St Olave's, both under the care of a sequestrator. Neither could really be afforded as they both produced a meagre stipend. It was, however, upon St Martin's that the axe was to fall, the building otherwise requiring considerable expenditure upon its continual repair and upkeep.

The fate determined for it was demolition, which was carried out in 1906. At the time, a number of surprise discoveries were made, mainly related to an earlier restoration that had been undertaken in 1804, financed by Martha Dear, a parishioner of St Martin's at that time. It was generally believed she had removed much of the older structure and, initially, progress on the demolition of the building seemed to prove this. When the pillars were removed, for instance, it was discovered that within the outer casing of wood panels, they contained no interior masonry or brickwork. Instead, a huge oak beam, much riddled with woodworm and rot, was responsible for supporting the entire weight of the roof. Furthermore, upon removal of the interior lath and plaster, it became clear that the south and west walls were of a fairly recent date. The surprise, however, was that the north and east walls of the nave were clearly of medieval origin. Although they, too, had been restored, the restoration appears to have dated to the sixteenth or early seventeenth century. This was confirmed by a further discovery of Gothic text from this period, arranged in tablet form, and plastered over in 1804.

As it happens, only the core of the building was removed, with the walls of the church left standing. Today, this forms a pleasant memorial garden which is in the keeping of the city council. At night the gates are locked, so helping ensure that this quiet and secluded retreat remains free of vandalism and despoliation. To remind those who enter the garden of the original church and its extensive restoration, there is a tablet to Martha Dear in the area of the former chancel.

Unfortunately, two scars disfigure the collective memory of these years: those of the major conflicts that occurred between 1899 and 1918. These are the Second Boer War (1899–1902) and the Great War (1914–18). Both took with them the lives of a number of young and promising Cicestrians. Among

South Street decorated for the Coronation of King George V. (*Photo courtesy Chichester District Museum*)

A feature of communal celebrations, especially important royal events, was the erection of decorated archways on the site of the former city gateways. This photograph shows the archway erected at Southgate to celebrate the coronation of George V.

the first to go to South Africa upon the outbreak of the first of these conflicts was the constituency's Conservative Member of Parliament, Lord Edmund Talbot. In October 1899, he made this surprising announcement to a packed meeting of party loyalists held at the Corn Exchange, so imbued with feelings of patriotism and 'a desire for the triumph' of national honour, that everyone present appears to have welcomed the move. A few days later, at a farewell gathering, Lord Talbot even received the support of his political opponents.

This particular incident of political bipartisanship was typical of the entire war. Within the city, over the next three years, there was limited discussion as to the rights and wrongs of the war. With a Conservative government in

The George V coronation day arch at Eastgate. (*Dela MacFarlane*)

power it might have been expected that the local Liberal party would act as a catalyst of anti-war feeling. This was not to be. Instead, they stood back from any form of opposition. In the general election of 1900 – known as the 'khaki election' – the Liberals failed to offer a candidate at Chichester. This was a surprising decision, given that the Conservatives had called the election to take advantage of the prevailing euphoria.

Following Lord Talbot's decision to fight in South Africa, it was the turn of the Chichester detachment of the Buffs. On 23 November 1899, led by their regimental drum and fife band, over 200 men marched from the barracks to the railway station. Here, a special train had been arranged to convey them to Portsmouth:

> When the whistle sounded for the departure, there was a sign of enlivening enthusiasm. The band of the 3rd Battalion Royal Sussex broke forth into the familiar strains of 'Auld Lang Syne' while the people on the platforms waved their hats and handkerchiefs and cheered again and again.

Over the following months, Chichester witnessed a number of similar scenes, the barracks having become an important assembly point for those posted to South Africa.

Although the war lasted much longer than had been predicted, support continued through to the bitter end. Returning battalions were cheered just as heartily as those leaving for the war. However, war-weariness certainly set in and it was with marked jubilation that the final series of victories were joyously celebrated. The relief of Ladysmith in February 1900 resulted in the raising of flags on all public buildings, the ringing of church bells and the holding of thanksgiving services in most of the city churches. But the long awaited relief of Mafeking easily topped all this. With news of the event reaching Chichester on the evening of 18 May 1900, many poured on to the four main streets of the city. Patriotic songs were sung and the crowd relieved its pent-up feelings by repeated outbursts of cheering. Over the following few days decorations sprang up everywhere, these blending into the commemorative celebrations held a few weeks later for the purpose of celebrating Queen Victoria's fifty-third year on the throne. For this reason, the Queen's initials, 'V.R.', and those of Baden-Powell (the hero of Mafeking), were to be found throughout the city. Once again, as with the report of the cinematographer at the Sloe Fair, the *Observer*'s reporter took a side-swipe at the borough's disinclination to introduce electric street lighting:

> All parts of the city were gay with colour; and in many cases preparations were also made for illumination by means of gas devices or oil lamps; Messrs Shippam also displayed the electric light, which they have installed, without waiting for the slow moving corporation to supply it.

Final victory was a further cause for celebration. On 1 June 1902 the welcome news arrived in the form of a telegram displayed outside the post

Student teachers at the Bishop Otter College enjoy their annual sports' day, *c.* 1910.

Staff and senior students of the Bishop Otter College, June 1912.

office. Shippam Ltd also displayed a copy outside their South Street shop while, more demonstratively, 'discharging a bomb'! Although the original telegram had arrived at 6.15 p.m., so rapidly did the news spread that the cathedral bells were being rung by 6.30 p.m. It was not until the following day, however, that the celebrations really got underway. During the afternoon, shops closed early while most of the main streets were decked out with flags and bunting. The highlight of the day was a huge military parade, with hundreds lining the streets 'and the more youthful, armed with trumpets, trying to make as much noise as possible'.

A vast crowd assembled in North Street to await the announcement of the general election result, January 1910. Once again, Edmund Talbot took the constituency for the Conservative party.

In the twelve-year period between the end of the Boer War and the outbreak of the Great War, Chichester received three important royal visits. In both 1906 and 1908 King Edward VII toured St Mary's Hospital, meeting a number of the patients. The second visit was particularly remembered as the king was, on that occasion, accompanied by Queen Alexandra and the then Prince and Princess of Wales. A further royal visit took place in August 1913 when George V bestowed the title 'Royal' upon the West Sussex Hospital. This was the occasion of the hospital's official reopening, a scheme of modernis-ation and enlargement having been completed. On the north side, sanitary blocks and an operating theatre had been built while a new outpatients' department had also been added.

The Great War, subsequently known as the First World War, broke out in August 1914. From the outset recruitment from within the city was far higher than that of the Boer War, with many hundreds of Cicestrians joining

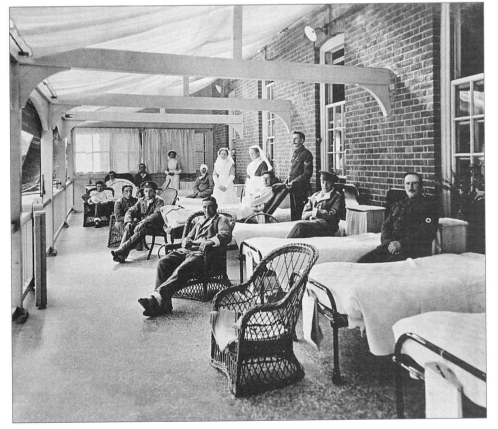

Troops march through St Pancras. Possibly taken at the outset of the First World War, the group may include a number of local volunteers. (*Photo courtesy of the late Dave Turner*)

During the First World War, Graylingwell became a military hospital and many thousands of wounded soldiers were brought here. This typical scene shows a group of convalescing soldiers sitting on one of the covered verandas. (*West Sussex Record Office*)

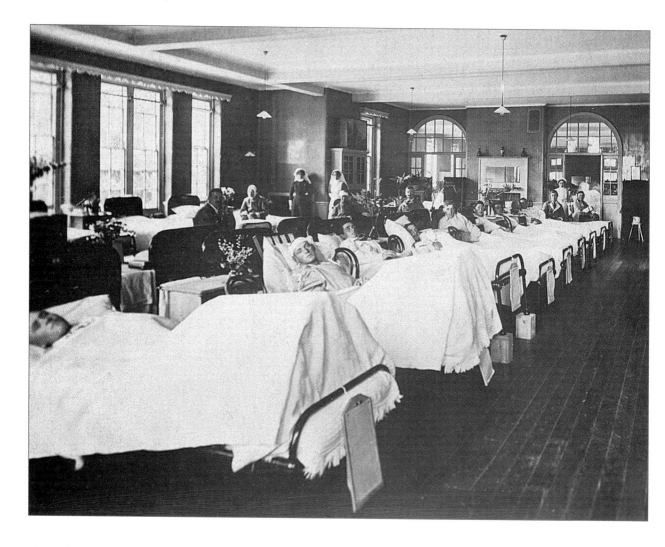

the colours during the first months of the war. Many, of course, volunteered for the county regiment but it seems that there were few other regiments who did not see a volunteer from Chichester within their ranks. Not surprisingly, this high level of recruitment also brought with it a heavy loss of life. In all, 333 of those serving were killed in action. Although the majority were from the army (with over a hundred serving in the Royal Sussex) a sizeable proportion had served in the navy. On board the battleship HMS *Formidable* in January 1915, the life of one of Chichester's youngest was claimed, that of Trevor Munro, a midshipman aged only 16. The sinking of the cruiser HMS *Hampshire*, while engaged in conveying Lord Kitchener to Russia, also claimed lives of those from Chichester. In June 1916, as a result of striking a mine off the Orkneys, three local sailors were drowned.

However, it was not just men of fighting age who were drawn into the conflict. Many others were also doing what they could. Among them were the nursing staffs of the Royal West Sussex and Graylingwell Hospitals, both institutions seeing military use. While the former also continued as a civilian hospital, setting aside fifty beds for the military, the latter was given over entirely to the war. This meant that in March 1915 all of the existing

One of the military wards at Graylingwell.

patients in Graylingwell were dispersed to other parts of the country, so creating space for a thousand wounded soldiers. Many of the existing doctors and nurses remained, however, with Dr Kidd, the medical superintendent, appointed to the rank of lieutenant-general. Even so, a considerable augmentation of skilled staff was required: a large number of resident surgeons had to be appointed by the War Office, with additional senior nurses drawn from hospitals in London. Providing invaluable assistance were a number of local volunteers, in particular members of the Red Cross and St John Ambulance, together with Boy Scouts who acted as messengers.

One little-known body created in Chichester at this time was the City Guard. Established in August 1914 by the mayor, it had certain parallels with the volunteers of the Napoleonic age. Outwardly, it was not supposed to be a military force, being available for any useful purpose (keeping order, road patrols and stretcher-bearing) that would aid the community. However, the undercurrent of feeling was that the City Guard should also have military training, so making it available in the event of an invasion. As part of their training, the new recruits were given access to a rifle range and regular training sessions were to be held. For their part, senior military officers were totally opposed to the scheme, pointing out that their use in any military situation might result in the City Guard being seen as 'non-belligerents' and hence, if captured, not entitled to the same treatment as a uniformed soldier.

Members of the Red Cross Society were brought to Graylingwell to make plans to deal with the impending wartime crisis, 1914.

Graylingwell convalescents, such as the man seen here, were given special uniforms to show that they were soldiers wounded in combat.

It was through local newspapers, in particular the *Observer and West Sussex Recorder*, that the full horrors of war were brought home to those living in the city. While national newspapers might report the various military attacks, whether a victory or a defeat, the *Observer* was much more personal in its approach. Every month, the total number of locally recruited volunteers was recorded, with a full roll-call of names listed in each edition. A further feature was the use of letters from the front line, local families encouraged to send to the newspaper copies of letters they may have received. Finally, and most tragic of all, were the weekly reports of those who had either died or sustained serious injury. Where possible, such reports were accompanied by a photograph, often showing the individual shortly after recruitment and resplendent in his new uniform.

A further feel for the war could be gained by a visit to Poole's Picture Palace or 'the Electric'. Both normally screened a series of short films together with some topical news stories. Mostly the films were light-hearted and featured the archetypal villain and a girl tied to a railway line. In October 1916, however, a much more important film came to Chichester, which was the official government-sponsored *The Battle of the Somme*, first shown at the Corn Exchange. Although filmed far away from the dangers of the front line, it gave an incredible appearance of reality, allowing the folks at home to get a far more realistic glimpse of exactly what was going on in France.

The Great War finally came to an end in November 1918. Scenes of jubilant celebration, even more enthusiastic than those that had marked the end of the Boer War, were witnessed throughout the city. Many, of course, gravitated towards the Cross, partly drawn in this direction by a 6in howitzer gun that had taken up position here. An unusual addition to the city, it was there for the purpose of encouraging donations in the ongoing 'Gun Week for War Bonds'. Nor did this gun prove superfluous, proving an ideal platform from which Alderman Turnbull, the deputy mayor, and the

A First World War tank, East Street, September 1919. Chichester, like many cities throughout the country, was provided with a presentation tank that was available for Cicestrians to either admire or ponder on the follies of war. (*Photo courtesy Chichester District Museum*)

Revd Mr Hannah, the dean of the cathedral, both gave speeches to the thronging mass.

The war to end all wars had brought great changes, with post-war Chichester irrevocably different from pre-war Chichester. Perhaps it was one of the contestants in the hastily called general election of 1918 that served as an initial indicator that the way of things was now very different. In most previous elections, the local contest had usually been fought between a Conservative and Liberal candidate. Now, things had changed. Although Lord Talbot was to be re-elected, having safely held Chichester for the Conservatives in every election since his return from South Africa, he was now confronted by an entirely new adversary. Instead of a Liberal, his opponent was the voice of the working man, Frederick Ernest Green of the Labour Party. This, indeed, was the first time that the party had contested the Chichester constituency (a vast area that encompassed Arundel, Bognor, Littlehampton and Midhurst), enabled to do so through its sponsorship by the

The unveiling of the city war memorial that originally stood in Eastgate Square 20 July 1921.

War memorial that stood within the main office and reception area of the Shippam Eastgate factory. Many local institutions and companies erected their own memorial to those lost in the First World War. (*Photo courtesy of Shippam's*)

locally powerful Agricultural Section of the Workers' Union. Campaigning on the issue of agricultural wages (which were lower in West Sussex than much of the rest of the country) and smallholdings for returning soldiers, Green netted 6,705 votes. It was not enough to win; far from it, for Lord Talbot gained 14,491 votes. However, it had, in this first election that saw women voting, changed the political outlook of the city, giving the radical working class of the area a voice that they had lacked since the days of Captain Swing.

THE SHIPPAM FAMILY FIRM

From 1750 (when it was founded) until 1975 (when it was incorporated into an international conglomerate), Shippam's was a family-run business. Famously, its links with the city go right back to the original inception of Shippam as a company, with Shipston Shippam having first established his shop in Westgate. A former sergeant in the 72nd Regiment of Foot, he was the one who hit upon the idea of bulk-buying bacon, cheese and butter in the West Country and then selling it through his new outlet. It was a superb success and allowed him to pass on this profitable venture to Charles, his eldest son.

From that moment onwards, the company never looked back. It was Charles who moved from the original shop to larger premises in North Street while also establishing profitable links with the Admiralty, directly

Work underway on the new Shippam's East Walls factory, 1911. This building was to become an important landmark for twentieth-century Chichester. (*Photo courtesy of Shippam's*)

selling to their purchasing agency, the Victualling Board. This resulted in the firm of Shippam being one of the suppliers to the Royal Navy during the bitter conflict with Napoleonic France.

The Shippam company board room photographed shortly after completion of the new factory and offices in 1912. (*Photo courtesy of Shippam's*)

Unlike many companies Shippam survived the period of post-war retrenchment and was eventually in a position to continue a programme of expansion. Another Charles Shippam was responsible for obtaining the larger East Street premises that were later extended along East Walls. Here, food processing was undertaken, an operation that made the company a household name throughout the length and breadth of the British Isles. At first, it was based on the packaging of various foods, including the famed Chichester Sausage, into hermetically self-sealing tins. These were then exported from Chichester, courtesy of the London, Brighton and South Coast Railway. In 1894, the company launched a high-quality meat paste range, sold in earthenware pots. This was not an instant success as the method of sealing, nothing more than a top layer of butter, gave the product a restricted shelf life. Soon after, however, a glass top was introduced, considerably extending the shelf life. Much more important, though, was the innovation of 1905 that saw the introduction of vacuum-sealed glass jars containing potted meat and fish.

Another event that seemed to suggest that the post-war world had changed was a royal visit in 1924. On that occasion it was Queen Mary, consort of George V, who came to Chichester, directing some of her attention to the previously invisible factory worker. Admittedly she also visited St Mary's Hospital but most of her time was spent at the East Walls meat paste factory owned by Messrs C. Shippam. For Chichester, it was a truly historic event,

undoubtedly fostered by the company's reputation as an employer of ex-servicemen. This was the real point of the Queen's visit: she wished to pay her respects to those who had fought for their country. In touring the kitchen, sausage room and boiler room, she was easily able to identify her quarry. The fifty ex-servicemen who Shippam's employed, bedecked in spotless white caps and aprons, were all proudly displaying their various medals. On reaching the boiler room, Queen Mary passed a few words with Frederick England, a former stoker on board HMS *Irresistible*, sunk near the Dardanelles. Later, she entered the sausage room and fell into conversation with George Farndale, a holder of the Military Medal:

> The Queen congratulated him on his award and asked him how long he had been in the service of the firm, to which he replied 'eighteen years, your Majesty'.

A distinctive feature of the factory was its collection of 20,000 wishbones, one of which was invariably given to any visitor to the factory. In being given a wishbone, the Queen was told that the collection had been started some years earlier when a party going round the building had refused to believe that chicken was included in certain lines of potted meat. In order to prove

Following a visit to Goodwood races, Queen Mary visited the Shippam's East Walls factory, July 1924. During her tour she not only gained an insight into the work of the factory but also spoke to a number of those employed on the shop floor. (*Photo courtesy of Shippam's*)

the case, the company chef decided that all wishbones should be preserved for exhibition.

Another aspect of the newly democratised Chichester was the expanding cinema, providing cheap entertainment for working class and middle class alike. A third cinema arrived in 1920. This was the Picturedrome, which was opened on 26 July. Situated in South Street, and renamed the Plaza in August 1929, it lacked the impressive façade of both 'the Electric' and the Corn Exchange. In fact, it was somewhat hidden away, tucked neatly behind Wren's Café and extending back through a narrow corridor. On the other hand, it did have the advantage of a central location, drawing audiences away from 'the Electric'. However, it was not for this reason that Chichester was soon reduced to two cinemas. Instead, it was the result of a fire, which broke out in the auditorium of 'The Electric' early on the morning of 6 February 1922, generally considered to have been caused by a discarded cigarette left over from the previous evening's performance.

And now back to the Selsey tram, still awaiting its passengers for an outward journey to the Manhood peninsula. Serving the community from its opening in 1897, it continued to perform this important task until 1935. In that year, having kept its superb reputation for unreliability, it finally faltered and collapsed. Quite simply, it could not cope with the increasing competition that was then being generated by motor buses. Whereas in 1919 the Selsey

A popular event with the Shippam staff was the annual charabanc trip. As always, a convoy of Southdown open-top coaches set out from East Walls to the chosen destination. (*Photo courtesy of Shippam's*)

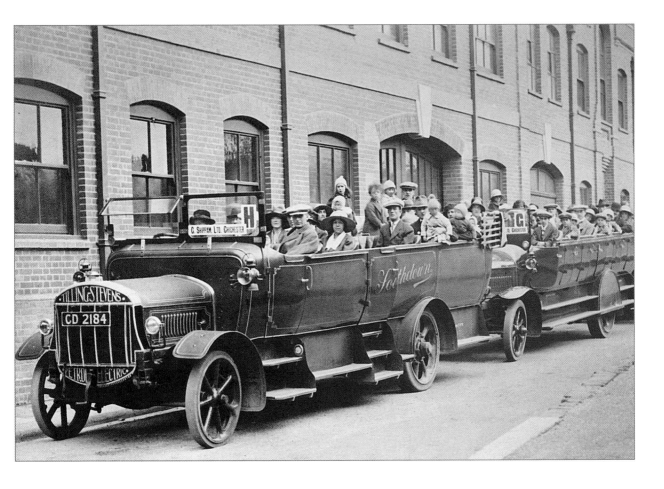

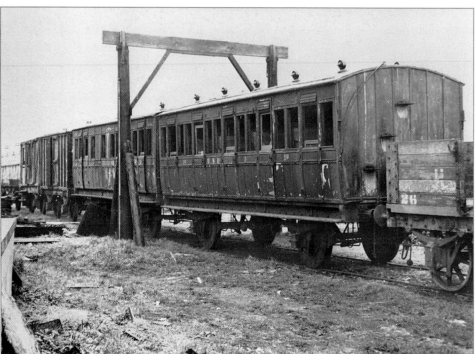

To help reduce overall operating costs, petrol-driven Shefflex rail buses were introduced to the Selsey tramway in 1925. Given that they could quickly be converted to road use, they provided the line with a certain comic absurdity. (*Photo courtesy Chichester District Museum*)

Abandoned and derelict, the final days of the Selsey tram.

tram had carried a total of 102,292 passengers, this number had diminished to a mere 21,088 by 1933.

Generally, it was the double-decker buses operated by the Southdown Bus Company that were taking most of this trade. Admittedly, in choosing to take the bus, passengers were having to pay higher fares, a single journey to Selsey costing 11d by bus and 8d by tramway; but the additional 3d seemed worthwhile. For a start, the buses were much more frequent, offering a regular hourly service throughout the day. In addition, they had far more stopping places. A typical bus journey to Selsey, for instance, started from right outside the main railway station, then proceeded towards the Cross, much more convenient for shoppers. From here, the bus began its outward journey to Hunston, Sidlesham and Selsey.

In such a situation, the Selsey tramway simply could not compete. To do so would have meant the building of more stations and a general modernisation of its rolling stock, which would in turn have meant spending money that the Hundred of Manhood and Selsey Tramway Company simply did not possess. Already it has been mentioned that every conceivable economy was taken right from the moment of the tramway's inception. This continued right through to the end: old and outdated locomotives continued to be bought, and the general rolling stock was no better. Indeed, during the 1920s, the tramway had even replaced many of its locomotives with rail-buses. These, in every way, were simply single-decker buses mounted on rail wheels. Assembled by the Shefflex Motor Company of Tinsley, Sheffield, they could, in a matter of minutes, be converted to road use. Absurd as they may have looked, they at least kept the tramway running for a few more years. However, the end was still inevitable: the era of the Selsey tram finally terminated on Saturday 12 January 1935.

11

Within Living Memory

The years immediately preceding the Second World War (1939–45) witnessed an intense period of building work in Chichester, much of it initiated by West Sussex County Council. Among buildings completed during this period were the county police station (1935), County Hall (1936), St Richard's Hospital (1937), the post office in West Street (1937) and the county court (1939). In addition, construction of the A27 Chichester bypass was commenced, although this project was not to be completed until after the war.

Although each of these new constructions undoubtedly attracted a degree of local interest, it was probably the arrival of a new cinema that was to have the greatest impact. This was the Gaumont, constructed in Eastgate Square, which had its official opening on 20 September 1937. Even before its opening, however, the new building was having an influence, with the County Cinema Company deciding to close the Plaza temporarily.

North Street, c. 1930. The Council House stands on the right while to the left motorists are invited to 'fill up' with Shell.

As it happens, the County Cinema Company was not surrendering to the competition, merely raising the stakes. The new, planned Gaumont was to be much larger than either of the two existing cinemas, having a seating capacity of 1,278. Furthermore, it would not only have the latest sound and projection equipment but it would be much more luxurious than either the Exchange or the Plaza. Its one drawback, that of its location in Eastgate, placed it outside the centre of the town but this was offset by the fact that it also had a car park.

To ensure that it could effectively compete with the new Gaumont, the temporarily closed Plaza was to be completely reconstructed within its existing walls. An enlarged screen and new sound and projection equipment, together with the latest-style seating, were all introduced. In addition, a balcony was added, bringing the number of seats to over a thousand. Perhaps the most striking feature, however, was on the outside. Here, the frontage was made much more noticeable by the introduction of a wide entrance and canopy. In later years, one who frequently visited this cinema was June Arnold (née Hickcox) whose sister, Jean, worked there as an usherette. She felt that this particular cinema had 'elegance', explaining that once you went through the entrance there were grand stairs leading to the doors of the auditorium, as well as further stairs leading up to the balcony.

It was shortly before Christmas 1936 that the Plaza reopened, giving sufficient time for the cinema to re-establish itself before the onslaught to be unleashed by its new competitor. To ensure maximum publicity, the reopening

Announcing the arrival of the Gaumont cinema in 1937.

GAUMONT
CHICHESTER
A GAUMONT - BRITISH THEATRE
TELEPHONE 948

The entire proceeds of the opening performance are being donated to *The Royal West Sussex Hospital*

GRAND GALA OPENING
MONDAY, 20th SEPTEMBER, at 7.45 p.m. Doors open 7 p.m.

THE OPENING CEREMONY WILL BE PERFORMED BY
HIS WORSHIP THE MAYOR OF CHICHESTER
(COUNCILLOR W. H. G. NAPPER)

Fanfare by the Herald Trumpeters

THE BAND OF HIS MAJESTY'S ROYAL MARINES (PORTSMOUTH DIVISION)
CONDUCTOR LIEUT. F. VIVIAN DUNN A.R.A.M., R.M., DIRECTOR OF MUSIC (by kind permission of BRIGADIER E. G. B. BOURNE, C.B., D.S.O., M.V.O., A.D.C.)

Personal appearance of **SIX GAUMONT BRITISH STARLETS**
THE STARS OF TOMORROW

ON THE SCREEN
MON. TUES. WEDS.

PAUL ROBESON
CEDRIC HARDWICKE
KING SOLOMON'S MINES (U)

DONALD WOODS
JEAN MUIR
ONCE A DOCTOR (A)

Special added attraction **THE FARR-LOUIS FIGHT** *Round by Round*

From Tuesday onwards continuous 2 to 10.30 p.m. Doors open 1.30

CAFE OPEN TO THE PUBLIC   ∴   **FREE CAR PARK**

on 18 December was turned into a gala event overseen by the Mayor of Chichester, Cllr W.H.G. Napper.

Of course the new Gaumont was not to be outdone, and its own opening event was even more lavish. Once again the mayor was invited to oversee the occasion, with music provided by buglers from the band of the Portsmouth Division of the Royal Marines. An additional attraction was the personal appearance of 'six Gaumont starlets', described as 'the stars of tomorrow'. Not surprisingly, a large number of people turned up to the opening and many were disappointed when there was insufficient room to admit them. Some of those who found themselves locked out managed to push open the doors and rushed in, so that the police had to be called and the foyer of the cinema forcibly cleared.

One small controversy emerged from Mayor Napper's having been requested to open these cinemas. After his appearance at the Plaza opening, he took it upon himself to act as a local film censor. In December 1936 he requested of the County Cinema Company that they should not show the film *Green Pastures*, believing that it would not 'be edifying' for Cicestrians. He was very much on his own: the film received excellent reviews and was later described by Graham Greene as 'as good a religious play as one is likely to get'. It was the portrayal of Jesus in this film that seems to have upset the mayor, although at the time of his attempt to ban the film, he had not actually seen it.

In theory, of course, it was the Exchange that should have suffered most from the arrival of the Gaumont. For one thing, there had been no attempt to modernise and improve the Exchange at this time, while it was also much nearer to the Gaumont: the two cinemas were virtually in sight of one another. However, what saved the Exchange, and allowed Chichester to retain three large cinemas for the next twenty years, was that it was on the national circuit of films released through Associated British Cinemas. This ensured that it had new and different films from those shown at the Plaza (part of the Odeon circuit) and the Gaumont (which had its own circuit). In May 1945, the Plaza was renamed the Odeon, so cementing its link with this particular circuit.

A further controversy that surrounded the city cinemas in the years immediately before the outbreak of war concerned the showing of films on Sundays. Since the first arrival of the cinema earlier in the century, the local council had placed

A 1938 newspaper advertisement for Sharp Garland, Chichester's longest surviving company. Unfortunately the Eastgate store (on the corner of East Walls and East Street) was demolished in 1964.

PHONE 407

EXCHANGE
CHICHESTER

—"SOUND COMFORT"—

ALL THIS WEEK—

FICTION'S MIGHTY HERO SWEEPS
TO GLORY ON THE SCREEN!

MICHAEL STROGOFF
COURIER OF THE CZAR (A)

with

| ANTON WALBROOK :: ELIZABETH ALLAN |
| MARGOT GRAHAME :: AKIM TAMIROFF |

3.25   6.30   9.30   JULES VERNE'S thrilling tale of romance and adventure

————ALSO————

BINKIE STUART

(The Sensational Child Performer of the Century) in

ROSE OF TRALEE (U)

MONDAY, SEPTEMBER 27th   **FOR SIX DAYS**

A Programme with full MARX!

THE MARX BROTHERS

GROUCHO :: HARPO :: CHICO

in

A DAY AT THE RACES

2.10   5.40   9.10

————ALSO————

VICTOR JORY *in*

ZANE GREY'S

RANGLE RIVER

4.0   7.30   (Please note times of screening)

A 1937 newspaper advertisement for the Exchange, the name (at that time) for the cinema operating from the Corn Exchange.

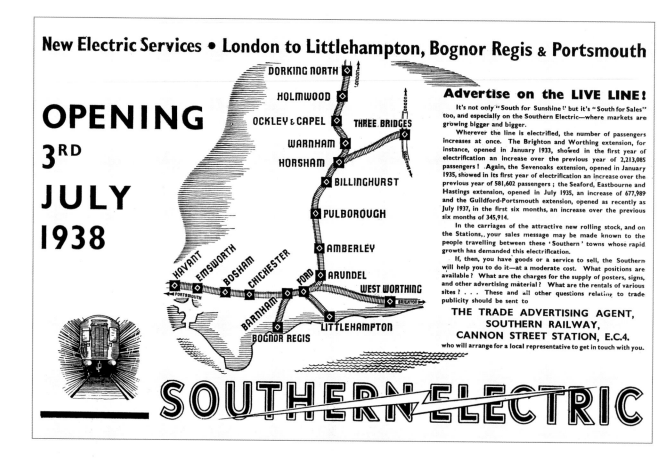

a clear restriction on the showing of films on the sabbath. At first, this was not considered particularly restrictive as most other authorities had introduced similar rules. Over the years, however, various neighbouring boroughs, including Portsmouth, Southampton and Havant, had rescinded such rules, with their cinemas open seven days a week. Within the city of Chichester, the proponents of Sunday openings were becoming increasingly vocal and were eventually able to force a local referendum. Taking place on 19 July 1937, with all local electors eligible to vote, the matter was finally settled once and for all. With 4,066 choosing to cast a vote (this representing about 50 per cent of the electorate), a clear majority, 2,934 (72.1 per cent), voted in favour of Sunday films.

While 'the silver screen', particularly with films screened seven days a week, may have provided a diversion, most in the city were aware that the nation was heading for a second global war. As early as May 1936 the city council had announced detailed plans for dealing with an aerial attack. Most important was the establishment of air-raid sirens, these to be placed at the barracks and the fire station (others, such as one at Portfield cemetery, were added later). In addition, an increased number of civilian air-raid wardens were to be recruited while first-aid posts were also to be established throughout the city. A particular concern of the report was the possibility of gas bombs being used against the city. For this reason, a decontamination centre, composed of a number of converted sheds, was to be created in the

Another important advance for the city during the 1930s was completion of work on electrifying the railway line that connected Chichester with Portsmouth and Brighton. As a result of electrification, the journey time from Chichester to London was reduced by 90 minutes on some services. This was a remarkable achievement that has not been available to rail travellers for many years. The fastest journey time to London is currently 1 hour and 50 minutes.

cattle market. Fortunately, this idea was quickly modified, with the city isolation hospital (built at Spitalfields) eventually being given over to this role. However, whether initial decontamination of victims was undertaken at the cattle market or isolation hospital, more serious cases would have to be dealt with elsewhere. It was decided that such cases would need to be transported out of the city and to facilities that were to be established at the Goodwood grandstand and the Goodwood House kennels.

To make the wider community fully aware of the dangers that they might have to confront, a range of activities was organised. Between 1936 and 1938 a number of lectures were given, these normally well attended. Later, in the summer of 1938, for a period of seven weeks, premises at 22 North Street, which had been given a gas-proof room, were available for public inspection. A few weeks later, in October 1938, a full-scale demonstration of an air raid was undertaken. It began with the sounding of the two sirens, followed by the supposed detonation of a high-explosive bomb in the cattle market. From their normal places of work, members of the ARP and medical personnel made their way to the market and attended to those who had sustained 'mock' injuries. Over a thousand Cicestrians gathered at the market to view the demonstration, being also shown how victims of mustard gas

Chichester railway station, *c.* 1935. (*Photo courtesy of the late Dave Turner*)

Bishop George Bell, seen at the opening of an extension to the Central Girl's School, Orchard Avenue. Throughout the Second World War he was a controversial figure who stuck rigidly to his Christian principles. (*Photo courtesy Chichester District Museum*)

would be decontaminated and treated. Finally, in July 1939, with war only two months away, a second full-scale ARP exercise was held, involving the 'blacking out' of the entire city and a number of mock bombing incidents. These were spread out across the city and included the Girls' High School, the Unicorn Inn and Westgate Brewery.

Despite the very real fear that existed within the town, the government in London did not perceive the city of Chichester as being at high risk. For this reason there was no attempt to evacuate the city in September 1939. Instead, 4,800 evacuees from London were actually brought to the city. Arriving on 2 September, they included 2,200 children and 2,600 adults. For their part, the adults (mostly teachers and mothers of very young children) were given overnight accommodation and communally fed in nearby halls. Unaccompanied children, on the other hand, were housed as family members in private homes while continuing their education in local schools. To help accommodate them, some schools operated a shift system, with evacuees using the school building at different times of the day from local children. This did not mean a shorter day for either group, those not in school receiving additional lessons in a local hall. Even so, there was a severe lack of school accommodation, with the Bishop's Palace converted to school use for pupils of a school in Streatham.

It was not until the day following the mass evacuation of London and other threatened cities that the nation actually found itself at war. From that evening onwards, the lights of Chichester were extinguished and the black-out was as rigorously enforced as anywhere else in the country. Air-raid wardens and police in military-style helmets patrolled the evening streets, beseeching all and sundry to 'put that light out!' Those who failed to darken their premises adequately were regularly taken to court, with a number of

Cicestrians duly fined. One of the earliest to be brought to court was an overenthusiastic gardener in Whyke Road who had lit an early-evening bonfire. On this occasion the magistrates were not unsympathetic, releasing him upon his payment of costs that amounted to 12*s* 6*d*. On other occasions, those accused of showing lights were normally fined 10*s* or £1.

Dela Warrington (later MacFarlane) tells of slightly different experiences in these early days of the black-out. At that time, with her father employed as superintendent and registrar at Portfield Cemetery, she lived with her family at the gatehouse. Apparently, they frequently received the visits of a policeman who was worried that the house was showing a chink of light. However, Dela puts it down to the fact that the policeman was young, she was good-looking and her father bottled his own wine.

The introduction of the black-out was to prove a particular problem for Canon Wells of the subdeanery. He knew that, without considerable expenditure, it would be impossible to cover effectively the very high windows that were a feature of this building. From October onwards, when evensong was held during the hours of darkness, it was decided that this service should be moved to All Saints'. This way, the two congregations could then share the costs of blacking out the much smaller windows of this building. Eventually, however, with the war continuing into the following year, the subdeanery church was blacked out, at a cost of £82. It was also during 1940 that the railings around the subdeanery were removed as part of the government's drive to collect scrap metal.

Another matter attended to upon the outbreak of war was construction of a number of communal shelters. Although most householders had some sort of air-raid shelter built either within the house (a Morrison shelter) or at the end of the garden (an Anderson shelter), these were of little use for those caught away from home when the sirens sounded. For this reason, the city council quickly erected twenty-one shelters, located in the Hornet, St Pancras and the four main streets of the city. In addition, the basements of retail premises, including Stringers of North Street and the Dolphin and Anchor in West Street, were also converted into shelters.

In the city hospitals other important developments were taking place. At both St Richard's and the Royal West Sussex Hospitals, the Emergency Medical Service installed a total of fifteen additional wards. These were in the form of temporary 'hutments' that, between them, provided bed space for a further 908 patients. Reserved for wounded military personnel, they could also be used for treating air-raid casualties.

In May 1940 the recruitment campaign for the Home Guard was initiated, with many Cicestrians joining in the very first weeks. Among them was 'Jack' Williams, chief cashier of Barclays Bank in East Street. As a First World War veteran who had fought in Turkey, he was given the rank of sergeant. In later years, he was to recall regular training sessions (at the East Walls drill hall), rifle practice at Funtington and endless patrols around the outskirts of Chichester. Within his Avenue Approach home, he appears to have collected an impressive armoury, Sergeant Williams often having to take home the occasional Sten gun and rifle, all duly locked away. June Hickcox's father,

Frank Hickcox, was also a member of the Home Guard and she remembers being given the task of cleaning his Home Guard buttons each week and receiving 6*d*. Both 'Jack' Williams and Frank Hickcox were members of the 1st Sussex (Chichester) Battalion of the Home Guard. Other Cicestrians in the Home Guard, however, were sometimes recruited into company units, with the 11th (GPO) and 12th (Southdown Bus Company) battalions active in Chichester. Only those employed by these companies joined such units, undertaking duties designed to protect property that related to their work.

As well as the Home Guard, many Cicestrians volunteered for other essential war work. Of particular importance was fire-watching. Often this involved sitting out the night in a high building and raising the alarm if a fire was spotted. This was an essential task as German raiders often carried incendiary bombs. Among those involved in fire-watching duties was Dela Warrington. Upon leaving the Lancastrian Girls' School at the age of 14, she had taken up an apprenticeship in a North Street draper's shop run by Mr Penny. Upon the outbreak of war she had volunteered for fire-watch duties. Together with staff employed in some of the other nearby shops, she patrolled the night-time streets (patrols were always in pairs) looking for any

Members of the 1st Sussex (Chichester) Battalion of the Home Guard marching along what appears to be Market Avenue. Corporal 'Jack' Williams is immediately to the left of the lead officer. Corporal Williams' son, Alan, was the young boy who remembers the Stuka dive-bombing raid on Tangmere. (*Alan Williams*) sign of fire. The only concession for such a dangerous task, given that there was always the chance of an unexpected raid, was that of being issued with a metal helmet.

Although the newly installed emergency medical facilities were busy treating evacuated troops from Dunkirk during May 1940, the city did not get its first real taste of war for a further few weeks. As the summer days lengthened, anyone looking up into the skies would often see the twisting vapour trails formed by aircraft engaged in mortal combat. On 16 August, from being a distant spectacle, it all suddenly came a lot closer. On that day, the nearby airfield of Tangmere was subjected to a massive bombing raid that inflicted considerable damage on both equipment and parked aircraft. Those in Chichester clearly heard the frequent explosions and the rata-tat-tat of German fighters that were also strafing the airfield. One who particularly remembers the event is Alan Williams, son of the Home Guard sergeant. Then a 9-year-old boy at Lindaneau School (next to Northgate House and now a hairdressers), he clearly remembers the terrifying noise of the Stuka dive-bombers, their underwing sirens screaming madly as they fell upon their intended targets.

It was as a result of this raid that the important airfield operations room at Tangmere was moved, for reasons of safety, into the centre of the city. Here, grouped around a large-scale map of the south of England, members of the Women's Auxiliary Air Force (later Women's Royal Air Force) would move counters variously representing attacking enemy aircraft and the defending

A more formal picture of the 1st Sussex Home Guard, this time photographed in the grounds of Priory Park. Corporal Williams is seated on the front row, third from the left. (*Alan Williams*)

fighters. Initially, the location of the operations room was a small building in Little London, but in early 1941 it was moved to St James's School. Later, and because of the increased activities that would be brought about by the Allies' invasion of Europe, the operations room was again moved, this time to Bishop Otter College.

That the Luftwaffe attack upon Tangmere had been so successful was a consequence of the airfield's fighter squadrons having been previously 'scrambled' to meet a series of attacks carried out elsewhere. Only during the course of the raid were they brought back to defend the airfield, with the Hurricanes and Spitfires of 43 and 602 Squadrons eventually destroying nine of the attacking Stukas. In the meantime, a damaged Hurricane from 601 Squadron attempted to land between the bomb craters. As it came to a stop, it was machine-gunned by an attacking aircraft and burst into flames. Although ground crew managed to release the 29-year-old pilot, he was already seriously burned, and was immediately taken to the Royal West Sussex Hospital. Pilot Officer William Meade Fiske III died in Chichester a few days later and was buried in the grounds of Boxgrove Priory. Pilot Officer Billy Fiske, a man of considerable charisma, was one of the first Americans in uniform to die in Europe during the Second World War. His death is likely to be the subject of a planned Hollywood film in which, if the plans come to fruition, Fiske will be played by the equally charismatic Tom Cruise.

Members of 601, Billy Fiske's squadron, would have been familiar faces in Chichester during the summer of 1940. Universally dubbed 'the millionaires' squadron', it was a magnet for the rich and famous. They, together with members of the other fighter squadrons based at Tangmere, regularly descended on their favourite pub – the Unicorn in Eastgate Square. Here, the landlord, Arthur King, did everything he could to make them welcome. For him, nothing was too much trouble, with late-night parties frequently arranged at short notice. If Fiske was present at any of these, then the clue would have been the nearby presence of his racing-green Bentley. That he always had petrol was easily explained. Rhodes Moorhouse, another member of 'the millionaires' squadron', had recently purchased a petrol station for the sole use of its members. When the station ran out of petrol, Loel Guinness, a Shell director and yet another member of the squadron, simply called up a petrol tanker and had it topped up!

This, indeed, is the interesting other side to the war. Those with money could always overcome any small hardship. While the 'millionaires' appear to have gone to extremes, others with money could always bulk up their rations by eating out. A number of fine restaurants remained open in Chichester and a good meal (without the need for coupons) was always to be had at a price. For those with less money, the British Restaurants were eventually introduced, these supplying a good wholesome set meal for a standard price of 6*d*.

At Chichester, this no-frills, government-run institution was to be found in the Assembly Rooms. Those who used these facilities recall that meals were served during the middle of the day and that the food was quite appetising. The only drawback was that there was no choice of menu, and fish was always served on Fridays. The use of the Assembly Rooms as a restaurant had developed out of its earlier use as one of the communal canteens established for evacuees. Shortly after its opening as a canteen on 9 October 1939, Queen Mary had made a point of visiting the evacuees in Chichester, herself purchasing a typical meal. This was on 7 December 1939 when she was served with stewed beef, vegetables and potatoes followed by bread jam tart and a drink of water.

As for the American pilot-hero, Billy Fiske, another story relating to him comes from the nurses of the Royal West Sussex Hospital. From them it was reported that the American, in spite of his horrendous injuries, was soon sitting up and joking with the staff. Yet, forty-eight hours later he had died 'from shock'. In being removed to Boxgrove, his body was laid in a coffin draped with both the Stars and Stripes and the Union Jack. Today, his last resting place is easily found. Lying under a tree in the south-east corner of the churchyard, it is not only well tended but is often given the addition of small flags representing both the country of his birth and the country for which he died.

The government in London were correct in their initial thinking that Chichester would be relatively safe for evacuees from London. The city suffered only three air raids, the first not until early 1942 when a number of houses near the Basin were destroyed. Approximately a year later, on 10 February 1943 at 4.45 p.m., a lone German daylight raider took the lives of five Cicestrians when it unloaded a cargo of bombs on St Martin's, Chapel

The aftermath of Chichester's worst air raid which occurred on 10 February 1943. Extensive damage was wrought on the St Martin's area, as seen here in St Martin's Street, with a number of residents in the road losing their lives. (*Picture courtesy of the* Chichester Observer)

and North Streets. At the same time, the blast from these bombs damaged the east window of the subdeanery church. It may well have been because of this second raid that the anti-aircraft defences of the city were reinforced through the addition of 4275 Anti-Aircraft Flight of the RAF Regiment. Equipped with 20mm Hispano guns, they operated alongside 'B' Troop of 364 Battery, Royal Artillery.

Expansion of the city's anti-aircraft defences could do little to avert the events of 11 May 1944. On that day a fully laden, four-engined Liberator bomber of the United States Army Air Force exploded over Velyn Avenue before crashing into the Electric Laundry (behind Cover's woodyard) near the Hornet. Already the crew had abandoned the aircraft, unable to control a fire in one of the engines. Before baling out, the pilot had set the Liberator on a course that should have taken it over the Channel. Unfortunately, the aeroplane had veered round, heading more or less for the cathedral. Indeed, with a fraction more height, it could well have hit the centre of Chichester, leading to an even-greater tragedy. As it was, there were injuries, among them Special Constable Leonard Price. The father of Bernard, who later came to write a number of books about the city, Leonard Price died of his injuries over a year later.

At the time of this incident, the city of Chichester was already involved in the build-up to D-Day. The barracks, in particular, was an important staging post, housing the 18th Battalion of the Durham Light Infantry together with

The February 1943 air raid also damaged St Mary's Hospital. (*Picture courtesy of the* Chichester Observer)

a number of specialist units. Among the latter were the 36th Beach group (whose task was to secure one of the beaches following the first assault) and members of the 30th United States Infantry Division Command Post. Graylingwell Hospital was also undergoing changes: it was to be used for intensive medical care, treating the wounded who were to be shipped from the beaches of Normandy. Overhead, there was also increased aerial activity. Advanced Landing Grounds (ALGs) had been established at Funtington, Selsey and Apuldram for the purpose of accommodating ground attack aircraft, which would be involved in the softening-up of German coastal defences in the weeks leading up to the invasion.

A few weeks before the crash of the American Liberator, General Eisenhower visited the city, staying for three nights at the Ship Hotel. The purpose was to inspect preparations taking place on this part of the south coast, his itinerary including both Tangmere and the new ALG established at Apuldram. Only a few days after his departure, the city received its third and final air raid, with bombs falling on Armadale and Bridge Roads. Again, there were a number of deaths and injuries while a swathe of houses was also destroyed. Twelve-year-old Rodney Gladman, living in Oving Road, was woken by this night-time raid, witnessing a number of fires in Armadale Road.

A controversial figure during this war time period was George Bell, Bishop of Chichester from 1929 to 1958. Uncompromisingly opposed to Hitler and all that he stood for, Bell was in the forefront of the pre-war campaign against the Nazis, drawing attention both to their persecution of Jews and arrests of leading churchmen. In particular, he highlighted the fate of Martin Niemöller, a Lutheran pastor who was imprisoned in the Dachau concentration camp. It was Bell's campaign that saved Niemöller's life. Although senior Nazis, such as Joseph Goebbels, wished to be rid of Niemöller, Hitler was convinced that such a move would provide his opponents, particularly the Bishop of Chichester, with a unique opportunity to attack the German government.

It was following the outbreak of war that Bell drew upon himself a degree of unpopularity. As a Christian he held strongly to his views, arguing against the indiscriminate internment of refugees from those countries with which Britain was now at war. Even more controversial, and ultimately responsible for his failure to be appointed to Canterbury (for which he was a major contender), was his opposition to area bombing.

In 1941, with Britain more or less fighting alone, the policy of saturation bombing (also known as terror bombing) had been adopted. Yet such bombing, especially when carried out at night, resulted in the deaths of countless numbers of civilians. It was in May 1941 that Bell made one of his most celebrated speeches, describing the 'night bombing of non-combatants as a degradation of the spirit for all who took part in it'.

Following the end of the war in 1945, considerable attention had to be given to the reconstruction and improvement of the city. Whereas the immediate pre-war years had seen the building of a range of municipal and public buildings the post-war years were given over to new housing. Between 1946 and 1951, the Whyke, Orlits and Parklands estates were built. All three used former German prisoners of war to carry out much of the construction work

The urgency of post-war housing needs initially led to the introduction of prefabs in Chichester. These were factory built and rapidly erected on vacant areas of land. Intended only as temporary accommodation they were later replaced by the Whyke, Parklands and Orlits estates. (*Photo courtesy Chichester District Museum*)

Former prisoners of war at work on the Whyke estate, October 1945. Alan Williams, aged 15 at this time, remembers that some of these former prisoners stayed in a house opposite where he lived and were employed on agricultural duties. He was surprised by just how ordinary they were. (*Photo courtesy Chichester District Museum*)

The building of the Whyke housing estate, October 1945. Many of the labourers employed were former prisoners of war, recognisable by their forage caps and prominent markings on the backs of their jackets. (*Photo courtesy Chichester District Museum*)

with the Orlits pioneering the use of prefabricated building materials to ensure rapidity of construction. As well as their involvement in the construction of new housing, a number of former prisoners of war, while housed in Chichester, were also employed on local farms and on a scheme to improve the city's water supply. This last involved the construction of a new pumping station at Funtington and the laying-down of the necessary pipes.

By the mid-1950s the town was beginning to get back to normal with the four main streets of the city having long since witnessed the first of the traffic jams that had inevitably followed the return of the private car. Fortunately, at this time, public transport was very competitive. Since July 1938, the railway had been electrified, so reducing journey time while increasing the frequency

Houses on the Orlits estate. Although intended to be permanent structures, similar methods of construction were used to erect these as the temporary prefabs. In other words, they were factory built houses and put up on site. (*Photo courtesy Chichester District Museum*)

of services. This had been carried out at a cost of £2.75m, and had included a lengthening of the station platforms to 820ft. Apart from the trains, frequent bus services were operated by Southdown from their newly built bus station in Southgate. This had been constructed in 1954 on the site of the earlier county police station. The buses themselves were highly distinctive, being in Southdown's light-green and cream livery. According to Stephanie Cecil (née Gladman), there was nothing more fun as a child, than catching the 31 bus to Bognor Regis. On a warm summer's day, as she clutched her bucket and spade, the fun was always heightened by the chance of being able to sit at the front of the bus.

Employment within the city was also high during these years. A number of long-established companies continued to trade, with Shippam's, of course, the most noticeable. In addition, Gibbings, Harrison & Co. Ltd of Westgate still carried out the ancient trade of tanning (the production of leather for shoes), while Sadlers, founded in 1866, were manufacturing cattle feed and dog food. Elsewhere, Bartholomews dealt in 'feeds, seeds and fertilizers' while handling vast quantities of barley used by Scotch whisky and London gin distillers. Pinks, with their factory in Melbourne Road, produced bottled ginger beer, lemonade and soda water while Chichester Dairies (established in 1889) was the main supplier of local milk. However, one particular long-time employer, the brewing firm of Henty and Constable, had closed in 1954. Situated at the Gatehouse Brewery in South Street and supplying pubs throughout the south of England, the firm had connections with Chichester that can be traced back to the early nineteenth century.

As well as the longer-established companies, the city also had a number of new industries, many of these having premises on the industrial estate to the south-west of the city. Among them was Hambling Industries (a manufacturer of components for typewriters, aircraft and diesel engines, which also

A bottle of Pinks Ginger Beer.

An advertisement for Pinks' products.

made model locomotives) and the Chichester Rubber Company (a manufacturer of toys, surgical supplies and household gloves). Also located on the industrial estate were Smith & Jewell (structural engineers), Carne's Mimeograph Company (manufacturers of duplicators) and the Beanstalk Shelving Company. In Kingsham Road was to be found Wingard Ltd, makers of motor car accessories (the former site now commemorated by Wingard Close), while in St Pancras the St Pancras Engineering Works specialised in equipment for the printing industry, trucks, concrete pipes and agricultural rollers.

This high number of small industries led Francis Steer, the compiler of the 1957 city guide, to assure visitors that 'Chichester is not industrial.'

Underlining the point, it was further stated that the city, 'is not smoky or noisy, and these (and other) firms have not lessened the city's attraction'.

The 1960s witnessed a number of important changes to the city. In 1961, the original Victorian railway booking office was replaced by a modern building that, itself, has become something of a local icon. Indeed, there are several architectural organisations that wish to see it listed, being a rare surviving example of a mid-twentieth-century railway building. Of particular note are its fine ceiling and period chandeliers. Another important building added to the city during the 1960s is the County Library in Tower Street. This was constructed in 1967, a circular-style building that replaced the original county library that had been located at Edes' House. For many, pedestrianis- ation must count as the most important change to the city's face. This, how- ever, was not to come until 1976. Much more important for the 1960s was completion of the inner ring road, this undertaken in 1965 and completely removing the heavy traffic that was then regularly passing through the centre of the town.

At the beginning of the 1960s Cicestrians had to confront the loss of two of their cinemas: the Gaumont and the Odeon. First to disappear was the Odeon, finally closing its doors in February 1960. Logically, or so it might be thought, this should have secured the future of the city's other super-cinema, the Gaumont. That was not to be. In October of the same year the Gaumont also closed its doors. Only the Granada Exchange, which had eventually been

Southgate, 1951. Looking towards Brighton on the railway line, the bus station has now replaced the nearby houses and the trees have made way for part of the one-way road system that weaves around the county court. (*Photo courtesy of the late Dave Turner*)

modernised and given a balcony in 1948, still remained. It was not to close until August 1980. Stephanie Cecil, who, as a teenager, occasionally visited this cinema during the 1970s, recalled something of its flavour:

To celebrate the coronation of Queen Elizabeth II residents of Castleman Road, on the Orlits Estate, organised a street party. (*Douglas Cecil*)

> You queued from the front to the right-hand side as you look at it and round the right side of the building. There was a post box on the corner and people had to post letters through the queue – most inconvenient. The entrance to the cinema had two front doors that led into a wide but not very deep foyer. You went in on the right-hand side and on the left was the ticket box and popcorn counter.
>
> After purchasing a ticket an usherette, at the entrance to the auditorium, would tear the ticket in half and then thread it on to a wire. Inside the auditorium, another usherette would show you to your seat using a tiny torch.
>
> The seats were all red and a bit worn with sections you pushed down to sit on and, when you stood up, they went up too. Sometimes we would sit on this part without pushing it down so as to see over any tall person in front. If you weren't careful, this could annoy people behind. You never sat in the back row because these were always occupied by kissing couples that never seemed to watch much of the film! About five rows in front of them was where the circle seats came out above you and you had to be careful, if sitting here, that nobody above threw bits of

West Street, *c.* 1950. Note the Belisha Beacon on the right and the existence of a two-way road system.

The Gaumont cinema in the years immediately before its closure. (*Dela MacFarlane*)

The Granada Exchange cinema, *c.* 1955. (*Photo courtesy of the late Dave Turner*)

popcorn on you. This only happened if there were schoolboys and uncouth youngsters sitting in the balcony. As it cost more to sit in the circle, this didn't happen too often.

The picture screen had thick red curtains in front and most films I can remember started with a short film about things like how toffee or chocolate was made or what it was like to be in the navy. I particularly remember the last, as on board one of the ships was a boy I recognised from school.

Another of the city institutions that Stephanie remembers is the cattle market. Here, up until 1990, livestock brought in by large lorries was auctioned each Wednesday.

All the animals were held in pens, about ten to fifteen in each. Everywhere was noisy, although the squealing pigs were the loudest. The cows made a lot of noise too and they were frequently covered in cow dung. The sheep were always following each other around in their pens.

The auction room had a circular floor and around this the cattle and bulls were paraded. As a child I could never understand what the auctioneer was saying. He spoke so fast, rattling off, I suppose, the numbers and amounts of money. Every so often I recognised the words 'five' or 'ten', these always clearer than the rest.

Down one side of the market was a long shed against the wall and which held the smaller animals: rabbits, chickens and pigeons. They were

all housed in hutches that were stacked on each other to a height of five
or six feet. Here, you could be looking and talking to a rabbit while a
poor chicken was having its neck wrung just a few short feet away.

Later, Stephanie took up employment at the Festival Theatre. Here she was
engaged at the front of the house as an usherette. Again she has a number of
interesting memories:

> I was 18 years old when I started working at the CFT and remained for
> about four years. You can't help but be a bit star-struck at that age and I
> was no exception. I met and worked with many of the acting fraternity
> during my time as an usherette. We had a different uniform each season,
> usually a long sleeveless dress, blouse and a scarf or tie that reflected the
> season's colours. We would arrive about an hour before doors opened, to
> prepare for that shift. Then, as now, there were two weekly matinees,
> these on Thursdays and Saturdays.
>   The front-of-house manager for two of my years there was the actor
> Michael Brennan, a fierce looking man who had often played 'hard
> men' in '007' and other films. He was particularly strict when it came
> to the playing of the national anthem. He would stand stock-still when
> it played at the end of a performance and, woe betide any of us if we
> dared move. I can remember the look he once gave when a couple of

On the way to market,
1962. Cattle, possibly
from a local Chichester
farm, are herded into
the nearby market.
The buildings in the
background include the
recently closed Odeon
cinema and St Pancras'
Church. (*Photo courtesy
of the late Dave Turner*)

patrons came running out while the anthem still played (obviously trying to beat the crowds to the car park); he was clearly saying, 'How dare you move at this time.' Yet, at other times, he was a really nice man who would talk about his life – he just had certain principles that he stuck to.

Some of the nicest actors I met were also the most famous, such as Gordon Jackson, Edward Woodward, Michelle Dotrice and even Patricia Routledge (before she became Mrs Bucket in the television comedy *Keeping Up Appearances*).

The genesis of the Chichester Festival Theatre can be traced to the year 1959. On a 'cold, blustery, January evening', former mayor of the city Leslie Evershed-Martin found himself watching a television programme that told the story of the newly created Shakespeare Theatre in Stratford, Ontario. One of those closely involved in the Canadian scheme, and interviewed on the programme, was Tyrone Guthrie, a well-respected theatrical producer. So taken was Evershed-Martin with the success of the Ontario project, that he determined upon a similar scheme for Chichester.

Over the following year, the former mayor used his organisational flair to involve many of the most influential and affluent in West Sussex. While this task was not easy, it must have been even more difficult to raise a similar level of support among the acting fraternity. Even Tyrone Power found himself

Nurses at the Royal Sussex Hospital receiving their certificates, December 1955. Front row, first right, is Cecily Williams. Looking back on her hospital memories, Cecily recalls strict cleanliness and the pride of wearing the uniform. All the nurses wore stiffly starched aprons over blue and white striped dresses. No cardigans were allowed as they were 'germ droppers'. One aspect of training that has certainly changed relates to the right of those in their third (or final) year of training to be brought breakfast in bed by the matron's maid! (*Cecily Williams*) drawn into the campaign, together with a number of other leading actors of the day. Undoubtedly, it was Sir Laurence Olivier's agreement to become the theatre's first artistic director that really ensured that Evershed-Martin's dream would be turned into a highly successful reality.

Nor should the enormity of the task be underestimated. At the time, the British theatre was in recession, with more theatres closing than opening. Furthermore, Evershed-Martin started at a base point of zero: there was neither money available for the project or a local tradition of theatre-going upon which to build. All this had to be reversed and it was Evershed-Martin's enthusiasm that was to achieve this. His approach to the architect, Philip Powell, was fairly typical. Choosing a man with Chichester connections, he nevertheless had to convince this highly skilled individual, with an immense reputation, that he should work for an organisation that had doubtful prospects and no guaranteed source of income. Philip Powell later described their first meeting:

> We [Philip Powell and his partner Hidalgo Moya] found ourselves in the position of being rather stodgy, sophisticated architects, pointing out all the horrible difficulties; but the more he talked about it, the more he looked like an excited schoolboy . . .

This excitement proved contagious, and after a few days of thought, the two architects agreed to produce designs for the new theatre. Their only condition

Regular customers at the Coach and Horses pose for a photograph, *c.* 1955. Judging by the clothes worn, it is a summer's day and they are about to board the coach behind for Bognor or some other local seaside resort. (*Photo courtesy of the late Dave Turner*)

Chichester Market, October 1990. This photograph was taken shortly before the closure of the cattle market. Houses in Whyke Lane can be seen immediately beyond the wall. (*Judith Hills*)

was that if the project failed they would not charge any fees; if it were successful, however, they would expect their full standard fee.

The support given by Chichester City Council, while crucial to the success of the project, was not to everyone's taste. In particular, various cost breaks (including provision of the site on a ninety-nine-year lease at a peppercorn rent) was contrasted with a second group also involved in the raising of money. They wished to build a swimming pool and had been told by the council that before they received any support they must raise 50 per cent of the estimated cost. At other times, this may have been readily achievable, but successful fund-raising for the new theatre seemed to be adversely affecting people's willingness to donate for the new swimming pool. Some acrimony was certainly in evidence. However, in the end, both groups achieved their objectives: the Festival Theatre opened in July 1962 and the swimming pool was also completed during the summer of that year. The latter building made use of the former Gaumont cinema and was to remain a valuable addition to the city until replaced by a new pool at the Westgate Centre. As for the Festival Theatre, this has gone from strength to strength: the 2004 festival programme opened on 29 April with Cole Porter's musical *Out of this World* and concluded in September with a performance of Christopher Marlowe's *Doctor Faustus*. Other plays during that season included *A Midsummer Night's Dream* and Mikhail Bulgakov's *The Master and Margarita*.

Another important change to the city took place in 1974 with the abolition of the Chichester City Council and its replacement by the Chichester District Council. At the same time, much of the area of the former Chichester Rural District Council was absorbed into the new body. There was a well-grounded local fear that the creation of this much more powerful authority would lead it to become divorced from those it served. Within many of the surrounding villages, the right to elect a parish council has long ensured a full representation of local opinion. For cities and towns, this option is rarely available. However, for Chichester an exception was made, the area within the city being allowed to retain both a council and mayor. This was both the recognition of city rights held from ancient times and the acceptance of an idea expressed by a large number of Cicestrians.

That the city of Chichester was, indeed, of an ancient standing, has been frequently shown through the unearthing of many medieval and Roman remains. Whenever foundations are being dug for a new building in the middle of the city, there is often a good chance that some exciting discovery will be made. Returning, for a moment, to the late 1930s, initial building work on the post office uncovered the base of a monument dedicated to the Roman god Jupiter. Generally, it is assumed that this statue was connected to the public forum that is thought to have been located on this side of West Street. Further evidence of the existence of this building was revealed in 1940 when the air-raid shelter within the cellars of the Dolphin and Anchor was under construction. At that time, workmen uncovered part of a buried wall, six feet thick, and at just the right depth to have formed part of the footings to the south side of the forum. That this wall ran in a westward direction towards Chapel Street was confirmed in the late 1970s when work was being undertaken on the laying of new gas mains.

Another important Roman building, the public baths, is thought to run below the Army and Navy Stores, the telephone exchange and subdeanery. Part of this building was excavated in 1960, a geometric mosaic similar to one found at Fishbourne being uncovered at that time. Clearly a building of some size, its northern extension, which runs along Tower Street, was the subject of an archaeological dig in 1974–5. This revealed both the piping that supplied the water for the baths and remains of a storage cistern. Left in situ, but carefully covered over, they remain, as if undisturbed, beneath the car park opposite the library.

While the 1980s may have passed off fairly quietly, this was not so with the 1990s. The middle part of the decade brought two major catastrophes to the city. The first was in October 1993 when the Sainsbury's superstore at Portfield was totally destroyed in an all-consuming fire. Only a few months later the River Lavant overflowed its banks, with both the Hornet and St Pancras areas of the city under flood-water. The situation might have been considerably worse had it not been for the valiant efforts of the county fire service. Using the Hornet as a base, they successfully diverted the flow of the Lavant by piping millions of gallons of water through a corridor of hoses that snaked around the city. In November 2000, when part of the city was again under flood-water, a similar plan was immediately put into action, with the centre of the city once again saved. It is to be hoped that flooding on the scale witnessed on those two occasions will not be repeated, a permanent flood protection scheme having now been completed.

In bringing a conclusion to this chapter, it is worth considering the changing fortunes of Shippam's. A firm that, for much of its existence, has been located within the city walls, it has now moved out of central Chichester. Furthermore, the former factory site, lying alongside East Walls, is

The packing department at Shippam's East Walls Factory, *c.* 1950. (*Shippam's*)

about to be redeveloped. It was this building, constructed in 1912–13, that Queen Mary toured in 1924. At the time of her visit, the factory building was undergoing modernisation, with the East Walls/East Street corner bays and Georgian-style entrance completed just a few weeks prior to the event.

It was as recently as August 2002 that Shippam's vacated their prime city-centre site, completely relocating to Terminus Road. Here, its branded pastes and sauces continued to be manufactured together with a range of similar products for most major retailers, including Tesco, Sainsbury's and Asda. In centring upon the Terminus Road factory, it is interesting to note that numbers employed were increased from 140 to 180, so ensuring that the company remains the largest single industrial employer in the area.

Apart from having vacated the East Walls site, Shippam's has also undergone a number of other major changes in the last few years. During the 1990s, the company was absorbed into Underwoods and, through further financial dealings, became part of the Grand Metropolitan Group. In the event, this was also a short-term holding as Grand Metropolitan wished only to develop one particular aspect of Shippam's, their rights to Old El Paso branded products. For this reason Shippam's was again sold on, this time acquired by the Princes Corporation. This was not an unnatural association as both Shippam's and Princes were once major competitors in the pastes and spreads market. Indeed, Shippam's had once indicated a desire to acquire Princes, but this never came about.

It is through this acquisition by Princes that the future of Shippam's in Chichester has been secured. Apart from the manufacture of their own branded pastes, the factory in Terminus Road is also a major producer of products bearing the Princes trademark. Thus, Chichester has clearly benefited from the new arrangement, ensuring the continuance of a relatively large-scale employer within the area of the city.

12

Sleepy Hollow

Chichester is a city with a remarkable past and an equally promising future. Yet it is rarely seen in such a light. Past commentators have often been quite scathing. Words such as 'dull', 'boring' and 'sedate' have often been thrown in its direction. It is a trend that possibly started in the early seventeenth century when Daniel Defoe, on visiting the city, recorded that he was unable to say much of the city other than that 'if six or seven good families were removed, there would not be much conversation'. To this, he added the simple but uninspiring comment, 'the cathedral here is not the finest in England, but is far from being the most ordinary'.

Matters had not improved by the nineteenth century when the area's most eminent resident, the 4th Duke of Richmond, chose to dismiss the city in somewhat disparaging tones. In 1857 he remarked upon the changes in Chichester, comparing it with the days of his youth. Apparently, the city had once offered some excitement but now things were very different. In fact, he could 'scarcely believe that [which] now prevails there. Many of the principal shops are closed, the barracks instead of being occupied by some crack infantry corps and two squadrons of cavalry, are now principally devoted to the sick of the Crimean army, and are only occasionally enlivened by the presence of a detachment of militia.'

In 1866 a cathedral prebendaryship holder, Charles Anthony Swainson, added his pennyworth: 'Let us look at what Chichester is. It has but few manufactures: one set of very important ironworks; one small but clever brass foundry; five or six breweries, some of great moment; one considerable tan yard; two or three curriers of differing importance – I do not remember anything else.'

Indeed, the city must have plunged into a torpidity trough during these years, with a queue of individuals wishing to confirm this. Dean Burgon (1875–87) would often give the name of his city of residence as 'Sleepy Hollow' while proclaiming 'half its citizens were fast asleep, and the other half walked on tip-toe so as not to wake them'. Another critic was Dean Francis Pigou (1888–1892), who wrote in his autobiography, published in 1899, 'I doubt if there is a city in England that can compare with the general drowsiness and sleepiness of Chichester.'

Some thirty years later Thurston Hopkins, in his *Sussex Revisited*, described Chichester as 'a dear, decorous Victorian lady of a town'. He went on to say that this was not meant 'as an expression of sarcasm but of admiration'. Somewhat more disparaging was Tyrone Guthrie's thrust at Chichester made in 1959. On learning that the city was the planned site of the future Festival Theatre, this noted theatrical producer simply asked, 'Why?' According to him, 'no one has ever died or even lived there; I mean, at least no notable like Shakespeare, so that you could call it a memorial and have pilgrimages to it.'

Over the years, of course, Chichester has undergone many changes. But does it still possess that nineteenth-century torpidity? Has it, indeed, thrown off its 'Sleepy Hollow' epithet? To this there can be no definitive answer. Talk to youngsters in the city and they will frequently veer towards the negative, drawn instead to the bright lights of Portsmouth. Shoppers, too, are often disparaging about the city, noting the lack of certain high-profile retail outlets. Again, these can be more easily found in Portsmouth and Brighton. Before examining these claims, and taking a glance at a few other pressing issues, I first wish to consider the question of access to the city's cultural heritage. This is an issue that can be as dynamic and as controversial as any other area of city life.

For my part, it was a passion for history that first brought me to Chichester in 1974. The city possessed everything for which I could possibly wish. It had Roman walls, the foundations of a Norman castle and a splendid array of Georgian buildings. Yet I was disappointed. The city had simply hidden away its valuable resources. It's not that I was unable to find some of the more obvious sites but more a matter of orientation and interpretation. There was much more that I could have seen, but as a casual visitor I needed direction. The situation still remains. Other towns will direct you; Chichester leaves you on your own.

The city does itself a disservice. In terms of tourism, it should be at the top of the tree. There should be no detractors and every cultural tourist should have it high on his or her list. In 1948 the city council commissioned an incisive report that described the essential spirit of this particular urban community:

The city around the cathedral has kept its old quality in a way that no other place in England has. Here, within a street pattern laid down by the Romans nearly two thousand years ago, are all the essential physical ingredients of a cathedral-city in a surprisingly pure, unadulterated form. Chichester is the least spoiled example now remaining in England of a naturally grown, as distinct from a deliberately planned, renaissance town. It is a living and lively as well as a lovely city, living a natural, busy, common everyday 20th century life in its uncommon 18th century streets; supplying the needs of the surrounding countryside; an energetic and thriving county town as well as a cathedral city. And that, perhaps, is its most special quality of all; being special in so many senses, it remains essentially natural and ordinary in the life that it lives and in the services it performs.

A local group, the Huckleberries, are seen performing at the cross, summer 2003.

Since that report there has been little change (other than a lessening of its contact with the countryside). Chichester is still 'the least spoiled example' of a naturally grown 'renaissance town'. Rather than hiding its treasures, the city should emphasise them.

The process need not be expensive. A starting point must be the museum, a long recognised fact. Every so often a new scheme emerges for the relocation or modernisation of this important element to the interpretation of Chichester's past. The most recent suggestion was its transfer to Tower Street. The idea was that in a joint private-public-funded project, the unique remains of the Roman bath-house that lies covered underneath the current ground-level car park would be thrown open to public view, with the museum providing a protective cover. Nothing has come of the idea and the car park provides not the slightest hint of the Roman treasure that lies below the parked chariots of the twentieth century.

And try finding the museum, should you be a visitor to the town. Apart from a few eccentrically dispersed waymarks that leave you guessing at essential turning points, there are few clues to its actual location. Indeed, some visitors must leave the city believing that it has no such institution.

Although not an alternative to a new museum venture, a less expensive measure could be the introduction of a clearly marked, themed 'history walk' that would take both resident and visitor to points of greatest interest. Some towns provide this through the use of marked paving stones (sometimes a painted line or, as in Portsmouth, the recently installed 'jubilee' markers). In such a way, Chichester's exciting past could be made much more accessible. What better way of appreciating the dark days of the castle siege, the taking of the town by Parliamentarian troops or the aspirations of those who partici-pated in famine and 'Swing' riots than by standing on the exact locations associated with these events? Instead of the city having but one defaced and heavily weathered historical information panel (this currently at the site of the amphitheatre), it should have smart new ones placed at a variety of different sites. To all this might well be added smaller plaques, in the style

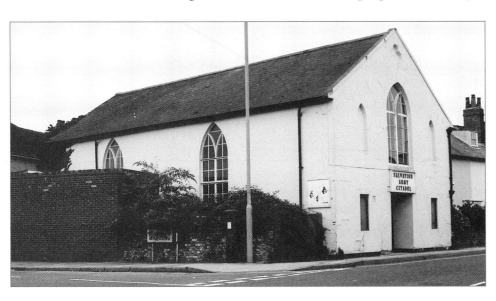

The Salvation Army citadel in Orchard Avenue. This building is facing demolition in 2004.

of the London blue plaque, placed on notable buildings. At the moment, the only plaques to be found on city buildings were erected to mark sites associated with the Quaker movement.

Furthermore, attention needs to be given to some of the more important historical sites in and around the city. The state of the motte in Priory Park is beyond belief. It is an overgrown, rubbish-strewn, tangled mass with not the slightest indication of its former significance. More could also be made of the numerous important archaeological sites that lie under the streets of Chichester.

Obviously, there is more to the city than just its history. I emphasise the town's treatment of its history because I am a historian writing a history of the town. But the present will, at some point, be tomorrow's history, so attention to other contemporary topics is also of importance. Currently, there are a number of heavily debated issues of which transport, housing and the future of inner-city retailing are among the most important.

A major problem that will have to be resolved is that of increasing traffic. Here, Chichester is a victim of circumstance. The district council on its own simply does not have the wherewithal to solve the problem in its entirety. Much depends on government and private enterprise. In this direction, the loss of the Selsey tram must be considered a major blow. What better link could be provided with the Manhood peninsula than an efficient and modernised tramway? Nowadays, and relying only upon narrow roads, the journey is slow and tedious while fraught with the potential for a road accident. A solution does exist to relieve some of this congestion, that of building a link road that will run south of Stockbridge to the Fishbourne roundabout, a project that is earmarked for 2006. As frequently happens, the solution is as problematic as the difficulty it is supposed to resolve: the loss of countryside consequent on the building of a further road will impact upon the overall quality of life.

The demands of the road lobby have become even more strident as a result of government policy that requires that the area around Chichester should provide space for a large number of new houses. Some of these, if built on the flood plain, would add to the already-existing problem of flooding. Once the houses are constructed, however, their occupants will be facing rush-hour gridlock on most local roads. This was one reason put forward for construction of a new road from Stockbridge to the A27. Just as worrying is the demand for a northern bypass. Again slicing through nearby open land, this would, if built, further deplete southern England's rapidly diminishing countryside. If a halt is not brought to road-building, then a logical outcome will be the demand of a future generation for an outer ring-road to bring relief to the still unbuilt (and hopefully unplanned) inner ring-road.

As for the meeting of other important demands, those associated with leisure activities and shopping, a few important strides have certainly been made in recent years. A major boost to the city's leisure venues came in 1987 with the opening of the Westgate Centre. Directed primarily to sporting and health activities, the centre receives an average of 625,000 customer visits each year. To ensure its continued popularity, Chichester district council

approved an £864,000 five-year refurbishment and development plan in May 2004. Another important contributor to this aspect of town life was the completion, in 2003, of the Chichester Gate complex, adjacent to Terminus Road. Apart from several restaurants, bars and a private sports centre, the complex also includes a bowling alley and Cineworld, a multiplex cinema with ten screens.

It is, perhaps, the Chichester Gate complex that has done most, in recent years, to destroy the city's 'Sleepy Hollow' image. Prior to its development, the city offered very little in terms of cinemas, boasting only the New Park Cinema. Although a worthy addition to the city, the New Park is nothing more than a converted school building that works best when showing films that have escaped the national circuit. In other words it is not, and has never been, a cinema designed for the 'blockbuster' movie.

Of course, the CFT should not be forgotten; it is an undoubted success – but somewhat exclusive. With a planned restaurant and other additions, it will soon ensure that those who want to see a play need never set foot within the main city area.

So what else did the city offer in those days before the Chichester Gate complex? In the seventies and eighties there were a few clubs and a number of popular bars. But these pale into insignificance when compared with the Slurping Toad and the controversies that often surrounded this particular once-trendy pub. Formerly a church, none other than the redundant

The corner bay and entrance to Shippam's. While much of the East Walls building was constructed in 1912–13, the entrance and attached four bays were completed shortly before the important royal visit of 1924. A key city landmark, there was much controversy over its possible demolition in 2003. It was proposed that a shopping complex would replace the factory site.

subdeanery, the Slurping Toad became, for a time, the meeting-place of the young and trendy. Unfortunately, because of its location opposite the cathedral, the eyes of the city elders were often upon it. A crisis point was reached in the run-up to Christmas 1999: the Slurping Toad was presented with a late-night Christmas Eve licence. This was too much. The fashionable pub would be in direct competition with the cathedral and its midnight mass. Worse still, congregation and party-goers would be forced to mingle at the conclusion of the two events. Despite attempts to rescind the licence, the Slurping Toad remained open and, inevitably, the city of Chichester survived.

Following close on the heels of the Chichester Gate project is an attempt to revitalise the city as a shopping centre. Unfortunately, the scheme appears to have one serious flaw: an undue stress on the need to bring into Chichester many of those shops that can be found everywhere else. Such an outcome would undermine Chichester's uniqueness. Different shops, preferably local in origin, would be much more imaginative. It is hoped that the planned redevelopment of the former Shippam's site on the corner of East Street and East Walls will not overemphasise the multinational aspect over that of the local entrepreneurs. Early signs are hopeful. To begin with, the complex will retain not only listed-building frontages in East Street but also a significant part of the Shippam's facade that runs along East Walls. Within the complex, which has room for both shops and housing, will be space for a number of small retail outlets, many of these to be removed from Sadlers Walk.

Conversion of the sub-deanery into a pub was a major controversy. Once known as the Slurping Toad, it has since become Wests.

In connection with this new complex, Chichester City Council, in March 2004, failed to acquire listed-building status for the former Shippam's entrance on the corner of East Street and East Walls. On advice given by English Heritage, this was turned down by the Secretary of State for Culture, Tessa Jowell, as being of a fairly standard style. A rather unfortunate decision perhaps. Apart from anything else, it failed to consider both the long and important association of Shippam's with Chichester and the fondness that many local residents have for this particular piece of architecture. Whether the Shippam's entrance façade will remain is a matter still undecided.

With this brief presentation of how Chichester is meeting the twenty-first century, it is up to the reader to decide whether the 'Sleepy Hollow' image has been finally thrown. On the positive side Chichester now has many new entertainment complexes and a planned shopping centre. On the downside, it has yet to solve transport and housing issues, which hang over the city like the proverbial sword of Damocles. An imaginative and environmentally sensitive approach is required, possibly encompassing the rebuilding of the original Selsey tramway. In the process, modern-style trams could be introduced, together with a number of linking branch lines. Finally, of course, a real decision needs to be made as to how the city should present its cultural heritage. Simply talking about a possible relocation of the museum is not enough. A unified and concerted approach is required, based on a coord-inated policy of interpretation and access.

Bibliography & Sources

Chapter 1: To the Victor the Spoils

Undoubtedly, the most useful source for any historian of Chichester considering the Roman and early medieval period is the nine-volume *Chichester Excavations* published between 1971 and 1996 and edited by Alec Down et al. (although not all directly relate to the city of Chichester). These provide a systematic record of the various archaeological digs carried out during the late twentieth century together with a general discussion of how any discoveries impact upon an understanding of the town. Particularly valuable for a consideration of the city walls were volumes 1 (1970), 2 (1974) and 8 (1993) while a useful note on the chapel of St Cyriac appears in volume 3 (1977). A further invaluable guide to the Roman period was Alec Down's *Roman Chichester* (Phillimore, 1988). Also of value was John Guy's *Castles in Sussex* (Phillimore, 1984). However, care has to be taken in reading this particular account of Chichester Castle. While some useful details and a site plan are included, a few errors are also detectable. He incorrectly dates the earth ramparts on the inner face of the wall to the eighteenth century, while loose wording of a photo caption creates confusion as to whether the entry into Orchard Street is a surviving gateway. Other books and papers consulted for this section were:

Fisher, E.A., *The Greater Anglo-Saxon Churches*, Faber, 1962
——, *Saxon Churches of Sussex*, Newton Abbot, David & Charles, 1970
Hills, G.M., 'Chichester; The City Walls' *Journal of the British Archaeology Association* 42 (1886), 119–36
Luxford, J.M., 'The Anglo-Saxon Nunnery at Chichester: a further source' *Sussex Archaeological Collections* 140 (2002), 150–1
Mainwaring Johnson, P., 'Earl Roger de Montgomery and the Battle of Hastings', *Sussex Archaeological Collections* 47 (1904), 109–12
Morris, J., *Domesday Book 2: Sussex*, Phillimore, 1962
Wacher, J., *The Towns of Roman Britain*, Batsford, 1974
Warner, P., *The Medieval Castle*, Weidenfeld & Nicolson, 1971

Chapter 2: A Centre of Trade and Prosperity

For an understanding of the early economic and constitutional developments within the city, the *Victoria County History of Sussex* volume 3, proved quite invaluable. In addition *Chichester City Charters* by Francis W. Steer (Chichester Paper 3, 1956) proved extremely useful. It was from here that I quoted the important city charter of

1135, Steer providing both the original Latin text and the translation that I used. As to references made to archaeological digs that uncovered the state of the walls during the reign of Edward III and the existence of a pottery outside the walls, these were based on reports to be found in *Chichester Excavations* volume 1 (Phillimore, 1970, 149–64) edited by Alec Down. In addition, *Chichester Excavations*, volume 3 (1978, 47), provides details of the temporary bell foundry. Details of the 1380 poll tax were drawn from W.D. Cooper's *Former Inhabitants of Chichester* (Sussex Archaeological Collections 24, 67–9). Other material drawn upon:

Schofield J. and Vince, A., *Medieval Towns*, Continuum 1994

Turner, E., 'The Merchant Guild of Chichester', *Sussex Archaeological Collections* 15 (1875), 165–77

Chapter 3: The Town Spiritual

For a full appreciation of Chichester cathedral during the medieval period there is nothing better than *Chichester Cathedral* (Phillimore, 1991) edited by Mary Hobbs. It contains detailed chapters on the early bishopric of Selsey and the workings of the cathedral in Chichester, as well as the building itself. A second valuable publication is Ian Nairn and Nikolaus Pevsner's *Sussex* (1965), published in the Penguin Buildings of England series. The latter is especially useful if read in conjunction with a visit to the cathedral, the precinct, St Mary's Hospital, Greyfriars and surviving medieval churches. For the purposes of trying to unravel the complexities of the numerous parishes of Chichester, I found 'The Parishes of the City of Chichester' by W.D. Peckham (*Sussex Archaeological Collections* 74, 65–97) of particular value. I have also adopted, for reasons argued by Peckham, his use of dedicatory names for the various churches of the city. Furthermore, Peckham provides a useful discussion on the authority of the dean over the various medieval parishes. In addition, volume 3 of the *Victoria County History of Sussex* contains much useful material on the cathedral and medieval churches of Chichester. Beyond these, the following books and articles were consulted:

Cavis-Brown, J., *An Old English Hospital: St Mary's, Chichester*, c. 1906

Down, A., (ed.), *Excavations in St Andrews, Oxmarket*, Chichester Excavations, no. 5, Phillimore, 1981

Fleming, L., *The Little Churches of Chichester*, Chichester Paper 5

Gudgeon, M., *The Story of St Richard*, Scalar Publishers, 2002

James, A., (ed.), *Past Matters*, Chichester District Council, December 2003. This is the first of an annual publication and contains a useful item on the application of new mapping technology to the burials associated with the hospital of St James and St Mary Magdalene.

Jones, D.J., 'The Cult of St Richard of Chichester in the Middle Ages', *Sussex Archaeological Collections* 121 (1983), 79–86

——, *Saint Richard of Chichester: the Sources for his Life*, Sussex Record Society, 1995

Munby, J., *St Mary's Hospital, Chichester: a Short History and Guide*, Trustees of St Mary's Hospital, 1987

Oswald, N., 'Care of the Sick and Elderly in Medieval Chichester from 1100 to 1400 AD', *West Sussex History* 62 (1998), 19–26

Palmer, C.F.R., 'The Black Friars of Sussex', *Sussex Archaeological Collections* 29 (1877), 39–45

Steer, F.W., *The Grey Friars in Chichester*, Chichester Paper 2, 1965

Swainson, C.A., 'The Hospital of Saint Mary, in Chichester', *Sussex Archaeological Collections* 24 (1872), 41–62

Chapter 4: The Reformation

Much of the material used in this chapter has been listed in the two earlier chapters: Revd J. Cavis-Brown *c.* 1906, Michael Gudgeon (2002), Julian Munby (1987), Francis W. Steer (1965), C.A. Swainson (1872). Of specific value to this period of Chichester's history was Neville Ollerenshaw's *The History of the Prebendal School* (Phillimore, 1984), which includes a good account of the school together with a complete translation of the original statutes of the school. In addition, *Chichester Cathedral* (1991) edited by Mary Hobbs provided details of the effect of the Reformation upon the cathedral. For details of the subsidy assessments of 1524, use was once again made of William Durrant Cooper's *Former Inhabitants of Chichester* (*Sussex Archaeological Collections* 24 (1884). Other material consulted:

Foster, P, (ed.), *A Jewel in Stone: Chichester Market Cross 1501–2001*, Otter Memorial Paper 15. Chichester, 2001

Lower, M.A., *The Sussex Martyrs*, nd

McCann, T.J., 'The Clergy' in M.J. Kitch (ed.), *Studies in Sussex Church History*, University of Sussex, 1981, 99–123

——, *Restricted Grandeur: Impressions of Chichester, 1586–1948*, West Sussex County Council, 1995

McGrath, P., *Papists and Puritans under Elizabeth I*, Blandford Press, 1967

Salzman, L.F., 'Sussex Religious at the Dissolution', *Sussex Archaeological Collections* 92 (1954), 24–36

Wilson, D., *The People and the Book: the Revolutionary Impact of the English Bible*, Barrie and Jenkins, 1976

Chapter 5: Civil War

The single most valuable consulted publication for this chapter was David Frampton's *The Siege of Chichester, 1642* (Partizan Press, 1996). Although it contains some interesting errors, such as the capture by Parliamentary forces of certain (not to be built until the nineteenth century) Portsmouth forts, its description of the siege of Chichester appears accurate. More important, however, is its verbatim inclusion of several contemporary documents. Among these are both Cawley and Waller's accounts. In addition, Reeves' account of the sacking of the cathedral can be found in both McCann (1995) and Thomas Stanford, *Sussex in the Great Civil War and Interregnum, 1642–1660* (1910). Details of the plague that came to Chichester in 1608 were mostly drawn from contemporary parish records held at the West Sussex Archives Office. Also consulted:

Boynton, L., *The Elizabethan Militia, 1558–1638*, David & Charles, 1971

Foster, A., 'The Dean and Chapter 1570–1660' in M. Hobbs (ed.), *Chichester Cathedral*, Phillimore, 1991

Hay, A., *The History of Chichester*, 1804

Hothersall, G., 'Petitions to West Sussex Quarter Sessions', *West Sussex History* 70 (Winter 2002), 20–8

McCann, T., 'The Catholic Recusancy of Dr John Bullacker of Chichester, 1574–1627', *Recusant History* (1971), 75–85

Parish, P., 'William Cawley, His Life and Times', *Chichester History* 15 (1999), 16–22

Chapter 6: Restoration

Several of the titles used in the writing of previous chapters proved useful: Hays (1804), McCann (1995), Parish (1999) and volume 3 of the *Victoria County History of Sussex*. The work of Oswald (1998) on epidemiology served as a starting point for research that I also chose to conduct into the health of Chichester during the seventeenth century. It was as a result of consulting the extant burial registers for all parishes of Chichester (held on microfiche at the West Sussex Archives Office) for the years 1600–1700 that I reached certain conclusions as to the extent of plague during 1659 and the mid-1660s. For Bishop Carleton's account of Monmouth's visit to Chichester I used a printed version of the letter that appeared in Volume 7 of *Sussex Archaeological Collections*, 168–172. The club that was formed to celebrate the accession of William III was known as the Corporation of St Pancras, a full account of its formation and history appearing in Francis W. Steer, *The Corporation of St Pancras*, Chichester (Chichester Paper 42, 1964). It met at the Unicorn Inn (St Pancras) every 4 November, the eve of the Gunpowder Plot, to wine and dine.

Other material consulted:

Defoe, D., *A Tour through the Whole Island of Great Britain*, Penguin, 1971

Flower, S.J., et al., *Pallant House*, Pallant House Gallery Trust

Green, K., 'The Duke of Monmouth at Chichester', *Chichester History* 3 (1987), no. 2, 7–8

Hothersall, G., 'Guy Carleton Bishop of Chichester 1679 to 1685', *West Sussex History* 67 (Spring 2001), 21–33

Hughes, P.J., *Oliver Whitby School*, Phillimore, 2002

Millington, A.G.E., 'The First Quaker Meeting House and Burial Ground in the Hornet', *Chichester History* 2 (1986), no. 2, 4–9

Morriss, C., *The Journeys of Celia Fiennes*, 1949

Steer, F.W., *The John Edes House, West Street, Chichester*, Chichester Paper 52, 1968

Swainson, C.A., 'The Hospital of St Mary, Chichester', *Sussex Archaeological Collections* 24 (1872), 41–62

Chapter 7: Transformation

The following primary sources, available at the West Sussex Archives Office, were drawn upon:

Chichester City Records, E1, the papers of the Board of Paving Commissioners, 1791–3.

——, WG5/1A/1-2, Minutes of the Chichester Workhouse Guardians, 1756–*c.* 1810

Of secondary published sources for the Georgian period, nothing proved of greater value than Emlyn Thomas's locally published three-volume *Georgian Chichester* (2001). Another useful publication was F.H.W. Shepherd's 'Street Administration in Chichester from the Sixteenth to the Nineteenth Century' (*Sussex Archaeological Collections*, 90, 1952). This provided a general account of street maintenance and improvements. Once again, several of the titles used in the writing of previous chapters proved useful: Hay (1804), Hughes (2002), McCann (1995) Parish (1999) and volume 3 of the *Victoria County History of Sussex*. Also referred to:

Dangerfield, M.E., *et al.*, 'Chichester Workhouse', *Sussex Archaeological Collections* 79 (1938), 131–66

Haines, W. and Arnold, F.H., 'Spershott's Memoirs of Chichester', *Sussex Archaeological Collections* 29 (1868), 219 ff.

Steer, F.W., *The Royal West Sussex Hospital*, Chichester Paper 15, 1960

——, *The Memoirs of James Spershott*, Chichester Paper 30, 1962

Swainson. C.A., 'The Hospital of St Mary, Chichester', *Sussex Archaeological Collections* 24 (1872), 41–62

Chapter 8: War and Peace

For the writing of this chapter considerable use was made of various contemporary accounts, especially those appearing in the *Sussex Weekly Advertiser*. Although published in Lewes, it was widely read in the city and provided regular accounts of any local activities considered newsworthy. The various protests over the price of food were covered in reasonable detail. Another particularly useful source for the wartime period was Hay's *History of Chichester*, this of particular value as it was published in 1804. In addition, reference was made to a number of government papers held at the National Archives (Kew). These included: HO42/27 (innkeepers' petition and the response of Henry Dundas); HO50/88-311 (correspondence of the Sussex Militia and records of Lord Lieutenancy meetings); MH12/12813 (26 March 1836, Edward Gilbert's account of the procedure for electing the Guardians); WO40/25 (details of barrack accommodation). George Loader's map of Chichester, dated 1812, is located at the West Sussex Record Office: PM219. Of published secondary sources, use was again made of Hughes (2002), Parish (1999) and Steer (1960) together with the following:

Emsley, C., *British Society and the French Wars, 1793–1815*, Macmillan Press, 1979

Hine, G.M., *The Lancastrian School for Girls, Chichester 1812–1962*, Chichester Paper 26, 1962

Vine, P.A.L., *London's Lost Route to Midhurst: The Earl of Egremont's Navigation*, Sutton Publishing, 1995

Wells, R., *Insurrection: The British Experience, 1795–1803*, Alan Sutton, 1986

——, *Wretched Faces: Famine in Wartime England, 1763–1803*, Alan Sutton, 1988

Chapter 9: An Age of Reform

A valuable insight to the many changes that occurred in Chichester during these years was provided by a little-known account of the city held at the West Sussex Record Office. This account consists of the recorded memories of William Hoare. Born in Chichester in 1817, he rarely left the area for more than a couple of days and subsequently set down his reflections on the changing city in 1887. As well as being in manuscript form at the Record Office (Add Ms 7729) they have also been transcribed by Ken Newbury and published by the Chichester Local History Society in *Chichester History* 12 (1996). The wording of the 1835 petition was drawn from T.G. Willis, *Records of Chichester* (1928). Of importance for my account of the work of the Guardians I drew heavily upon material held at the National Archives (Kew), in particular MH12/12813, the correspondence of the Guardians. Material relating to the health of the town was partly drawn from further material held at the National Archives: MH12/12823-5. However, proving of particular value was Barbara Stewart Ely's comprehensive study of Dr Frederick John Freeland. This appeared as 'The Struggle for Public Health in Chichester' and was published in *Chichester History* 10 (1994). For times of stagecoaches to Brighton I relied on Pigot's *Royal National and Commercial Directory and Topography of the Counties of Kent, Surrey and Sussex* (1839). Also consulted was the Chichester Corporation Water Act 1897, 60 Vict. xlvii, together with the following publications:

Berriman, H., 'The Census and the City: the relationship between social status and mobility in Chichester 1871/1891, *Chichester History* 17 (2000)

Elleray, D.R., *The Victorian Churches of Sussex*, Phillimore, 1981

Foster, P., (ed.), *Chichester Cathedral Spire: The Collapse* (1861), Otter Memorial Paper 13, 2001

Hobsbawm, E.J. and Rude, G., *Captain Swing*, Penguin, 1973

Knott, J., *Popular Opposition to the 1834 Poor Law*, Croom Helm, 1986

Moloney, M., *et al.*, *Aspects of Whyke through the Ages*, Whyke Residents' Association, 2000

Nairn, I., and Pevsner, N., *Sussex*, 1965

Newbury, K., 'The 1851 Census of Rumboldswyke' *Chichester History* 13 (1997)

——, 'The Eastgate Development Area' *Chichester History* 10 (1994)

Vickers, J.A., *The Religious Census of Sussex 1851*, Sussex Record Society, 1989

White, H.P., *Southern England, A Regional History of the Railways of Great Britain*, no. 2, David & Charles, 1969

Chapter 10: The Era of the Selsey Tram

In this chapter considerable use was made of contemporary newspaper accounts, particularly those appearing in the *Observer and West Sussex Recorder* (various issues) and *West Sussex Advertiser* (various issues). For details relating to the attempted abolition of the Sloe Fair, papers relating to this can be found at the National Archives: HO45/10060/B1622. Books and articles referred to:

Bathurst, D., *The Selsey Tram*, Phillimore, 1992

Eyles, A., *et al.*, *Cinema West Sussex: The First Hundred Years*, Phillimore, 1996

Howell-Thomas, D., *Socialism in West Sussex: A History of the Chichester Constituency Labour Party*, 1983

Garrett, S., 'The Selsey Tramway in its Last Days', the Colonel Stephens website: www.hfstephens-museum.org.uk

Greig, I., *et al, D-Day West Sussex*, West Sussex Record Office, 2004

Chapter 11: Within Living Memory

Much of this chapter was based on interviews with a number of Cicestrians who were kind enough to share their memories of the late-twentieth-century city. In addition, I also drew upon various newspapers and, in particular, the *Chichester Observer*. Of special value were a series of articles that appeared in the *Observer* during the latter part of 1938, these describing the city's major industrial enterprises. From the National Archives (Kew), and relating to the positioning of anti-aircraft guns in 1941, reference was made to AIR29/884. Among published accounts referred to:

Evershed-Martin, L., *The Impossible Theatre*, Phillimore, 1971

Hylton, S., *Their Darkest Hour: The Hidden History of the Home Front 1939–1945*, Sutton Publishing, 2001

Steer, F.W., *The City of Chichester*, Chichester City Council, 1957

Index